Transparent Simulacra

TRANSPARENT SIMULACRA
Spanish Fiction, 1902–1926

Robert C. Spires

University of Missouri Press
Columbia, 1988

University of Missouri Press, Columbia, Missouri 65211
Printed and bound in the United States of America

Library of Congress Cataloging-in-Publication Data

Spires, Robert C.

Transparent simulacra : Spanish fiction from 1902–1926 /
Robert C. Spires.
p. cm.
Bibliography: p.
Includes index.
ISBN 0-8262-0695-6 (alk. paper)
1. Spanish fiction—20th century—History and criticism.
I. Title.
PQ6144.S66 1988 88-4882
863'.62'09—dc19 CIP

∞™ This paper meets the minimum requirements of
the American National Standard for Permanence of Paper
for Printed Library Materials, Z39.48, 1984.

To my parents

Preface

The title *Transparent Simulacra* responds to what may constitute a truism but is somehow often overlooked. Fiction does not recreate reality; it provides illusions by means of verbal images. Beginning most dramatically in 1902 and culminating, at least artistically, in 1926, Spanish fiction was inspired by an effort to unmask the illusion that the word is the object to which it refers, that the imaginary world of fiction is somehow real. The analyses in this volume all focus on the textual strategies employed to expose the representations for what they are, to render transparent the verbal simulacra that define fiction itself.

This book is intended to provide a new view of a selected body of well-known fiction. On the one hand it aspires to open some closed categories, and on the other to provide fresh readings of several canonized fictional works. The type of textual analysis represented by this study can be and has been attacked as excessively insular. The charge is often made that the work of literature in studies of this type is treated as if it had been created in a sociocultural vacuum; the history of ideas and social change is sacrificed for the sake of the mechanical process of identifying and defining formalistic elements. Without question, at least some validity exists in such criticisms. Yet one can argue in response that sociophilosophical orientations have tended to reduce texts to documents; rather than analyze them as dynamic works of art, critics have displayed them as static artifacts. Fortunately, such reductions on either side of the issue have been the exception rather than the rule; I hope that my study manages to avoid the pitfalls of mechanical formalism and cultural isolation.

Others have attended to the danger of excessively isolating the works of fiction analyzed here. A large and distinguished body of literature treats the philosophical roots and the social implications of the Generation of '98 and the European and Spanish-American sources of and correlations with the Spanish vanguard movement. I have attempted not only to identify these studies but also in many cases to relate their findings to the textual strategies being applied. In addition, I have perused most of the principal newspapers and magazines of the period in an effort to acquire and convey a feeling for the sociopolitical atmosphere. As for the issue of a mechanical process of identifying and defining techniques, the emphasis here falls on how certain strategies make the text *work*; in other words, it is a question of explaining how the reader's experience is created rather than of providing catalogues for technical terms. Readers will have to judge for themselves, however, the degree to which this book successfully avoids the charges so often leveled against textual criticism.

The basic thesis for my study grew out of graduate courses; accordingly, a long list of University of Kansas students over the past several years deserves credit for whatever virtues the book may have. Those students were instrumental in changing my views regarding the traditional distinctions between the fiction of the Generation of '98 and of the vanguard movement. They were my teachers. If the presentation here of the lesson they taught me is defective, in this case all blame lies with the pupil, not with the instructors.

The book is divided into three primary chapters, with a date for each title. The dates are arbitrary, as are the selections. That is to say, in each case there is a justification provided for why a particular work was chosen for analysis; yet, with few exceptions, those choices are subject to challenge. My hope is that even with other selections and therefore different dates for chapter heads, the picture that I project of Spanish fiction during these three decades would not change appreciably. In sum, the dates are designed to convey the process of evolution in textual strategies forming the thesis for this study.

In addition to the graduate students at the University of Kansas, I would like to thank Dian Fox for reading the entire manuscript and offering many thoughtful and invaluable suggestions, and Roberta Spires for doing that and much more. I would like to express my appreciation also to the General Research Fund of the University of Kansas for a grant to help me do the final editing, and to the staff of the Spencer Research Library at the University for providing me with a study in which to do the preliminary research. For the support to do the primary research and writing in Spain, I am indebted to the U.S.–Spanish Joint Committee for Cultural and Educational Cooperation, without whose fellowship this book could not have been written.

R. C. S.
Lawrence, Kans.
February 1988

Contents

Introduction

In his study of vanguard fiction, Gustavo Pérez Firmat contends, "Before 1926 there was no general awareness of the genre, nor was there a corpus of works that could have engendered it."[1] My study challenges that statement by tracing the development of some basic textual strategies from 1902 to 1926. I argue that a body of works capable of engendering vanguard fiction began to develop in 1902, and also that the vanguard movement is a direct and perhaps inevitable extension of that development. This book, then, is not a study of the Generation of '98 nor of vanguardism, but rather of the evolution of novelistic techniques that link those two movements.

When I note that I will be challenging Pérez Firmat's statement cited above, I would like to emphasize that I do not dispute his entire study. In fact, my work ends with the very year Pérez Firmat's *Idle Fictions* begins and is therefore designed to complement it, to be in a collegial dialogue rather than a contentious dispute with *Idle Fictions,* as well as with other studies. Since I consider criticism to be a community effort, any virtues my study may have would be diminished significantly without the contribution of the works with which it sometimes takes issue.

If one were limited to the statements and manifestoes of those identified with the vanguard movement, one might conclude that their textual strategies were completely new[2]; they talk as though they were the first to react against the canons of nineteenth-century romanticism and realism. Based on their statements, one receives the impression that vanguardism was unique in its campaign to renovate fiction.[3] Yet the aesthetics that the vanguardists describe as the enemy is essentially the same as the one that members of the Generation of '98 rejected twenty years earlier. One is inclined to conclude, therefore, that the continued popularity of realistic and romantic fiction—the latter in the form of the *novela rosa*—inspired the vanguard claims of pioneering the effort of renovation.[4] Thus the poetics being advocated by the new group was in fact almost identical to that developed by Unamuno, Azorín, Valle-Inclán, Pérez de Ayala, and to a lesser degree even Baroja. Both groups reacted against the realistic/romantic tradition that from the turn of the century through the 1920s defined popular literature in Spain. In short, two different groups of artists existed, but with a common cause. This book examines selected works from each group, reflecting the evolution of strategies designed to redefine Spanish fiction in the twentieth century.

In an effort to establish the major points of this new definition, I have selected what I consider to be representative works spanning the twenty-four-year period. Again, emphasizing that my goal is to trace the development of textual strategies from 1902 until 1926 and not to survey the two movements involved, I have chosen what are generally recognized as canonized works from each of the three decades. In doing so I have avoided, even at the expense of strengthening my own thesis, works that represent exceptions rather than the rule.

The year 1902 is fundamental to the efforts of renovating Spanish fiction, and I have included analyses of the four famous novels published that year: Baroja's *Camino de perfección,* Martínez Ruiz's *La voluntad,* Unamuno's *Amor y pedagogía,* and Valle-Inclán's *Sonata de otoño.* Although many critics refer to the significance of these four novels appearing in the same year, until now no one has attempted to compare them by subjecting each to a close reading.

From the next decade the selection was less obvious. First, I replace Pío Baroja with Pérez de Ayala, since Baroja became less experimental in his fiction after writing *Camino de perfección.* Consequently, we have the case of a charter member of the Generation of '98 shedding at an early stage in his career one of the fundamental traits defining the generation. Pérez de Ayala, on the other hand, is universally recognized as one of the primary innovators in Spanish fiction in the second and third decades of this century,[5] yet many deny him membership in the Generation of '98. Since this is not intended as a study of the Generation of '98, I had no qualms about replacing Baroja with Pérez de Ayala. The selection of *Las novelas poemáticas,* and specifically of "La caída de los Limones" from that collection, is perhaps more subject to second-guessing.[6] Indeed, *Belarmino y Apolonio,*[7] with its long introductory self-analysis, or the combination *Tigre Juan* and *El curandero de su honra,*[8] with the double-column attempt to reflect temporally simultaneous but spatially separated action, would perhaps have made my task easier. I feel, however, that the three novellas are better known and the results consequently more felicitous. Unamuno's "Nada menos que todo un hombre" was selected by virtue of its proximity to *Niebla,* in terms of both chronology and textual strategy. Having dealt with *Niebla* in a previous book,[9] I did not want to repeat myself here. Perhaps *Abel Sánchez* could have served just as well as "Nada menos que todo un hombre" to demonstrate how a character assumes authorial control of a novel, but again temporal proximity finally dictated the choice.

There is no question concerning the secure position in the canon of the next two novels analyzed: *Doña Inés* and *Tirano Banderas,* by Martínez Ruiz and Valle-Inclán respectively. It is all but impossible to conceive of a study of Spanish fiction of the first three decades of this century that could justifiably omit these two modern masterpieces. When the focus then moves to works identified with the vanguard movement, the canon is not so clearly defined. First I looked for works written by 1926, since my purpose is to establish the contact point between the two movements. Then I chose the three names most prominent among the initiators of the Spanish vanguard movement in fiction: Ramón Gómez de la Serna, Benjamín Jarnés, and Pedro Salinas. The choice of Gómez de la Serna's *El novelista* (1923) was relatively easy. Although there is no clear consensus, most critics consider it one of his best novels, if not the best. In the case of Jarnés, my choice was dictated in part by availability. *El convidado de papel* (dated 1924 although not published until 1928) is the only Jarnés novel that has been reprinted in recent years, and consequently copies are reasonably available. In addition to this practical and pedagogical motive, I selected it on the basis that the novel is generally recognized as one of his three or four best efforts. Finally, then, Salinas's *Víspera del gozo* (1926) only very recently has achieved the degree of recognition to secure it a position in the canon. I suspect we can thank the recent edition of the stories cited in this study, plus Pérez Firmat's perspicacious reading of "Mundo cerrado,"[10] for this long-overdue recognition.

Perhaps most conspicuously absent from the list above is Gabriel Miró. Although the reasoning may be subject to challenge, I found it difficult to identify any particular textual strategy in Miró's novels and stories that was not also evident in the works of the other writers.[11] Particularly his *Libro de Sigüenza* deserves special recognition, but neither it nor his novels seems to fit the focus of this study.[12]

I have employed the noun *dialogue* or its adjective *dialogic,* and as most may have already guessed, I have a very specific referent: *The Dialogic Imagination: Four Essays by M. M. Bakhtin.*[13] As Bakhtin makes clear, he does not offer a system of analysis, but rather a way of looking at a work of fiction that, used in conjunction with a system, can lead to new and significant insights. Although my critical approach is eclectic and includes poststructural concepts, it owes a great deal to the structuralists.[14] Since I have attempted to incorporate into my approach only some aspects of Bakhtin's vision, just which aspects I will treat and how I interpret them deserves a word of explanation.

The concept of dialogue is central to Bakhtin's thesis: "Everything means, is understood, as a part of a greater whole— there is a constant interaction between meanings, all of which have the potential of conditioning others" (p. 426). In its largest sense, every literary work is in dialogue with all preceding and future texts, and also with many nonliterary works. For example, the fictions examined in this study are first of all in very self-conscious dialogue with their precursors from the previous century. Also in a very obvious way the works of fiction of the Generation of '98 are in dialogue with several philosophical treatises (by Nietzsche, Schopenhauer, Kierkegaard, and others). And since the members of the generation and of the vanguard movement proposed a renovation of fictional form, all the works are in dialogue with their anticipated progenies.

Within the fictional text the dialogue takes the form of double-voicing and refraction. For example, as the characters speak to one another, the narrator speaks to the narratee. The discourses of the characters are, therefore, double-voiced. That is to say, the narrator who constructed the dialogic situation speaks—refractedly—by means of it to his narratee. Consequently, in so-called dramatic dialogue the message does not involve merely what one character says to another, but also and more fundamentally what the narrator says to his reader by means of the personages' dialogue.

Of course, since narrators can also address their narratees directly, they are not dependent exclusively on double-voicing as a means of communication. Authors, on the other hand, are totally limited to double-voicing for conveying their messages—with the exception of any explanations or analyses they may add about that work of fiction after its completion. In such cases they speak as privileged readers, but nevertheless from outside the text. Bakhtin discusses the posited author rather than the real author because he is interested only in the authorial image created by the work itself.[15] To approximate that image, or rather, the message emanating from it and directed to the posited reader,[16] requires a consideration of how all the discourses of the work enter into dialogue with one another. The central character in this dialogue, therefore, is the narrator.

Whether it is a case of a first-person protagonist or witness or of a third-person omniscient voice, behind each narrator's discourse is the doubled and refracted voice of the posited author. In the same way that narrators speak refractedly through their characters, posited authors speak refractedly through their narrators, or in effect through the works themselves. The medium for posited authors, therefore, is the fictional text. Any voice within that fiction that is identified with a source, even if that source is an assertion of authorship, is merely a refraction of the posited author. The Unamuno, for example, who appears in the novel *Niebla* is but a refracted image of the posited author of the novel, who in turn is a refracted image of the real author.[17] Authors cannot appear, nor can they express their voices directly, in a work of fiction.

As noted earlier, double-voicing is not a system of analysis, but rather a way of looking at fiction. In one sense it is a misnomer, since the word *double* suggests a numerical limitation. As I read Bakhtin, however, he is projecting an infinite rather than a limited process. In effect, for each second or doubled voice identified, there must be another voice. By way of example, as already noted, the narrator's voice is doubled over that of the characters', and the posited author's over that of the narrator's. Logically, then, a series of voices is doubled over that of the posited author. Indeed, a large portion of the scholarship on the novelists of the Generation of '98 is dedicated to identifying the philosophical voice behind the author's. Those studies in effect concern a type of double-voicing. By the same token, many influence-studies are dedicated to identifying the literary source for a given work. Again, that is a type of double-voicing. Yet in all these cases one is tempted to ask whose voice is behind the one identified as the source. If Nietzsche is the voice behind the posited Pío Baroja of *Camino de perfección,* who is the voice behind Nietzsche? What I am suggesting, and what I believe Bakhtin is saying, is that double-voicing is itself a type of infinite deferral. The dialogue that Bakhtin seeks to define does not lead to closure but to aperture: "A word, discourse, language or culture undergoes 'dialogization' when it becomes relativized, de-privileged, aware of competing definitions for the same things. Undialogized language is authoritative or absolute" (p. 427).

Finally, then, my study aspires to dialogue; it is intended to open the categories "Generation of '98" and "vanguard fiction" within which we tend to enclose authors and works of literature. And when I say *open,* I do not mean *destroy.* Not only would it be absurdly presumptuous on my part to think that I could erase these two time-honored categories,[18] but it would be counterproductive, since they serve useful purposes. My goal, again, is merely to "dialogize" them, continuing in the process the dialogue initiated by others over the years, and perhaps even contributing to some new ones in the future.

1 1902

Since 1913 when José Martínez Ruiz (Azorín) is credited with coining the label "the Generation of '98," critics have been trying to define its essential characteristics. One of the vintage definitions that has held its age well was proposed by Angel del Río. According to del Río, the writers of the Generation of '98 were concerned with three fundamental problems: Spain, the individual, and art.[1] To a large degree everything said before and since about the generation merely refines and expands on del Río's definition.[2]

Although preceding by several years Azorín's term, the intellectual and spiritual force behind the movement manifested itself in a series of short-lived magazines that members of the generation either founded or were regular contributors to: *Germinal* (1897–1899), *Vida Nueva* (1898–1900), *Revista Nueva* (1899), *Juventud* (1901–1902), *Alma Española* (1903–1904), and *Helios* (1903–1904).[3] The last two are significant since many believe that *Alma Española ola* represents the final phase of the magazine life of the generation and that *Helios* emerged as the new standard bearer of modernism. In short, the magazine phase of the Generation of '98 ended the year after the novelistic expression began. The conclusion, therefore, seems to be that the magazines served to project the attitudes that were to characterize this group of writers and to afford them a medium for refining and previewing their new approaches. By 1902 its primary members were ready to offer their finished products to the public. With the transition from theory to practice, from rehearsal to performance, the need for this type of magazine had passed.[4]

Although the magazines provided a forum, it is all but impossible to point to anything in them that qualified as a poetics manifesto for the Generation of '98 (as opposed to the many vanguard manifestoes that appeared in selected journals). In regard to fictional modes, the criteria that emerge are defined more often indirectly than directly; a definition of the new novel surfaces by means of the critical comments leveled at other novels, or by means of the stories and fragments of novels written by the new novelists themselves. And although the definition emerging from such an indirect method is vague at best, a few characteristics seem clear: a rejection of the rhetorical excesses of romanticism, the pseudoscientific cause-and-effect emphasis of realism/naturalism, and in general the excessively paradigmatic nature of nineteenth-century fiction.[5] The analyses that follow are designed to demonstrate the artistic expression of these new criteria in the four landmark novels published in 1902.

Camino de perfección

Pío Baroja's *Camino de perfección* represents a break from nineteenth-century novelistic conventions, but a less radical departure than that represented by the other three 1902 novels studied here. At the time of publication it was the center of much critical acclaim, most of which tended to stress the novel's adherence to realistic principles.[6] In fact, the reception of Baroja's novel seems to have been more favorable than that afforded the other three 1902 novels under discussion, perhaps precisely because readers felt that *Camino de perfección* was less unconventional than *La voluntad, Amor y pedagogía,* and *Sonata de otoño.* And apart from the other three novelists, who became progressively experimental, Baroja continued, indeed intensified, his commitment to realistic canons in subsequent years. Baroja's *Camino de perfección* is important, nevertheless, for it reflects how Spanish fiction at the turn of the century was dedicated to developing new modes of expression.[7]

Critics inevitably speak of the presence of Baroja's voice when commenting on *Camino de perfección* and then insist on identifying that voice with a single spokesman within the novel. Yet they seldom agree as to who that spokesman is. Some identify Baroja with the witness narrator who speaks in the first person at the beginning of the novel, others with the third person omniscient narrator who recounts most of the action, and still others with the protagonist, who also narrates for several chapters.[8] Yet as Bakhtin states, an author's voice is always refracted; it cannot be traced to any single speaker or discourse within the work but rather emerges as the sum of speakers and discourses.[9] Because of double-voicing, then, the posited author's voice is heard behind every speaker in *Camino de perfección*; moreover, by examining how the authorial voice is refracted by each speaker, we can better understand the way in which *Camino de perfección* redefines the fictional canons of the previous century as it rejects conventional realism for its own brand of subjective realism.

Anecdotally, *Camino de perfección* deals with Fernando Ossorio's search for authentic values in what he feels is a society almost devoid of such values. His peregrination leads him from Madrid, to Segovia and the surrounding area, to Toledo, to Yecla (called Yécora in the novel), and finally to a Mediterranean village near Castellón. In his search for existential fulfillment he encounters a variety of characters, both male and female, who define the society in which he lives and ultimately determine the road he chooses. Indeed, this travel tale has been likened to a mythic search consisting of separation, a series of trials, illumination, and apparent transcendence.[10] But whatever reading one ascribes to the story (myth, social commentary, or *bildungsroman*), the function within the novel of voice and vision[11] represents the key to Baroja's contribution to a new concept of the Spanish novel for the twentieth century.[12] The importance of voice and vision to the reader's experience is underscored by the various narrators whom Baroja employs to tell the protagonist's story. The novel begins with an intradiegetic witness narrator speaking in the first person, only to switch in Chapter 3 to an extradiegetic third-person narrator. Then at the beginning of Chapter 46 the narrator again intrudes in the first person to state that he is merely transcribing what he found in a notebook. At this point the narrating voice is turned over to the protagonist, who tells his own story until Chapter 62, at which point the extradiegetic narrator once again assumes the narrating responsibility.[13]

The radical changes in narrative level and voice serve to emphasize the dialogic relationship between each distinct narrator and the posited author; as each narrator speaks, the posited author speaks through him. The posited author's voice, then, comes to us in refracted form as the total of the narrative voices in the novel. The posited author conveys the message of the novel, but since that message is also refracted, it resists any unequivocal interpretation. To read *Camino de perfección* is to confront the ambiguity and even apparent contradiction of its multiple voices, which in turn project a new and subjective view of reality.

The first voice we hear in the novel is that of an intradiegetic witness narrator: "Entre los compañeros que estudiaron medicina conmigo, ninguno tan extraño y digno de observación como Fernando Ossorio" ("Among the friends who studied medicine with me, none was so strange and so worthy of observation as Fernando Ossorio").[14] As the narrator then describes Fernando, he notes that his classmate is something of a heretic because he esteems Pantoja de la Cruz, Sánchez Coello, and El Greco over Velázquez and Murillo as painters. In spite of the heretical nature of these views on art, the narrator notes: "a mí me parecían excelentes" (p. 8; "they seemed excellent to me"). As a result of such a declaration, the narrator immediately bestows superior credibility upon Fernando. We now look to Fernando, rather than to the narrator, as the authoritative voice in the initial part of the novel.

The protagonist's narrative authority is demonstrated when the narrator, upon examining some of Fernando's sketches, remarks that they do not really resemble their referents, to which Fernando replies:

> —El arte no debe ser nunca natural.
>
> —El arte debe ser la representación de la naturaleza, matizada al reflejarse en un temperamento—decía yo que estaba entonces entusiasmado con las ideas de Zola.
>
> —No. El arte es la misma Naturaleza. Dios murmura en la cascada y canta en el poeta. Los sentimientos refinados son tan reales como los toscos, pero aquéllos son menos torpes. Por eso hay que buscar algo agudo, algo finamente torturado. (pp. 8–9)
>
> (Art should never be natural.
>
> Art should be a representation of nature shaded by the temperament of the artist, I said then, since I was enthusiastic about the ideas of Zola.
>
> No. Art is Nature itself. God whispers in the waterfall and sings in the poet. Refined are as real as gross sentiments, but the former are less awkward. Thus we must look for something piercing, something daintily tortured.)

With the discussion abruptly ending at this point, it is clear that Fernando's and not the intradiegetic narrator's ideas on art are to be afforded more credibility. What that means is that the discourses of both speakers are double-voiced. Precisely through the juxtaposition of a defense of Zola's concept of naturalism with Fernando's defense of a subjective realism are we able to hear the posited author's voice telling his posited reader how to read the novel. And by virtue of Fernando's superior credibility, the implied message is that the novel at hand represents a break from the nineteenth-century pseudo-objective conventions. In doing so, it pretends to create a new subjective concept of reality.[15] Behind the discourses of the two characters who address one another, therefore, is the voice of the posited author who, refracted by those discourses, defines a new aesthetic for the novel.

Another kind of double-voicing, one based on vision as well as dialogue, occurs in Chapter 2, in which the action takes place several years later. The same witness narrator is examining one of Fernando's paintings at an exhibition when the former classmate suddenly appears. As they begin to discuss the painting, Fernando once again offers his definition of art: "—Lo que sí creo es que el arte, eso que nosotros llamamos así con cierta veneración, no es un conjunto de reglas, ni nada, sino que es la vida: el espíritu de las cosas reflejado en el espíritu del hombre. Lo demás, eso de la técnica y el estudio, todo eso es m . . ." (p. 14; "What I do believe is that art, what we call art with a certain veneration, is not a group of rules; it is nothing but life: the spirit of things reflected in the spirit of man. Furthermore, all that about technique and study, all that is sh——"). The similarity between these ideas and those Fernando expressed in the previous chapter again suggests the hidden presence of the posited author, who is again using a character's dialogue to define the novel the reader holds in his hands. Yet double-voicing in this instance assumes a new dimension as the two men then decide to leave the gallery and pause at the doorway to observe the setting sun. We are offered a vision through the eyes of the witness narrator:

> El cielo estaba puro, limpio, azul, transparente. A lo lejos, por detrás de una fila de altos chopos del Hipódromo, se ocultaba el sol, echando sus últimos resplandores anaranjados sobre las copas verdes de los árboles, sobre los cerros próximos, desnudos, arenosos, a los que daba un color cobrizo y de oro pálido.
>
> La sierra se destacaba como una mancha azul violácea, suave en la faja del horizonte cercana al suelo, que era de una amarillez de ópalo, y sobre aquella ancha lista opalina, en aquel fondo de místico retablo, se perfilaban claramente, como en los cuadros de los viejos y concienzudos maestros, la silueta recortada de una torre, de una chimenea, de un árbol. Hacia la ciudad, el humo de una fábrica manchaba el cielo azul, infinito, inmaculado. (pp. 15–16)

> (The sky was pure, clean, blue, transparent. Far away behind a line of high poplars of the Hippodrome, the setting sun was casting its final orange radiance over the green tops of the trees, over the nearby naked and sandy hills, which it tinted copper and pale gold.

The mountains were silhouetted like a blue violet stain, gently swathed in the low horizon of opulent yellow; and over that wide opaline strip, in the depths of that mystic altar, the profile was as clear as in the paintings of the old and meticulous Masters, the silhouette, cut by a tower, a chimney, a tree. Towards the city, the smoke of a factory stained the blue, infinite, immaculate sky.)

The voice and the vision here belong to the anonymous witness narrator. Yet the voice seems to echo Fernando's previous definition of art as "el espíritu de las cosas reflejado en el espíritu del hombre." This is a case of double-voicing on top of double-voicing. First we detect Fernando's voice behind the witness narrator's vision. Then as we re-examine Fernando's verbal definition that, in effect, seems to predetermine this vision, we cannot ignore the voice of the posited author. This double refraction of the posited author's voice both defines and demonstrates how *Camino de perfección* projects its own concept of subjective realism as a response to mimetic criteria of the previous century.[16] And although the departure may not strike us today as so radical as the posited author suggests, there can be no question concerning his intention in 1902 to redefine the novelistic canons of the previous century.

The switch to an extradiegetic narrator at the beginning of the third chapter offers the reader yet another type of double voicing, which in turn further defines the concept of subjective realism. Whereas up to now Fernando's dialogue has provided the primary vehicle through which the posited author's voice asserts itself, beginning with the third chapter Fernando's perspective combines with the narrator's voice to provide that vehicle: as we look through Fernando's eyes we listen directly to the voice of the extradiegetic narrator. Yet behind both Fernando's visions and the narrator's words stands the posited author. The authorial voice, therefore, comes to us refracted by two distinct sources, one seemingly visual and the other manifestly verbal.

The switch from dialogue to intradiegetic vision and extradiegetic voice is apparent when Fernando attends a party at Retiro Park:

En la obscuridad, entre el negruzco follaje verde lustroso, brillaban focos eléctricos y farolillos de papel. Los puestos, adornados con percalinas de colores nacionales y banderolas, también amarillas y encarnadas, estaban llenos de cachivaches colocados en los estantes. Una fila de señoritas en pie, sofocadas, rojas, sacaban papeletas de unas urnas y se las daban a los elegantes caballeros, que iban dejando al mismo tiempo monedas y billetes en una bandeja. (pp. 21–22)

(In the darkness, the electric lights and tiny paper lanterns sparkled between the blackish-green, lustrous foliage. Each booth, adorned with percalines of the national colors and the flag, yellow and blood-red, was full of dangling trinkets. A line of women standing, stifled and red, plucked papers from vases and gave them to elegant gentlemen, who at the same time left coins and bills in a tray.)

We see through Fernando's eyes a scene characterized by artificial adornments—the lights, the percalines covering the stands, the flags, the trinkets, and the elegantly attired guests. The message, as a result, seems to concern the superficiality not just of the people attending the party but of the society they represent. And it is precisely this superficiality that so disgusts Fernando that he promptly leaves the fete in a state of deep depression.

Soon after the party the brother of Fernando's grandfather dies, and his aunt Laura asks him to come to her home where the other relatives have gathered for the funeral. Fernando finds a house full of bourgeois people concerned with the division of the dead man's estate, with family gossip, or in the case of the house staff, with what effect the death may have on future employment, all this while the corpse lies forgotten in another room:

> En el despacho se seguía hablando de la cuestión del aceite; en la sala se comentaba en voz baja los escándalos de la Nini; los criados andaban alborotados por si les despedían o no de la casa, y mientras tanto, el tío abuelo, solo, bien solo sin que nadie le molestara con gritos ni lamentos, ni otras tonterías por el estilo, se pudría tranquilamente en su ataúd, y de su cara gruesa, carnosa, abultada, no se veía a través del cristal más que una mezcla de sangre rojiza y negra, y en las narices y en la boca, algunos puntos blancos de pus. (p. 34)
>
> (In the study they continued discussing the oil business, and in the living room they commented softly on the scandals of Nini; the servants wandered anxiously for fear they would be fired, and all the while, the grandfather, alone, with no one to bother him with screams or laments, or other foolishness, rotted away tranquilly in his coffin. You could only see through the window a mixture of red and black blood on his thick, fleshy, massive face, and on his nose and mouth some white dots of pus.)

Such a description resonates with naturalistic techniques. Yet rather than reflecting the cause-and-effect relationship quintessential to naturalism, this description seems designed merely to shock, to stand in glaring juxtaposition with the scenes in the rest of the house. Again, as Fernando explained in the first chapter, "Los sentimientos refinados son tan reales como los toscos, pero aquéllos son menos torpes. Por eso hay que buscar algo agudo, algo finamente torturado" (pp. 8–9; "Refined are as real as gross sentiments, but the former are less awkward. Thus we must look for something piercing, something daintily tortured"). By virtue of Fernando's function as the viewing source in the novel, and in conjunction with the extradiegetic narrator's voice, the reader experiences the need for "algo agudo" to contrast with the refinement of society. Apparently only by means of such a juxtaposition, of a mixture of the refined with the grotesque,[17] can a "realistic" view of the world be projected. And so once again the voice of the posited author emerges from behind the scene Fernando observes (or rather imagines) and looms over the voice of the extradiegetic narrator who describes the scene, to redefine the prevailing concept of reality in a work of fiction.

Fernando's decision to leave Madrid and embark upon a real journey is inspired first by the discovery that Laura is involved in a lesbian affair with her servant, and then by the disgust he experiences from his own sexual involvement with his aunt.[18] Madrid becomes identified with what Fernando considers a corrupt and false society and perverted sexuality. Only by leaving the capital can he hope to find a free, natural, and meaningful existence. With his departure the novel enters into a new structural unit in which the emphasis falls on the conflict between nature and the natural order on one side, and religion and the restraints it imposes upon the natural order on the other.[19]

This second structural unit is set in Segovia and Toledo. In the province of Segovia, Fernando meets Schultze, a German who serves as defender for a Nietzschean approach to existence.[20] But although Schultze defends Nietzsche, he does not really define what Nietzschean thesis he is defending. That thesis is expressed only indirectly through Fernando's eyes as he and Schultze gaze at the evening sky from a mountainside:

> Comenzaba a caer la tarde. Rendidos, se tendieron en el suelo. A su lado corría un torrente, saltando, cayendo desde grandes alturas como cinta de plata, pasaban nubes blancas por el cielo, y se agrupaban formando montes coronados de nieve y de púrpura; a lo lejos, nubes grises e inmóviles parecían islas perdidas en el mar del espacio con sus playas desiertas. Los montes que enfrente cerraban el valle tenían un color violáceo con manchas verdes de las praderas; por encima de ellos brotaban nubes con encendidos núcleos fundidos por el sol al rojo blanco. De las laderas subían hacia las cumbres, trepando, escalando los riscos, jirones de espesa niebla que cambiaban de forma, y al encontrar una oquedad hacían allí su nido y se amontonaban unos sobre otros. (p. 99)
>
> (Evening began to fall. Exhausted, they sprawled out on the ground. On one side ran a stream, jumping and falling from the grand heights, like a silver belt. The white clouds passed through the sky, forming mountains crowned with snow and purple; in the distance, the clouds, gray and immobile, looked like lost islands with deserted beaches in the sea of space. The mountains that closed the valley in front were a violet color, stained green by the meadows; above, the clouds sprouted with their centers fused by the sun to a white redness. On the mountainsides the thick fog climbed in shreds to the pinnacles, trimming and scaling the cliffs, changing in form and, as soon as it found a hollow, building a nest as one layer adhered to another.)

By virtue of the contrasting imagery, we experience a conflict between the beauty and vitality of nature on the one hand and the sensation of static desolation and death on the other. Beauty and vitality are conveyed above all with images such as "un torrente, saltando, cayendo desde grandes alturas como cinta de plata . . . pasaban nubes y se agrupaban formando montes coronados de nieve y de púrpura . . . color violáceo con manchas verdes de las praderas . . . brotaban nubes con encendidos núcleos fundidos." Interwoven with this positive imagery are connotations of desolation and death:

"nubes grises e inmóviles parecían islas perdidas en el mar del espacio con sus playas desiertas . . . sol al rojo blanco . . . jirones de espesa niebla que cambiaban de forma, y al encontrar una oquedad hacían allí su nido y se amontonaban unos sobre otros." By first documenting Baroja's role in translating "Nietzsche, íntimo" at approximately the same time that he was writing *Camino de perfección,* Gonzalo Sobejano concludes that this episode with Schultze "se produce en Fernando una pugna entre la religión cristiana y la libre vitalidad natural, junto con el presagio, casi la convicción, de que la muerte de aquélla es necesaria para la plenitud de ésta. Y, aunque la herida cristiana resulte incurable ya para él, en el hijo de su carne soñará hacer valedero su proyecto"[21] ("produces in Fernando a struggle between Christian religion and a free, natural vitality, joined with the portent, almost a conviction, that the death of the former is necessary for the plenitude of the latter. And, even though the injured Christianity is irreconcilable for him, in the son of his flesh he will dream that his project is made valid"). When Sobejano uses this passage and the Schultze episode in general to arrive at his Nietzschean nature-versus-religion reading, he is practicing another form of double-voicing. Although the passage conveys conflict, it is difficult to see how anything in it or in the Schultze episode in itself would lead directly to the particular Nietzschean thesis Sobejano proposes. Yet by drawing on biographical data Sobejano convincingly argues for the nature-versus-religion theme. Without wishing to diminish in any way Sobejano's scholarly contribution, we could reach the same conclusion by limiting ourselves to the text at hand— including in the analysis what anecdotally follows the Schultze episode. As we saw above, the reader experiences from the Schultze episode, and specifically from the descriptive passage cited, a conflict, between life and vitality on the one hand and death and sterility on the other. Since Schultze prefaces the description with a reference to Nietzsche, the stage is set for defining this conflict in Nietzschean terms. Thus when Fernando then leaves Segovia to go to Toledo, religion as the opposing force to the natural order becomes the dominant theme. And so whether relying on biographical or textual evidence, there seems to be a convincing case for detecting Nietzsche's voice superimposed upon the narrative. Of course the challenge to the posited reader is not so much to identify the source as to decode the message.[22] Toledo, in conjunction with the title of the novel itself, seems to represent the key to that message.

Historically, Toledo served as the seat of the church in Spain, and Fernando goes there apparently believing he can find the inspiration for a mystic transcendence. What he finds instead is an institution dedicated to suppressing and controlling human instinct through fear and threats, and through rewards appealing to vainglory. He concludes that the mysticism he seeks has no place in the church as it now exists:

Pero que no le explicaran, que no le dijeran que todo aquello se hacía para no ir al

> infierno y no quemarse en lagos de azufre líquido y calderas de pez derretida; que no le hablasen, que no le razonasen, porque la palabra es el enemigo del sentimiento; que no trataran de imbuirle un dogma; que no le dijeran que todo aquello era para sentarse en el paraíso al lado de Dios, porque él, en su fuero interno, se reía de los lagos de azufre y de las calderas de pez, tanto como de los sillones del paraíso. (p. 158)
>
> (But don't explain to him, don't tell him that it was all done just so a person would not go to hell and burn in the lakes of liquid sulfur and the cauldrons of melted tar; don't talk to him, don't reason with him, because words are the enemy of feeling; don't try to imbue him with dogma; don't let them tell him that all that was just so he could sit down in paradise at the side of God, because he, in his conscience, laughed at the lakes of sulfur and the cauldrons of tar, as well as at the comfortable armchairs of paradise.)

Fernando longed for spiritual freedom, and Catholic mysticism seemed to symbolize the type of freedom he was seeking. Now with the conviction that such a Catholicism no longer exists, if it ever did, he sees religion as an obstacle rather than a path to authentic spiritual freedom, a freedom that he now realizes exists only in natural freedom. Toledo represents the turning point from a conventional to a personal, highly subjective spiritual search. He abandons Catholic mysticism as a possible solution, and in so doing identifies religion as the major opposing force to his search for a means of integrating himself into the natural order.

Yet it is also in Toledo that Fernando transcends his instincts by refusing to seduce Adela, an innocent young woman to whom he is attracted. This victory over himself, inspired by personal, subjective morality rather than external restraints, forms a direct link to the next geographical setting, as the episode reminds Fernando of a similar situation years earlier in his native village where instinct won over moral conviction. This memory prompts him to leave Toledo and return to Yécora, where he proposes to pursue his newly discovered subjective moral code.

Whereas in the Toledo phase the emphasis is on Fernando as the source of focalization—that is, we look through his eyes and surmise from the scene he observes what he thinks and feels—in the Yécora section Fernando is primarily the object of the focalization: the emphasis now falls directly on his thoughts and feelings. This switch in the object of focalization plays a fundamental role as Fernando's personal conflict between freedom and religion reaches a climactic point.

Fernando's first efforts in Yécora are to find Ascensión, the young woman whom he seduced years earlier, and beg her forgiveness. She, however, refuses to forgive him and in fact blames him for the unhappy marital situation in which she now finds herself—a situation for which he is logically not to blame. Fernando is totally disillusioned by Ascensión's refusal to set aside personal grievances and imitate the type of moral transcendence he displayed toward Adela (indeed, the irony of Ascensión's name ranks as one of the less subtle ploys in the novel). Shortly thereafter, Fernando quarrels with a local priest intent on proselytizing him. Even before this unpleasant debate, the protagonist had drawn a conclusion about the role of religion in human existence: "Allí comprendía, como en ninguna parte, la religión católica en sus últimas fases jesuíticas, seca, adusta, fría, sin arte, sin corazón, sin entrañas" (pp. 244–45; "There he understood, as in no other place, the Catholic religion in its most recent Jesuitic phases, dry, austere, cold, without art, without heart, without guts").

With Fernando's thoughts now the object of focalization, voice rather than vision begins to dominate the text, and with the emphasis on voice, we begin to feel even more strongly the presence of the posited author. In addition, the messages now seem to fuse as Fernando's thoughts become identical with the posited author's attitude toward Spanish society, provincial life, and above all Catholicism. Behind the posited author's voice, we hear even more clearly now the voice of Nietzsche and the conflict between Christian repression and the need for individual freedom. In addition to a subjective view of reality, the novel projects a subjective conceptualization of religion.

The final structural unit of the novel is set in the province of Castellón, where Fernando's search for a path to an existential solution culminates. While some would argue that the path leads to the haven of perfection he has been seeking, the manipulation of voices suggests that the message is somewhat more equivocal. In fact, the importance of the switch in voices for decoding the message is underscored by the introduction to this final structural segment:

> ¿Fue manuscrito o colección de cartas? No sé; después de todo, ¿qué importa? En el cuaderno de donde yo copio esto, la narración continúa, sólo que el narrador parece ser, en las páginas siguientes, el mismo personaje.
>
> . . . .
>
> . . . . (p. 277)
>
> (Was it a manuscript or a collection of letters? I do not know; after all, what does it matter? In the notebook from which I copy this, the narration continues, but in the following pages the narrator seems to be the character himself.
>
> . . . .
>
> . . . .)

This sudden shift in narrative level changes the focus from what is narrated to the act of narrating. Whereas before the narrator was merely an anonymous voice removed from the events he was narrating, now he switches the focus to himself, thus calling attention to his presence as the voice behind the events. As he ostensibly cedes to Fernando the role of narrator, he in fact asserts his presence and authority; as we listen to Fernando's voice, we are now alerted to the hidden presence of the narrator—visually signaled by the two lines of dots—who is allowing the character to speak for himself. The final effect of this narrative strategy is to mark a clear distinction between character and narrator. Whereas up to this point there has been a tendency toward fusing the voices of Fernando, the narrator, and the posited author, in this final section Fernando's voice is separated from the other two. This separation, in turn, plays a fundamental role in decoding the concluding message of the novel.

As Fernando ostensibly assumes the narrating role, the first note that emerges is one of optimism. Fernando believes that he has found a solution to his problems by virtue of his move from Yécora to the Mediterranean shore: "Estoy alegre, satisfechísimo de encontrarme aquí . . . todo es jugoso, claro y definido, pero alegre" (p. 278; "I am happy, really satisfied to find myself here . . . everything is juicy, clear and defined, but happy"). Yet as he describes the countryside, another voice emerges: "Enfrente, brillan al sol campos de verdura; las amapolas rojas salpican con manchas sangrientas los extensos bancales de trigo que se extienden, se delatan como lagos verdes con su oleaje de ondulación" (p. 278; "Before me the sun shines on the verdant countryside; the red poppies splash the golden wheat fields with blood-red stains; they outline themselves like green lakes with their undulating surf"). The red color of the poppies, likened to blood as it stains the golden wheat, and then projected into infinity with the simile of the undulating surf, strikes a discordant note in Fernando's hymn of fulfillment. It is by means of this disharmony, then, that the reader hears an echo of the narrator who so pointedly separated himself from Fernando. His act of separating himself from this Utopian dream only underscores the illusory essence of Fernando's discovery.

Following Fernando's narration of his meeting, courtship, and marriage proposal to Dolores, a woman who seems to incarnate the natural virtues he has been seeking,[23] we find another switch to an extradiegetic narrator. This final switch in narrating voice dramatically emphasizes the separation between Fernando and the narrator. Whereas in the preceding chapters the narrator's dissenting voice to Fernando's declarations of fulfilled perfection is merely implicit in the imagery, as we approach the denouement that voice of dissent is made explicit as the narrator usurps Fernando's narrating role. As the resolution of Fernando's quest nears, there is a separation not only between Fernando and the narrator, but also between the narrator and the posited author. The final message emerges as a compromise between those projected by Fernando and by the extradiegetic narrator. The final message, in short, is refracted by these two conflicting and intervening messages.

Once again the imagery provides the first contradiction to Fernando's pronouncements of ultimate happiness. As he and Dolores travel by train along the seashore, they marvel at the sight of the moon shining on the water until suddenly their view is interrupted: "De pronto penetró el tren en un túnel. A la salida se vio la noche negra; se había ocultado la luna. El tren pareció apresurar su marcha" (p. 327; "Suddenly the train entered the tunnel. As it exited one saw the black night; the moon had descended. The train seemed to pick up its pace").

Corroborating this shadowing are the events that occur in this last section of the novel. Fernando's and Dolores's first child dies shortly after birth, and Fernando blames himself for offering the infant such a brief, miserable existence. The second child, a boy, does survive, and Fernando presumes to see for his son a future free of the religious turmoil that characterized his own life: "El le dejaría vivir en el seno de la Naturaleza; él le dejaría saborear el jugo del placer y de la fuerza en la ubre repleta de la vida, la vida que para su hijo no tendría misterios dolorosos, sino serenidades inefables" (pp. 334–35; "He would allow him to live in the bosom of Nature; he would allow him to taste the juice of pleasure and strength in the teat full of life, the life that, for his son, would have no painful mysteries, only indescribable serenities"). Not only does Fernando seem to back away from his previous claims of ultimate happiness by placing hope in his son rather than in himself, but the extradiegetic narrator even contradicts this hope as he notes, "Y mientras Fernando pensaba, la madre de Dolores cosía en la faja que había de poner al niño una hoja doblada del Evangelio" (p. 335; "And while Fernando was pondering, Dolores's mother stitched a folded page from the Gospel on the swathe that the baby was to wear").

If at first glance the narrator seems to negate Fernando's dream of the future for his son, it can also be argued that the posited author's message softens, if not negates, the narrator's cynicism. Since the posited author's voice cannot be pinpointed to a single speaking voice within the novel, the reader must consider the entire novel in order to arrive at the posited author's message. By analyzing the novel as a whole, we find some conclusions that seem indisputable. Fernando is closer to happiness now with Dolores than he was at the beginning of the novel; also, he has not found personal perfection, nor apparently will his son.[24] The implicit conclusion, therefore, is that the quest for perfection, even though doomed to failure, is the best and perhaps only salvation possible for mortals. In this sense, the novel makes a mockery of the mystic religious experience conveyed by the title. Indeed, the posited author seems both to affirm and to negate the messages of the vehicles within the novel through whom he refractedly speaks. Particularly in this affirmation through contradiction, Baroja can be seen as a precursor for many of our contemporary artists.

From the preceding analysis it is apparent that the posited author of *Camino de perfección* intended his novel as an alternative to nineteenth-century novelistic canons. His primary textual strategy for effecting such an alternative is the use of multiple narrating voices, which in turn project a very subjective image of reality. As a result of this subjective rather than mimetic image, the final message is so refracted that it invites conflicting interpretations. *Camino de perfección* plays a fundamental role in making 1902 such a key year in the renovation of Spanish fiction in the twentieth century.

The next novel we will examine from that year, *La voluntad,* is similar in many ways to *Camino de perfección.* Whereas Baroja limits himself to conveying a subjective view of reality, Martínez Ruiz takes a significant step toward directing the novelistic focus to art itself. As he does so, Martínez Ruiz not only widens the fissure between the realist tradition and the Generation of '98 already discernible in *Camino de perfección,* but he also points toward the fusion between the Generation of '98 and the vanguard movement.

La voluntad

Whereas reception of Baroja's *Camino de perfección* at the time of its publication was almost universally positive, Martínez Ruiz's less conventional *La voluntad* netted considerably more mixed reviews. Even when the critics reacted favorably to the novel, they invariably prefaced their praise with the admonition that it was not a novel in the conventional, or realistic, sense of the term. For example, one such review begins with the following remarks: "Este segundo tomo de la *Biblioteca de novelistas del siglo XX,* muy poco o nada tiene de novela, si por novela se entiende aquella 'epopeya bastardeada' de que hablaba Schlegel"[25] ("This second volume of the *Library of Novelists of the 20th Century* has very little, if anything, to do with a novel, if by novel it is understood that 'bastardized epic' mentioned by Schlegel"). In fact, Martínez Ruiz's *La voluntad* represents a many-faceted attack on the tenets of realistic fiction, an attack that goes far beyond Baroja's and points even more directly at vanguard fiction of the 1920s and 1930s.

Perhaps the most obvious departure from novelistic convention involves transforming the prevailing concept of description that conformed to the canons of the previous century. As opposed to that century's emphasis on physical surroundings as a mirror image of the human subject (humans are the product of the ambience in which they live), Martínez Ruiz employs impressionistic descriptions to suggest the viewing subject's state of mind; the relationship between observer and surroundings is affective, not causal; the reader surmises what the character experiences by sharing his or her view rather than by being told what the character thinks or feels.[26] The function of tensive action is also transformed. Rather than a clearly defined cause-and-effect sequence culminating in a dramatic event, in *La voluntad* only minimal causal relationships exist, and key moments are often summarized after the fact, as opposed to being presented as an immediate scene. Martínez Ruiz's innovative use of description and action has been noted and documented, but very little attention has been directed to his use of a shifting narrative perspective in *La voluntad.* This shifting narrative perspective, with its resultant multiple voices, radically challenges the conventional concept of a fictional protagonist. As the protagonist is effaced, the focus shifts from character study to art itself. In the final analysis, this combination of the effacement of the protagonist[27] and a shift in focus to art itself points directly at Martínez Ruiz's later masterpiece, *Doña Inés* (1925), and most significantly at textual strategies of the vanguard movement.

Since change in narrative perspective is the key to effacing character and to foregrounding art itself, I should note that it is not merely a question of what is commonly termed point of view. As used here, narrative perspective involves both voice and vision. Rather than establishing a stable point from which action is reported and observed, in *La voluntad* the voice and vision shift from extradiegetic to intradiegetic, or vice-versa, or there is a combination in which the voice is extradiegetic and the vision intradiegetic. Such shifts in narrative perspective give rise to various types of double-voicing, and the double-voicing in turn diminishes any potentially melodramatic effects associated with the protagonist's destiny. Consequently, the conventional function of the protagonist is undermined and redefined, and in that process the focus shifts to the creative process itself in the final sections of the novel.

The novel tells the story of a young man whose willpower is broken by the pettiness of the society in which he lives and by the strong-willed woman whom he marries. The protagonist Antonio Azorín (Azorín of course is the pen name José Martínez Ruiz later adopted)[28] is coming of age in Yecla, his native provincial city, under the tutelage of Yuste, a sixty-year-old mentor who offers him long and frequent discourses on various aspects of existence.[29] Antonio is in love with Justina, a young woman whose uncle, a priest, objects to Antonio as a match for his niece. Eventually she enters a convent, where she dies, and apparently in the same time span Yuste also dies. Antonio then moves to Madrid, where he pursues a writing career and engages in lengthy philosophical and aesthetic discussions with a fellow writer named Olaiz. Eventually Antonio tires of what he considers to be the phony intellectual atmosphere of the Madrid literary scene and moves back to the province. Disillusioned with provincial life also, he seeks refuge in marriage with Iluminada, a strong-willed friend of the deceased Justina. Antonio hopes that she will allow him to fulfill his life by providing him with the strength, energy, and drive that he lacks. In an epilogue we are told that, contrary to his hopes, Antonio's willpower has been destroyed as he has become totally subordinate to Iluminada. Their life is characterized by squealing children, squalid living conditions, and bourgeois pettiness. The Antonio of the concluding part is but a vague shadow of the young intellectual protagonist we met at the beginning of the novel.

The exterior structure of *La voluntad* is composed of a prologue, a body in three parts, and an epilogue. In the prologue the voice is an anonymous intradiegetic narrator (he exists on the same level as the narrated material). In Part 2 the voice continues to be that of an anonymous narrator, but he is now extradiegetic since he does not form a part of the novelistic world. In Part 2 the voice remains the same (extradiegetic), but the viewing angle is now through the eyes of the protagonist (intradiegetic). The protagonist assumes the role of narrator in Part 3, and therefore the voice and the view are from within the novelistic world. Finally, the epilogue is another example of internal voice and vision, but in this case they belong to a dramatized author who narrates his encounter with the protagonist.[30] The final effect of these shifts in voice and vision is to foreground the narrating instance at the expense of what is narrated; rather than the conventional *bildungsroman, La voluntad* becomes a novel about art itself.

Essentially the prologue is an example of historical narrative describing in detail the stages of construction of a church in Yecla. It is a process marked by inconstancy: "En 1775 la primera piedra es colocada . . . y en 1804 cesa el trabajo . . . en 1847 las obras recomienzan . . . las obras languidecen . . . en 1857 las obras cobran impulso poderoso . . . de Enero a Junio, 18.415 pies cúbicos de piedra son tallados en las canteras. Los veintinueve carpinteros de la ciudad trabajan gratis en la obra. Y mientras las campanas voltean jocundas, la multitud arrastra en triunfo enormes bloques de 600 arrobas"[31] ("In 1775 the first stone is put in place . . . and in 1804 the work ceases . . . in 1847 the work recommences . . . the work diminishes . . . in 1857 the work is undertaken with new vigor . . . from January to June, 18,415 square feet of stone are carved in the quarry. The twenty-nine carpenters of the city work without wages. And while the bells peal happily, the crowd triumphantly drags enormous blocks of 600 tons"). Notwithstanding the emphasis on statistical documentation,[32] the use of the historical present tense introduces a somewhat subjective note into what otherwise seems to be an impersonal historical narrative. As a result of this verb tense, we have the first hint of the presence of the speaker behind the factual information.

If the speaker's presence is only implicit in the verb tense, it soon becomes explicit when reference is made to another construction delay in 1858: "Y el autor de un *Diario* inédito, de donde yo tomo estas notas, escribe sordamente irritado" (p. 58; "And the author of the unedited *Diary,* from which I take these notes, writes with muffled irritation"). This insertion of a personal comment on the one hand reinforces the conventional role of a prologue by providing the fiction with a link to reality, while on the other hand it represents a break from narrative convention. Since the mode is historical narrative, the voice should be impersonal.[33] The use of personal markers in an impersonal narrative form, therefore, changes that form; the historical narrative becomes a narrating act committed by a personal speaker intent on conveying a message. The historical present can then be seen as a sign pointing at the eternal repetition of life in Yecla with Antonio's story forming an inevitable link in that repetition. The construction of the church provides another important link in the novel. Periods of feverish activity are suddenly interrupted and followed by inactivity and neglect; the will to finish the church is difficult to sustain, and when it is finally completed it does not really represent something new but rather an unconscious imitation of a pagan temple existing twenty-five centuries earlier. Finally, then, the edifice serves as a sign that points at both the protagonist—who lacks sustaining willpower—and society—the latter in the context of the paradoxical power and impotence of the church in provincial Spain.[34]

The use of an intradiegetic narrator for historical narrative calls attention to language's double-voicing essence; the prologue alerts us to the need to listen for both voices as we move from the general—life over the centuries in Yecla—to the specific—the coming-of-age of Antonio Azorín in Yecla.

By virtue of the techniques that transform impersonal narrative into a fictional narrating act, the prologue in effect is superimposed on the framed construct that follows. As the perspective shifts, then, from the intradiegetic vantage point of the prologue to an exterior or extradiegetic vantage point in Part 1, we still have as an informing image the construction of the church of Yecla, and its double-voiced significance.

Whereas the intradiegetic narrator serves as the primary textual strategy for personalizing the potentially impersonal mode of the prologue, the shift to an extradiegetic narrator in Part 1 serves as a distancing device; it offsets the more personal, and therefore potentially melodramatic, story material. The vision is from some unspecified point external to the level of the characters, and we tend to observe their actions rather than to be told their thoughts and feelings.

The emphasis on observation from an undefined external point is evident with the description at the beginning of Part 1. It is a description of glaring contradictions:

> Dos, cuatro, seis blancos vellones que brotan de la negrura, crecen, se ensanchan, se desparraman en cendales tenues . . . poco a poco la lechosa claror del horizonte se tiñe en verde pálido . . . largas vetas blanquecinas, anchas, estrechas, rectas, serpenteantes, se entrecruzan sobre el ancho manchón negruzco . . . el cielo, de verdes tintas pasa a encendidas nacaradas tintas . . . surge majestuosa la blanca mole de la iglesia Nueva, coronada por gigantesca cúpula listada en blancos y azules espirales . . . aquí y allá, en el mar gris de los tejados uniformes, emergen las notas rojas, amarillas, azules, verdes, de pintorescas fachadas . . . en primer término destacan los dorados muros de la iglesia Vieja. (pp. 61–62)
>
> (Two, four, six white tufts that spring from the blackness, growing, expanding, spreading in a thin silky gauze . . . little by little the milky light of the horizon becomes a pale green . . . long whitish seams, wide, stretching, straight, serpentine, interlacing over the wide black stain . . . the sky changes from green tint to a fiery pearl shade . . . the white bulk of the New Church emerges majestically, crowned by the striped cupola of white and blue spirals . . . here and there, in the sea gray of the uniform weavings, emerge the shades of reds, yellows, blues, and greens of the picturesque façade . . . in the foreground, the golden walls of the Old Church, emerge sharp and clear.)

As the narrator presents the opening scene, we visually experience the complexity and contradictory essence of this provincial setting. The black-and-white contrast, the threatening green tint of the sky giving way to a rainbow of colors, and finally the imposing white presence of the church with its gilded walls, all suggest the contradictory essence of the setting for this first section of the novel. The atmosphere is simultaneously hostile and inviting, depressing and cheerful, austere and luxurious. The description, then, does not pretend to document reality but to transform it into sensations that create tension by virtue of their contrasting nature.

The visual experience of contrast is also evident in the introduction of Justina, the young woman with whom Antonio falls in love: "Justina es una moza fina y blanca. A través de su epidermis transparente, resalta la tenue red de las venillas azuladas. Cercan sus ojos llameantes anchas ojeras. Y sus rizados bucles rubios asoman por la negrura del manto, que se contrae ligeramente al cuello y cae luego sobre la espalda en amplia oleada" (p. 67; "Justine is a delicate and white young woman. Through her transparent skin protrudes a faint network of bluish veins. Outlining her flaming eyes are wide dark circles. And her blonde curly ringlets are visible through the black of her scarf, pulled together at the collar, as it falls over her back in ample waves"). Similar to the descriptions of nature that create tension through contrast, this description of the heroine is a strange mixture of parody and portent. On the one hand Justina is so coded that she is a literary convention: "moza fina y blanca . . . ojos llameantes anchas ojeras . . . rizados bucles rubios." Yet the convention is accompanied by portentous aspects: "a través de su epidermis transparente, resalta la tenue red de las venillas azuladas . . . la negrura del manto, que se contrae ligeramente al cuello." Without ever indicating what she feels or thinks, the narrator seems to mock Justine and at the same time to foreshadow her tragic demise. By virtue of the parodic tone and the exterior view, the reader remains distanced from her.[35] Whatever Justine's fate in the story, she remains an abstraction, a literary construct not easily confused with a real person—in short, the antithesis of the heroine of the previous century.

Whereas external focalization serves as the textual strategy for creating emotional distance between Justine and the reader, the narrator's voice becomes the primary strategy for creating a similar distance in the case of the protagonist Antonio. He is the ostensible hero with whom the reader should identify. His is the voice that seems to echo the author, Martínez Ruiz. He is the victim of Justina's friend, Iluminada. Yet the narrator seems intent on controlling reader identification even in this case. Antonio, as the would-be hero, appears in the setting of his home, yet the narrator's voice rather than the protagonist's vision dominates the scene: "Aquí es donde Azorín pasa sus hondas y trascendentales cavilaciones, y va leyendo a los clásicos y a los modernos, a los nacionales y a los extranjeros" (p. 94; "Here is where Azorín passes his transcendental ruminations and continues reading classic and modern works, the Spanish and the foreign authors"). Although the tone is not glaringly ironic, the anteplacement of the adjectives "hondas" and "trascendentales" creates at least a hint of mockery.

It is not long before this hint of mockery is corroborated, and again it is the narrator's voice rather than the vision he offers that provides the corroboration: "No lejos de su cuarto está la biblioteca, que es una gran habitación a teja vana, con el techo bajo e inclinado, con las vigas toscas, desiguales, con grandes nudos. Los estantes cubren casi todas las paredes, y en ellos reposan sabiamente los sabios y discretos libros" (p. 94; "Not far from his room is the library, a grand room with a roof of tiles, low, slanting, with crude, uneven beams, filled with big knots. The shelves cover almost all the walls, and wisely resting there are the discrete and knowledgeable books"). The adverb *sabiamente* followed immediately by the adjective *sabios* combine to mock the young intellectual and his dedicated search for knowledge. The scornful tone reaches a climactic point as the description of the house draws to a conclusion: "Entre estante y estante hay grandes arcas de blanca madera de pino—donde acaso se guardan ropas de la familia—y encima multitud de vasos, potes, jícaras, tazas, platos, con dulces conservas y mermeladas, que sin duda se ha creído conveniente poner a secar en la biblioteca por seguir la indicación del buen Horacio, que aconseja que se ponga lo *dulce junto a lo útil*" (p. 94; "Between each bookcase there are great arches of white pinewood—where the clothes of the family are stored—and on top are various vases, pots, cups, glasses, plates, and sweet preserves and marmalades, which without a doubt have been placed there in the belief that they are following the advice of Horace, who counsels that *the sweet should be placed alongside the practical*"). Although no book titles are provided, the narrator feels obliged to specify pantry items, thus suggesting their privileged status. Then, the quotation from Horace totally ridicules the supposed esteem that learning enjoys in the household: it is difficult to imagine that the Latin poet had in mind putting jams and marmalades in a library when he spoke of placing "*lo dulce junto a lo útil*." And so this double-voicing by means of the quotation serves to mock Antonio and the pseudo-intellectual atmosphere in which he was raised. In this way the narrator assures that a sufficient distance will be maintained to facilitate aesthetic appreciation. The reader is not to be caught up in a story or in the personality of the protagonists, but in how the story is told or how characterization is achieved. In the case of Justine, exterior focalization creates the distance; in the case of Antonio, the narrator's voice, as doubled, accomplishes a similar effect.[36]

In addition to using vision and voice to maintain distance between the reader and the characters, the extradiegetic narrator employs the same techniques all but to eliminate any dramatic element from the action. For example, the romantic conflict involving Antonio and Justine, with her uncle as the obstacle, is ripe with potential melodrama. Based on her actions (since we rarely have access to her thoughts and feelings), Justine is apparently torn between her love for Antonio and her obedience to her uncle, who insists that she enter a convent. When the climactic moment of decision arrives, the narrator seems to set the stage for the drama: "Azorín mientras recorren la ancha calle, habla con Justina. Acaso sea esta la última vez que hable con ella; acaso va a quedar rota para siempre esta simpatía melancólica—más que amor—de un espíritu por otro espíritu" (p. 137; "While crossing the wide street, Azorín speaks with Justine. Perhaps it will be the last time he speaks with her; maybe this melancholy—more than love this sympathetic melancholy of one spirit for another—is going to be broken forever"). Reader expectations are foiled, however, for rather than a dramatic scene, we are offered only the narrator's summary: "El diálogo entre Azorín y Justina—entrecortado de largos silencios, esos largos y enfermizos silencios del dialogar yeclano—ha cesado. Y llega *lo irreparable,* la ruptura dulce, suave, pero absoluta, definitiva. Y se ha realizado todo sin frases expresas, sin palabras terminantes, sin repeticiones enojosas . . . en alusiones lejanas, casi en presentimientos, en ese diálogo instintivo y silencioso de dos almas que se sienten y que apenas necesitan incoar una palabra, esbozar un gesto" (p. 138; "The dialogue between Azorín and Justine—interrupted by long silences, those long and sickening silences typical of people from Yecla—has ceased. And the 'irreparable' arrives, that sweet rupture, gentle, but absolute and definitive. And all is realized without expressive phrases, without words, without maddening repetition . . . in distant allusions, in that instinctive and silent dialogue of two souls who feel and hardly need to initiate a word, to feign a gesture"). The potential drama of the moment is sacrificed to the voice of the narrator. And it is not just a question of eschewing a scene in favor of summary; this summary is embellished with irony. The narrative parodies dramatic dialogue—"sin frases expresas, sin palabras terminantes, sin repeticiones enojosas . . . en ese diálogo instintivo y silencioso . . . apenas necesitan incoar una palabra, esbozar un gesto." Such double-voicing with its ironic effect draws attention to the extradiegetic narrator's voice as he subverts the convention of dramatic dialogue, a subversion all the more striking if one considers the emphasis on philosophical dialogues between Antonio and his mentor Yuste. In effect, the philosophical dialogues represent yet another strategy designed to minimize the dramatic element in the novel.

The subversion of drama is not limited to irony and metaphysical discussions, however. After Justine makes her decision to enter the convent, we observe a decline in her physical appearance: "Y su cara está cada vez más blanca y sus manos más transparentes" (p. 172; "And her face grows more and more white and her hands more transparent"), and later: "Justina está pálida; su cuerpo es tenue; sus manos son transparentes; sus ojos miran ávidos" (p. 187; "Justine is pale; her body is frail; her hands are transparent; her eyes have an anxious gaze"). The significance of these signs of physical deterioration is not given until the beginning of Part 2: "Azorín, a raíz de la muerte de Justina, abandonó el pueblo y vino a Madrid" (p. 195; "After the death of Justine, Azorín left the town and came to Madrid"). What is potentially another climactic moment in the plot becomes a subordinate clause explaining a change in the location of the action. Justine's death is anticlimactic. By virtue of the emotional distance thus created, characters and action are subordinated to ideas and to aesthetic expression.

Part 2 reflects a shift not only in setting, but also in focalization. The narrator or the voice we listen to is still extradiegetic, but the vision fluctuates between an external and an internal view, with the latter originating from the eyes of the protagonist. The section begins, then, with Antonio once again the object of focalization as the narrator summarizes the young intellectual's thoughts upon arriving in Madrid: "Azorín ha llegado demasiado pronto para alcanzar estas bienandanzas. Su espíritu anda ávido y perplejo de una parte a otra; no tiene plan de vida; no es capaz del esfuerzo sostenido; mariposea en torno a todas las ideas; trata de gustar todas las sensaciones" (p. 196; "Azorín has arrived too soon to obtain happiness. His spirit wanders here and there, anxious and perplexed; he does not have a purpose in life; he is not capable of a sustained effort; he is like a butterfly flitting around every idea; he tries to enjoy every sensation and experience"). What we are offered here is a summary analysis. We listen and observe from a level beyond the level of the action.

The switch to an interior point of focalization occurs at the very beginning of the second chapter:

> A la derecha, la rojiza mole de la plaza de Toros, destacando en el azul luminoso, espléndido; a la izquierda, los diminutos hoteles del Madrid Moderno, en pintarrajeado conjunto de muros chafarrinados en viras rojas y amarillas, balaustradas con jarrones, cristales azules y verdes, cupulillas, sórdidas ventanas, techumbres encarnadas y negras . . . todo chillón, pequeño, presuntuoso, procaz, frágil, de un mal gusto agresivo, de una vanidad cacareante, propia de un pueblo de tenderos y burócratas. La tarde es tibia y radiante: se sienten los primeros hálitos confortadores de la primavera que llega. El sol baña la ancha vía. Y Azorín camina por ella lentamente, hacia las Ventas. (p. 197)
>
> (To the right, the reddish, massive Plaza de Toros, silhouetted in the splendid, luminous blue; to the left, the small hotels of modern Madrid, in painted splotches, together with walls colored with red and yellow cloth, banisters with vases, blue crystal and green copulas, dirty windows, roofs, alive and black . . . all is sharp, small, presumptuous, insolent, fragile, in an aggressive bad taste, vain and ostentatious, fitting for a town of merchants and bureaucrats. The afternoon is cool and radiant; one feels the first breath of the coming spring. The sun bathes the road. And Azorín walks along it, slowly, towards the Ventas).

The beginning of the passage is visual, with a close if undefined vantage point. As we share the observation with the still anonymous viewer, we are led from an array of brilliant colors to the conflicting drabness and garishness of the city. The vision then gives way once again to the voice as we become listeners rather than viewers—"todo chillón, pequeño, presentuoso, procaz, frágil, de un mal gusto agresivo, de una vanidad cacareante, propia de un pueblo de tenderos y burócratas." With a reference to sensations, we move back inside the viewer, until the voice of the narrator intrudes to reveal that Antonio is the source of what we see. It is a question, then, of the narrator's voice and Antonio's vision. Such a textual strategy creates a bond between character and narrator, but a bond that still allows the narrator to maintain a position of superiority over, and therefore a certain distance from, the character.

The narrator reaffirms his superiority in a very significant way as this second chapter of Part 2 comes to an end: "Y ya en Madrid, rendido, anonadado, postrado de la emoción tremenda de esta pesadilla de la Lujuria, el Dolor y la Muerte, Azorín piensa un momento en la dolorosa, inútil y estúpida evolución de los mundos hacia la Nada" (p. 200; "And now in Madrid, humbled, destroyed, done in by the tremendous emotion of this nightmare of Lechery, Pain, and Death, Azorín contemplates for a moment the painful, useless and stupid evolution of the continents toward Nothingness"). A paradox results from this clear separation between the protagonist, who forms a part of the action, and the narrator, who stands above and removed from it as he comments on the protagonist's state of mind. Yet this summary of Antonio's attitude clearly echoes attitudes already expressed by the narrator himself. As a result, Antonio functions as a vehicle for the narrator, thus representing another example of double-voicing. Even the protagonist's philosophical/aesthetic discussions with his friend Olaiz, which compose the majority of Part 2, assume the function of narrative statements rather than character dialogue. In short, Antonio is but an extension of the narrator's voice in this section.[37]

In addition to his spoken statements, the protagonist's view also identifies him with the narrator. For example, as he walks along the streets of Madrid we recognize a familiar scene:

Aparece un coche blanco, con una cajita blanca . . . Luego, detrás viene otro coche, negro, con una caja negra . . . Pasa un coche fúnebre blanco, pasa un coche fúnebre negro. . . Pasa un coche fúnebre negro, pasa un coche fúnebre blanco . . . vuelven precipitados coches negros, coches blancos . . . Van y vienen coches negros, coches blancos. (pp. 198–200)

(A white coach appears, with a little white box . . . Later, behind, comes another coach, black, with a black box . . . A white funeral coach passes, a black funeral coach passes . . . a black funeral coach passes, a white funeral coach passes . . . they return in haste, black coaches, white coaches . . . They come and go, black coaches, white coaches).

The repetition of black and white contrasts resounds throughout the first section of the novel. In that first section, however, the narrator was the focalizing source. The shift, therefore, from an external viewing position in Part 1 to an internal one here in Part 2 is not designed to change the emphasis of the novel from ideas to characterization. The message implicit in what happens to Antonio in Madrid, in what he says and in what he allows us to see, is double-voiced, since it has more to do with the nature of existence as defined by the narrator than with Antonio's particular personality. In the final analysis, Antonio himself seems to be merely the narrator's textual strategy for demonstrating the "inútil y estúpida evolución de los mundos hacia la Nada."

Part 3 represents a significant change both in the protagonist/narrator relationship and in the narrating voice. Rather than united in a common bond, in this section these two are separated: the protagonist becomes his own first person narrator. Yet as in the previous examples this apparent single voice must be heard as two, therein lying the key to a switch in focus from what is narrated to the act of narrating.

As Part 3 begins and the extradiegetic narrator turns over the narrating duties to the protagonist, he first foregrounds his own narrating instance: "Esta parte del libro la constituyen fragmentos sueltos escritos a ratos perdidos por Azorín. El autor decide publicarlos para que se vea mejor la complicada psicología de este espíritu perplejo" (p. 257; "This part of the book is composed of loose, fragmented writings by Azorín in his spare moments. The author decides to publish them so that one can better see the complicated psychology of this perplexed spirit"). In spite of ostensibly removing himself, the narrator has in effect imposed himself even more; rather than an anonymous voice, he is now a character, the dramatized author of the novel. Furthermore, by announcing that *he* has decided to present the fragments exactly as the protagonist wrote them, the dramatized author makes clear that he is doing so with a very specific purpose in mind: "para que se vea mejor la complicada psicología de este espíritu perplejo." When he served as the focalizing point, the protagonist was in effect an extension of the speaker. Now that the protagonist is going to do his own narrating, a new type of double-voicing comes into play. Every time the protagonist speaks, we know that what he says is meant to be interpreted not merely with his own intention in mind, but also and even primarily with the dramatized author's intention in mind. The protagonist no longer serves as an extension of the dramatized author. In these final sections the two work largely at cross-purposes; they are the conveyers of basically opposing messages.

As Part 3 unfolds and the protagonist narrates his experiences upon returning to Yecla, the message is clear: he is bored by the pettiness of small town politicians and pseudo-intellectuals. He consciously incurs the derision of both types as he not only confesses, but takes pride in his ignorance of local politics and popular commercial writers. He left Madrid to escape its phony intellectual atmosphere, only to find an equally phony atmosphere in his own home town. Up to this point the protagonist's and the dramatized author's messages seem to be the same. Only when the protagonist decides to visit Iluminada, an old friend only briefly mentioned in the first section, do we note a marked difference in the two messages.

Antonio reacts strongly at the first sight of Iluminada after so many years: "Ella se pone roja y yo me pongo pálido. Ella avanza erguida e imperiosa: yo permanezco inmóvil y silencioso. Al aparecer en la puerta la he visto cómo vacilaba, sorprendida, temerosa, durante un segundo; pero ahora ya es la de siempre y la veo ante mí fuerte y jovial" (p. 281; "She turns red and I turn pale. She advances erect and imperious: I remain immobile and silent. When she appeared in the door I saw how she hesitated, surprised, frightened, for a second; but now she is as always, and I see her before me strong and jovial"). Although the contrasts point out her assertiveness as opposed to his passivity, he thinks he notes an indication of insecurity and weakness on her part with the implication that perhaps he has finally found a kindred spirit. But if that is indeed his message, there is another negating message conveyed by the ensuing narrative: "Entonces ella me pone las manos sobre los hombros y me hace sentar en el banco con un vigoroso impulso" (p. 281; "Then she puts her hands on my shoulders and with a powerful shove makes me sit on the bench"). The reader senses a spirit in Iluminada that is totally out of harmony with Antonio's passivity and obsessive soul-searching. In other words, the reader is influenced by the dramatized author's silent voice: his message is "voiced" by his strategy of allowing Antonio to speak for himself.

The suggestion in the previous example that the dramatized author is sending a message in opposition to that of the protagonist is corroborated by Antonio's narration of his attendance at mass with Iluminada: "Ella está jovial como siempre; yo, en estos campos anchos, con este ambiente primaveral, me siento un poco redivivo . . . Entramos en la ermita; Iluminada se pone a mi lado y me hace arrodillar, levantarme, sentarme. Casi a la fuerza, como si se tratara de un muñeco. En el fondo, yo siento cierta complacencia de este automatismo, y me dejo llevar y traer, a su antojo" (p. 283; "She is happy, like always, and I feel revived in this spring-like atmosphere . . . We enter the sanctuary; Iluminada places me at her side and makes me kneel, rise and then sit down. She treats me as if I were a doll. Down deep I feel a certain complacency in this automation, and I allow myself to be led by her whims"). The protagonist declares that he feels "un poco redivivo" and "cierta complacencia," but the reader cannot ignore another voice emerging from the same narration: "me hace arrodillar . . . casi a la fuerza, como si se tratara de un muñeco . . . este automatismo, y me dejo llevar y traer, a su antojo." Although there is one speaker, there are two voices. The message the reader receives is not the one intended by Antonio. Clearly the dramatized author wants his reader to see Antonio as an unsuspecting victim of a domineering woman. And the key to such a message is the dramatized author's preface to this chapter in which he informs us that he is publishing the fragments just as Antonio wrote them. So as he removes himself from the narrative, he also asserts himself; when Antonio speaks, the dramatized author is speaking through him and contradicting the message being sent by the ingenuous protagonist.

The epilogue offers the final manipulation of voice and vision as a strategy for redefining the protagonist (and reader) conventions of the previous century. It consists of three letters addressed to Pío Baroja, all signed with the name of the real author. On the surface, this use of the names of real people seems designed to lend an air of authenticity to the fiction, and in this sense the epilogue would appear to conform to convention. Yet in another and more fundamental sense, such a textual strategy represents a culmination of the overall effort in the novel to break from established conventions as the dramatized author usurps the protagonist's role in the novel.

The vehicle in the epilogue for redefining the protagonist's role is the ostensibly conventional epistolary form: "Querido Baroja: Tenía que ir a Murcia, y me he acordado de que en Yecla vive nuestro antiguo compañero Antonio Azorín. He hecho en su obsequio y en el mío un pequeño alto en mi itinerario" (p. 285; "Dear Baroja: I had to go to Murcia, and I remembered that our old friend Antonio Azorín lives in Yecla. I made in your consideration and mine a brief pause in my itinerary"). By assuming the identity of dramatized author, the narrator reaffirms for himself ultimate authority over the text. In addition, by virtue of this narrative shift in which he is now one of the characters of the fictitious world, he competes for attention with the protagonist; it is now the speaker's reaction to Antonio as much as Antonio himself that serves as the object of attention.

The shift of the spotlight from the protagonist to the dramatized author begins with the latter's arrival in Yecla and his efforts to locate his long-time friend Antonio. At this point the story concerns his search rather than what is happening to Antonio. There is a momentary shift of focus to the protagonist, however, when the dramatized author finally asks a local couple if they can tell him where don Antonio Azorín lives: "—Antonio . . . Antonio—murmura la mujer. —Don Antonio Azorín . . . Don Antonio Azorín ¡Antoñico! Antoñico, el que está casado con doña Iluminada . . . ¡Como decía usted don Antonio!" (p. 286; " 'Antonio . . . Antonio,' murmurs the woman. 'Don Antonio Azorín . . . Don Antonio Azorín.' And then: 'Oh, of course! Antoñico! Antoñico, the one married to Iluminada . . . No wonder I didn't recognize him. You said Don Antonio!' ") This woman, by announcing a new name for Antonio, signals the final phase of his effacement as protagonist of the novel. That process intensifies when the speaker expresses his shock upon hearing that his friend is not only married, but that he has two children: "Y vuelvo a quedarme doblemente estupefacto. Después, repuesto convenientemente, para no inquietar a los vecinos, salgo a la calle y me dirijo a la casa Azorín." (p. 286; "I am doubly stupefied. Afterwards, conveniently having regained my composure so as not to worry the neighbors, I go out to the street and head in the direction of Azorín's house"). Rather than double voicing, this might be called an example of double-imaging. On the one hand we have the implicit image of the once highly respected intellectual and writer, now known only by the pejorative nickname Antoñico, his only claim to fame being that of husband to *Doña* Illuminada. On the other hand we have the verbal self-image of the speaker's shock. The focus of attention is now shifting to the dramatized author as Antonio loses stature, both anecdotally and structurally.

The new focus is even more evident when the dramatized author arrives at the Azorín household and describes what he sees. After first noting the humble furnishings of the house, diapers lying everywhere, two infants crying, and an overweight and unkempt woman attending them, the narrator turns his gaze to the man of the house: "Sentado ante la mesa, está un hombre joven; tiene el bigote lacio; la barba sin afeitar de una semana; el traje, sucio. ¡Es Azorín!" (p. 288; "Seated in front of the table is a young man. He has a thin mustache, an unshaven face and his clothes are dirty. It's Azorín!"). This description—again, the speaker's reaction competing with the image of Antonio for reader attention—inspires a narrative comment underscoring the strategy of making the speaker one of the characters of the novel: "Yo no sé al llegar aquí, querido Baroja, cómo expresar la emoción que he sentido, la honda tristeza que he experimentado al hallarme frente a frente de este hombre a quien tanto y tan de corazón todos hemos estimado" (p. 288; "I don't know how to express, dear Baroja, the emotion I felt, the wave of sadness that I experienced, finding myself face to face with this man whom we all so admired"). The tragedy of the protagonist's personal degeneration tends to assume a secondary importance to the disillusionment experienced by the dramatized author. That disillusionment is particularly relevant to the dramatized (or fictionalized) Pío Baroja as the recipient of these letters: bourgeois values are a particular menace to artists and intellectuals. Society, so the message seems to say, destroys creative willpower, and as Antonio demonstrates, "la falta de voluntad ha acabado por arruinar la inteligencia" (p. 297; "the lack of willpower has finally destroyed his intelligence").[38]

Yet the lesson to the fictionalized Pío Baroja does not end with this warning. If society and women[39] represent the constraints to creative willpower, then art represents a means of transcending those constraints. The idea of art as a liberating force emerges when the dramatized author voices the opinion that Antonio will not remain subjugated to Iluminada forever. He then proposes that a new story could be written entitled, "*La segunda vida de Antonio Azorín*" (p. 300; "The second life of Antonio Azorín"). Since Antonio is his creation, this dramatized author has the license to recreate his character. And even if the same fate eventually befalls the new creation, "¿qué importa? La idea está lanzada, el movimiento está incoado. ¡Y nada se pierde en la fecunda, en la eterna, en la inexorable evolución de las cosas!" (p. 301; "What does it matter? The idea is launched, the movement is underway. And nothing is lost in the fertile, eternal, inexorable evolution of objects!") At this point Antonio is completely effaced as protagonist in the conventional sense of the term. The façade of his supposed reality is stripped away to expose him for what he is: a novelistic simulacrum of a person whose fate is decided by the whims of his author-creator. Artistic creation itself is now the center of the reader's focus.

Because he lacks the will to resist, Antonio Azorín falls victim to the "dolorosa, inútil y estúpida evolución de los mundos hacia la Nada" (p. 200; "painful, useless and stupid evolution toward Nothingness"). Because he still possesses the will to create, the fictionalized J. Martínez Ruiz has found the key to transforming this evolution into the creative force represented by any work of literature. The title itself, *La voluntad,* is therefore also double-voiced. Suggesting the story of the destructive effects of Antonio's lack of volition, the title also signals the creative force behind that story. In short, *La voluntad* redefines the concept of the protagonist by proposing that art itself is the real protagonist of the novel.[40]

In spite of its innovations, *La voluntad* is far from a total artistic success. Most of the innovations in fictional modes are eclipsed by the preponderance of philosophical dialogue. Although in 1902 Martínez Ruiz was interested in novelistic form, his commitment to ideas was obviously greater. Without question he was still searching for a new mode of expression in this his first real novel.[41] The author's reliance on philosophical discussions in the form of dialogue seems to be more of a carry-over from the previous century than an innovation. Significantly, one distinguishing trait of his later masterpiece, *Doña Inés,* is an almost total absence of dialogue.

As the preceding analysis has demonstrated, *La voluntad* represents a more radical break from the conventions of the previous century than does *Camino de perfección.* Especially in the last part of his novel, Martínez Ruiz evinces more of a commitment to exploring new modes of novelistic expression than does Pío Baroja. By effacing the conventional role of the protagonist and foregrounding the creative process of art, *La voluntad* anticipates two of the distinguishing characteristics of vanguard fiction in the 1920s and 1930s: decharacterization and transparent narrating.[42] But *La voluntad* was not the only novel published in 1902 that projected new novelistic concepts. Unamuno's *Amor y pedagogía* is even more radical in its effort to redefine the canons from the previous century.

Amor y pedagogía

As the preceding analysis demonstrated, in *La voluntad* several strategies redefine the concept of the protagonist. Miguel de Unamuno's *Amor y peda-*

gogía also strives to redefine the protagonist, but the redefinition proposed by Unamuno bears little resemblance to Martínez Ruiz's model. In *La voluntad* the focus switches from the fictional world to art itself as Martínez Ruiz proposes to transform art itself into the character of his novel. In *Amor y pedagogía* the fictional world becomes confused with the real world as Unamuno attempts to make the author the character of his own creation. But the key to Unamuno's redefinition of the canons of fiction is his focus on language itself. As a result of his initial effort to challenge the fictional paradigms of the previous century, he creates a hybrid genre that critics to this day have had trouble defining.

"*Amor y pedagogía* is very evidently a literary oddity, even within the work of a writer so determinedly unorthodox as Unamuno."[43] This quotation, taken from a relatively recent article on the novel, could very well serve as a summary of the reception it was afforded by critics upon publication. Generally, reviewers praised *Amor y pedagogía* for its intellectual content but expressed varying degrees of reservation concerning its unorthodox style and structure.[44]

As was the case in *Camino de perfección*, and especially in *La voluntad*, the redefinition of the canons in *Amor y pedagogía* was a result of conscious artistic design; the novel represented a fundamental turning point in Unamuno's novelistic approach. Although his use of the famous terms "oviparous/viviparous" appeared after the publication of *Amor y pedagogía*,[45] by his own admission this novel actually represented his first attempt to write what were to become known as his "nivolas vivíparas."[46] Since both terms were appropriated to convey a new type of novel that represented a radical departure from nineteenth-century realism, *Amor y pedagogía* became a key to the renovation of novelistic techniques beginning at the turn of the century and culminating in what is known as the vanguard fiction of the 1920s and 1930s. Similar in exterior structure to *La voluntad*, Unamuno's novel features a frame consisting of a prologue and, in this case, two epilogues. Critical attention, not too surprisingly, has centered almost exclusively on the framed body, and particularly on the sociological and ontological themes projected there. The frame itself has essentially been ignored. Yet the frame is the source of the most radical attacks on novelistic convention, as it not only confuses the boundary separating reality and fiction but also foregrounds the concept of language itself. It is the logical focal point, therefore, for this analysis.

Directly related to the concept of language in a work of fiction is that of authoritative versus nonauthoritative discourse. Bakhtin, for example, categorically declares that "Authoritative discourse cannot be represented—it is only transmitted" (p. 344). Unamuno, however, creates the illusion in *Amor y pedagogía* that authoritative discourse is represented. He does so by dramatizing or fictionalizing the author of the prologue, who in turn criticizes the author of the novel. Then in the epilogue there is a dramatization or fictionalization of the author of the novel. Since both the author of the prologue and the author of the epilogue are fictional characters, their discourse is not really authoritative. In point of fact, then, dramatization of the authors in the frame of *Amor y pedagogía* challenges the very concept of authoritative discourse and represents a textual strategy designed to underscore the polysemic essence of all discourse.[47]

The story within the frame concerns the attempt by Don Avito Carrascal to become the progenitor of a son whom he would raise scientifically to be a perfect human being. From the beginning his plan seems to be doomed, since he selects the future mother of his progeny inductively rather than deductively. They produce an offspring whom Don Avito names Apolodoro and whose scientific education he entrusts to his philosopher friend Don Fulgencio Entrambosmares. The experiment fails, however, as Apolodoro proves himself to be considerably less than perfect; after being jilted by the woman he loves, he commits suicide. Anecdotally, then, the novel represents an attack on sociological theories that attempt to reduce human existence to formulas. On a deeper level, the framed body confronts the ontological question of dualism and antithesis, of the conflict between form and matter.[48] Yet the frame presents its own ontological question concerning the equivocal essence of language and how it relates to the conflict between fiction and reality.

The prologue, or initial section of the frame, introduces the concept of the equivocal nature of language through a dramatized author.[49] This author, moreover, creates a problem of identity in the initial passage of the prologue: "Hay quien cree, y pudiera ser con fundamento, que esta obra es una lamentable, lamentabilísima equivocación de su autor"[50] ("There are those who believe, and it could be with reason, that this work is a lamentable, a very lamentable mistake by its author"). By employing the words "su autor," the speaker separates himself from the author of the novel. Yet since it is not entirely unusual in normal speech to refer to oneself in the third person, especially when self-criticism is involved, the device here creates only a minor confusion concerning authorial identity. It seems to be merely an author talking about his own work. Very soon, however, who is speaking and with what authority becomes a central issue.

The question of identity and authority becomes crucial when the speaker directs even more severe criticism at the novel: "El capricho y la impaciencia, tan mal consejero el uno como la otra, han debido de dictarle esta novela o lo que fuere, pues no nos atrevemos a clasificarla. No se sabe bien qué es lo que en ella se ha propuesto el autor y tal es la razón de los más de sus defectos" (p. 7; "Caprice and impatience, one as bad an advisor as the other, must have dictated this novel or whatever it is, for we don't dare to classify it. One cannot tell what the author has proposed to do in it, and that's the basis of most of its defects"). If in the initial sentence the separation between the speaker and the author of the work seemed natural, conveying the impression that they are really the same person, this second sentence establishes a clear distinction between them. There is the first-person plural marker ("no nos atrevemos") juxtaposed with the third-person marker ("el autor"). Such shifts in person underscore the distinction between speaker and author; whoever is speaking here clearly does not want his or her identity confused with "el autor" of this ill-conceived work that defies classification. It is a case of one author—the one of the prologue—pitting his authority against that of another author—the one of the novel itself (or the fictional author as he will be called in future references).

The textual strategy just analyzed seems designed to confuse the very issue of authoritative discourse. In what could be considered a direct challenge to Bakhtin's thesis, there is a representation of authoritative discourse—the references to the fictional author of the novel—and then the authority of that representation is undermined by yet another authority.

In an effort to further dialogize or deauthoritize the fictional author, the speaker unwittingly weakens his own authority as he persists in criticizing other techniques of the novel: "Diríase que el autor, no atreviéndose a expresar por propia cuenta ciertos desatinos, adopta el cómodo artificio de ponerlos en boca de personajes grotescos y absurdos, soltando así en broma lo que acaso piensa en serio" (p. 8; "One could say that the author, not daring to express as his own certain outlandish statements, adopts the artificial pose of putting them in the mouths of his grotesque and absurd characters, disguising as a joke what he perhaps means seriously").[51] In exposing the double-voiced essence of character speech, the prologue author unmasks the whole artifice of the verisimilitude of fictional dialogue; characters, we are told, do not speak with their own voices but with those structured by the narrator, who in turn is a creation of the posited author. Every voice in the work of fiction is a refracted authorial voice. And so if on the one hand the exposure of the artifice seems to lend authority to the fictional author—he presumably is at the top of the hierarchy—on the other hand the act of exposing the artifice negates his privileged position; the author of the prologue attempts to supplant the fictional author of the work as the final voice in the novel. Yet it will not have escaped attention that in discrediting the fictional author, the dramatized author of the prologue in effect has subverted his own authority over the text.

What undermines the authority of the voice in the prologue is double-voicing itself; behind the dramatized author of the prologue there must also be another voice. Indeed, when this dramatized author criticizes the novel by maintaining that "the fictional author does not dare to express as his own certain outlandish statements," the characters are not the only vehicles of expression that come to mind; the speaker himself is a discursive device by which his creator alerts the reader to this game of double voices. In other words, the message is not what this speaker says, but what his creator (the posited author of the prologue and the novel as a whole) says through him;

whereas the speaker is criticizing the novel, the posited author is explaining how to read it. When the dramatized author of the prologue speaks, therefore, he projects two voices and two distinct messages.

Just as reality extends beyond visual surfaces, so language should not be interpreted solely on the basis of surface meaning. In reaction to what the previous novelistic generation tried to project, Unamuno here is rejecting the univocal function of language. He is probing beneath the surface and forcing his reader to confront language in all its polysemic and contradictory essence. That essence is never more apparent than when the prologue speaker, praising what he considers one of the novel's few virtues, dramatically turns his argument against himself: "Hay en ella elementos y partes que la hacen recomendable. Y no precisamente por lo que el autor ha querido poner en ella, sino por lo que a pesar suyo no ha podido dejar de poner. Es casi seguro que lo valioso de esta novela es lo que en ella tiene por poco menos que desdeñable su autor, siendo en cambio de lamentar la inclusión de todo aquello otro en que parece haberse esmerado más éste" (p. 13; "In it there are elements and parts that make it recommendable, and not exactly as a result of what the author tried to put into it, but rather as a result of what in spite of himself he has not been able to avoid including. It's almost certain that the value of this novel lies in the parts that the author most disdains, and on the other hand the weakest parts are those on which he placed his greatest efforts"). His message, that language not only serves to communicate what speakers want it to communicate, but that it also expresses what speakers may not even realize they are expressing, applies to his very discourse. The speaker of the prologue in effect is ridiculing himself as he voices his thesis; in criticizing the novel he is unwittingly criticizing his own existence. Indeed, for most readers, the prologue itself, along with the epilogues, are the clearest examples of "todo aquello otro" on which the author seemed to have placed his greatest efforts but that could and should have been omitted. That is to say, the frame does not conform to what readers expect in a work of fiction, and most view it as totally extraneous to the novel, or a type of authorial intrusion.[52] But of course the frame is part of the novel and the author within it is a fiction. In fact all these censoring comments are a game, a textual strategy designed to bring the multiple levels of language and meaning in a work of fiction into the foreground. Each voice is but an artifice behind which the posited author of the work hides; characters and speakers are disguises for the posited author that inevitably refract his true ideas and opinions. And whereas realistic novelists also wear these same masks, they normally do so unconsciously. In his prologue to *Amor y pedagogía,* Unamuno regales his reader with transparent masquerades. As he does so, he assigns an added responsibility to the reader who has been signaled that it is his task to bring into focus the refracted image that is being projected.

The reader's responsibility in the game of fiction is underscored by the dedication that precedes the prologue:

> Al Lector,
> dedica esta obra,
> El Autor. (p. 6)
>
> (The Author
> dedicates this work
> to The Reader.)

Since in effect every piece of fiction published is dedicated to its reader,[53] this dedication once again seems to be designed to make explicit what by convention is implicit. And the fictitious author's awareness of his reader does not pass unnoticed by the speaker in the prologue: "Parece fatalmente arrastrado por el funesto prurito de perturbar al lector más que de divertirle y sobre todo de burlarse de los que no comprenden la burla" (p. 8; "He seems fatally drawn by his ill-fated urge to disturb the reader more than entertain him, and above all to make fun of those who do not understand the joke"). The joke, of course, is the game of fiction itself. The reader who does not recognize that fiction is a game, a verbal illusion of real people and events, becomes the target of the joke; the one who does recognize the game, who sees through the simulacrum, becomes an active participant in it. Yet ultimately the participant may also see the game turn against him as he is forced to recognize the fictional nature of his own existence. Along with the blurring of authorial identities, there is a blurring of the distinction between fiction and reality. As a result, readers also may find themselves characters in the novel.

The similarity between fiction and reality became, after *Amor y pedagogía*, a constant in Unamuno's novels, and in this case it is tied to the common misconception that language is a direct and undistorted reflection of its source. The confusion of authors in the prologue of *Amor y pedagogía* allows the reader to see that language does not lead directly to its source, that every attempt to reach the "real author," whether speaking in biographical or ontological terms, will merely lead to another level of deflected and therefore distorted images.

Whereas the prologue offers a speaker who separates himself from the fictional author of the novel by referring to the latter in the third person, the epilogue complicates the process as a new first-person speaker asserts himself: "Mi primer propósito al ponerme a escribir esta novela fue publicarla por mi cuenta y riesgo, como hice, y por cierto con buen éxito, con mi otra" (p. 203; "My first purpose in writing this novel was to publish it on my own and at my own risk, as I did, and it turned out well, along with my other one"). The referent for "mi otra" would logically be *Paz en la guerra*, the novel that Unamuno published just prior to *Amor y pedagogía*. As a result, the speaker here appears to be Unamuno himself, or the unmasked author of the novel. A subsequent statement, however, casts doubt on such an initial assumption: "Ya yo por mi parte, previendo que la obra resultara demasiado breve para los propósitos del editor, la hinché mediante el prólogo que la precede y con tal objeto se lo puse, mas ni aun así parece que he llegado a la medida" (p. 203; "Then taking it on myself, since I knew that the work would be too brief for the purposes of the editor, I enlarged it by adding a prologue, but even with that I didn't achieve the necessary length"). Since this speaker admits to being the author of the prologue, he must be the same person who speaks in the prologue. Yet as already noted, that speaker referred to the author of the novel in the third person. This person, or voice, not only speaks in the first person, but makes it clear that he is also the author of the novel to which the prologue was added. The voice here in the epilogue, therefore, seems to represent some kind of fusion of the dramatized author of the prologue, and the fictional author of the novel referred to in the prologue. As a result, the distinction between fiction and reality is further blurred, and the question of linguistic and philosophical sources becomes even more problematic.

An even greater confusion between fiction and reality occurs when the epilogue speaker mentions a familiar name: "Sólo quiero desarrollar brevemente un principio que oí asentar en cierta ocasión a don Fulgencio" (p. 206; "I only want to develop briefly a principle that I heard Don Fulgencio posit on a certain occasion"). Later he refers to the same person when justifying his response to commercial pressures: "He aquí la doctrina que bajo la inspiración de mi don Fulgencio he excogitado para explicar y justificar los móviles mercantiles y de negocio que me incitan a poner estrambote a una obra de arte" (p. 210; "Here is the doctrine that, inspired by Don Fulgencio, I have thought up in order to explain and justify the business motives that inspire me to put an additional couplet on a work of art"). Since Don Fulgencio is one of the fictitious characters from the novel, this speaker must also exist in the realm of fiction. Rather than master of his creations, he is merely their equal. If the author exists on the same ontological level as the characters, then so does the reader. The implication of author/character/reader equality is corroborated by the speaker himself when he explains why he did not change the ending in which Apolodoro kills himself, even though he considered doing so: "Y en cuanto a cambiar de desenlace no me era posible; no soy yo quien ha dado vida a don Avito, a Marina, a Apolodoro, sino son ellos los que han prendido vida en mí después de haber andado errantes por los limbos de la inexistencia" (p. 211; "And, as for changing the ending, it was not possible; I am not the one who has given life to Don Avito, to Marina, to Apolodoro, but rather they have taken life within me after having wandered along the borders of nonexistence"). If this passage is justifiably cited by critics as evidence of Unamuno's change from creating traditional or oviparous characters to autonomous or viviparous ones, it also deserves to be cited for what it implies vis-à-vis the concept of voice in the novel. If author/character/reader exist on the same ontological level, no one speaks with innate authority. The author in the conventional sense of the word ceases to exist.

If we compare the prologue to this epilogue, it becomes clear that Unamuno is deauthorizing himself, that he is in effect erasing his own authorial identity. The speaker of the prologue, the author to whom that speaker refers, and the first-person speaker of the epilogue all pretend to be the author. Yet each identity is false; the verbal construct cannot become the object it represents; all characters, even those posited as authors, are fictions; all voices are doubled. Nevertheless, the game goes on, for following the epilogue we have another section entitled, "Apuntes para un tratado de cocotología," and yet another author in Don Fulgencio.

Initially the voice of the treatise seems clearly that of Don Fulgencio. Very quickly there is the hint of another voice, that of the fictional author, since the neologism, "cocotología," tends to mock Don Fulgencio's scientific pretensions—the term refers to the art of making paper birds, a popular children's pastime in Spain.[54] To add to the irony implicit in the term itself, this section is subdivided into pseudo-scientific categories (Preamble, History, Justification of Method, Etymology, etc.), along with diagrams demonstrating how to make paper birds. This pseudo-scientific format further mocks Don Fulgencio and his devotion to analytical approaches to reality. The same problem occurs here as within the novel: Don Fulgencio alternately appears as a buffoon and as an apparent spokesman for the real author's ideas.[55]

The change from buffoon to spokesman occurs rapidly. In the section entitled Etymology, the speaker develops a theory on the role of names in our existence. First he traces the Latin root of the noun *nombre*: "NOMEN GNOMEN es la raíz misma, GNO—del verbo gnosco, cognosco, conocer, y que esta raíz GNO es hermana de la raíz GEN—de signo, engendrar; nombrar es conocer y conocer es engendrar, nombrar es engendrar las cosas" (p. 242; "NOMEN GNOMEN is the root, GNO—of the verb *gnosco, cognosco, conocer,* and this root GNO is related to the root GEN—of sign, engender; to name is to know, to meet and to know is to engender, to name is to give life"). Since it is well known that Unamuno was a professor of Greek and Latin, this linguistic lesson seems to bear a clear imprint of the real author. But beyond the Latin is also a philosophical link between this character's words and Unamuno's ideas, since the capacity of language to create reality is one of the philosopher's favorite themes. For example, in *Del sentimiento trágico de la vida* Unamuno declares, "El lenguaje es el que nos da la realidad, y no como un mero vehículo de ella, sino como su verdadera carne, de que todo lo otro, la representación muda o inarticulada, no es sino esqueleto"[56] ("Language is what gives us reality, and not as a mere vehicle of it, but as its true flesh, of which everything else, the unarticulated or mute representation, is nothing but the skeleton"). Now we have the supposed author of this treatise echoing the same idea: "No ya sólo el lenguaje común todo, sino la ciencia y la poesía mismas, no son otra cosa, si lo examinas, que un exacto nombrar" (p. 243; "It is not only a question of all common language, but science and poetry themselves are only a process of naming"). Behind the voice of the fictitious character we hear the refracted voice of Unamuno, or more accurately, one of his voices. Paradoxically, therefore, we seem to be closer to the real Unamuno when the represented voice belongs to someone else; Don Fulgencio sounds more like the author than the voices identified as those of the author. Yet we dare not fall too easily into the trap of simplification. With an end to the treatise on paper birds, the fictional author's voice reasserts itself:

> Aquí termina bruscamente el manuscrito de los "Apuntes para un tratado de cocotología" del ilustre don Fulgencio, y es lástima que este nuestro primer cocotólogo, el primero en orden de tiempo y de preminencia, no haya podido llevar a cabo su proyecto de escribir en definitiva un tratado completo de la nueva ciencia. Me ha asegurado que piensa refundirla en su gran obra de *Ars magna combinatoria,* y aun parece ser que fue la cocotología lo que primero le sugirió tan considerable monumento de sabiduría. (p. 267)
>
> (Here the manuscript of "Notes for a Treatment of Cocotology," by the illustrious Don Fulgencio, ends abruptly. It is a shame that our first "cocotologist," first in terms of both chronology and eminence, was not able to finish his project of writing a definitive treatise on the new science. He has assured me that he is considering rewriting it in his great *Ars magna combinatoria,* and it seems that it was cocotology that first suggested such a considerable monument of knowledge to him.)

Once again, the ironic tone transforms Don Fulgencio into a buffoon. The represented author, therefore, in effect mocks what seems to be the clearest spokesman for the real Unamuno.

From the preceding analysis it is clear that the point is not which voice is the real Unamuno, for the textual strategy of multiple authorial voices suggests that the voice is never the actual person. The novel projects a refracted image of the author behind it because that author exists in a different medium. Whether in fiction or in real life, moreover, humans rely on verbal masks as an inevitable expression of their manifold personalities. The polysemy of language, as a reflection of the multiplicity of human personality, is one of the messages conveyed by *Amor y pedagogía*.[57]

Amor y pedagogía's most significant break from the realist tradition involves switching the focus from the object represented to the means of representation; rather than placing the emphasis on what is simulated, it shifts attention to the medium for simulating, to language. And by confusing the issue of authorial source, it challenges the very concept of logos. The author becomes his own character. The producer is in effect the product. Reality is a fiction. Yet Unamuno's game also turns against itself. A dramatized author is just as much a simulacrum as is a character from realistic fiction. No matter how many authorial representations Unamuno projects, he is always the one responsible for the projections, his voice is doubled in the fictional voice behind which he hides. Although the source may be indeterminate, at least in the world of fiction, there is always a source.

The emphasis on authorial representations in *Amor y pedagogía* anticipates what will become in *Niebla* and "Nada menos que todo un hombre" a whole new concept of a fictional protagonist. From an attempt in the former novel to make the author the protagonist, Unamuno will in the latter works transform the protagonists into their own authors. To arrive at that point, he first felt the need to foreground language as a distorted rather than direct reflection of its source. He achieves this new focus in *Amor y pedagogía* by projecting conflicting authorial figures in the frame of the novel.

Whereas Unamuno's textual strategies are more radical than those of Baroja and Martínez Ruiz, Valle-Inclán represents perhaps a more subtle but ultimately even more subversive attack on the prevailing novelistic canons. In *Sonata de otoño,* the final novel from 1902 to be analyzed here, Valle-Inclán transforms Christian terminology into textual signs. Anticipating the semioticians' celebration of the pleasure of the text, Valle-Inclán in *Sonata de otoño* transforms aesthetic sensuality into a sybaritic Eucharist.

Sonata de otoño

While in *Amor y pedagogía* Unamuno creates contradictory authorial masks, Valle-Inclán in his *Sonata de otoño* offers yet another strategy for redefining the prevailing conventions of fiction. Valle-Inclán transforms the Christian concepts of confession, repentance, and salvation into signs pointing at the glory of the text rather than of God. On the story level *Sonata de otoño* concerns the Marqués de Bradomín's confessional memories of his seduction of a dying lover, and then of his cousin on the same night the lover dies. On the discoursing level these incidents project a message concerning the seducing effect of the narrating act. The advantage the marquis takes of the two women is nothing compared to that which the fictional narrator of this novel takes of reader expectations; the women in the story are seduced, but reader expectations, founded on a long Judeo-Christian tradition, are violated.

The violation of reader expectations in *Sonata de otoño* begins with the confessional form of the novel and the concept of a confession itself. It embodies a conventional expectation, perhaps even stronger in Catholic societies, that when past deeds of moral misconduct are recounted they are done so in the spirit of repentance. And even though the epigraph to the memoirs that characterizes the protagonist as "feo, católico y sentimental"[58] ("ugly, Catholic, and sentimental") should give the reader pause, until proven otherwise reader expectations still incline toward the convention. The memoir form of

Sonata de otoño, therefore, emphasizes from the beginning the convention of the confessional mode as a stratagem for subverting that very convention.[59]

The narration of the memoirs encompasses several temporal levels. First is the narrative present in which the first-person narrator, the Marqués de Bradomín, confesses in his advancing years his past peccadillos. From this narrative present the narrator reverts to the past, to a specific autumn where the primary story line is set. His former lover, Concha, writes begging him to return to the Palacio de Brandeso, where she lies on her deathbed. The marquis returns to the palace and in spite of Concha's physical condition and moral scruples—she is a practicing Catholic, married, and has two young daughters—they resume their torrid love affair interrupted two years earlier. In response to Concha's urgings, the marquis recalls the even more distant past of their shared childhood experiences and of family histories passed along to them. The events of the primary story line culminate with Concha's visit one night to the marquis's room, where, despite her protestations that the next day she must go to confession, she succumbs to his persistence and they make love. The sexual passion is too much, and Concha dies. When he then goes to the room of his cousin Isabel to tell her the tragic news, he promptly seduces her as well, after which he carries the body of Concha back to her own room, where it is discovered the next day. The marquis's role in Concha's demise is never known, except of course to his reader, who apparently shares with the narrator a privileged viewing position in the narrative present. Yet the supposed privileged position of the reader is precisely the primary target in this novel's efforts to subvert conventional reader expectations.

The reader's time-honored prerogative is undermined by a series of textual contradictions. The marquis presents himself in the past as an innocent victim, yet in the present he appears as a cynical opportunist; his past self expresses nostalgia for a bygone era, while his present narrating being mocks that same era.[60] As a result of such contradictions, narrator and reader are adversaries rather than the confidants of conventional storytelling; readers must resolve the discrepancies on their own, as it were, and the key to the resolution is provided by the posited author's voice. That voice, although always present, rings most clearly when the narrator resorts to Christian terminology while narrating his escapades.

The contradiction between victimization and exploitation arises with the narrator's first sojourn into the distant past, to a past more remote than the time of his return to the dying Concha. This journey is inspired by the mention in her letter of the Palacio de Brandeso, which conjures up images of shared childhood experiences: "Yo recordaba vagamente el Palacio de Brandeso, donde había estado de niño con mi madre, y su antiguo jardín, y su laberinto que me asustaba y me atraía. Al cabo de los años, volvía llamado por aquella niña con quien había jugado tantas veces en el viejo jardín sin flores" (p. 90; "I vaguely remembered the Palace of Brandeso, where as a child I had been with my mother, the old garden, and the labyrinth that frightened and attracted me. After a period of time I would return, beckoned again by that child with whom I had played so many times in the old flowerless garden"). The reference to his mother and the confession of his childish fear of and attraction to the labyrinth communicate vulnerability. When the speaker then notes that he always returned at the request of Concha, "con quien había jugado tantas veces," a metonymic relationship is established between the labyrinth and Concha; suddenly his vulnerable masculinity contrasts with Concha's insidious femininity.[61] Apparently, he would have his reader believe, she bewitched him when they were children and at least to some extent has continued to do so: "Al cabo de los años, volví llamado por aquella niña."

The suggestion that Concha not only manipulated the marquis when they were children but also wishes to continue her seductive enchantment over him during their reunion in the palace soon becomes a dominant theme. Her strategy, the narrator suggests, consists of appealing to his nostalgia as she continually refers to their common childhood: "Como la pobre Concha tenía el culto de los recuerdos, quiso que recorriésemos el Palacio evocando otro tiempo, cuando yo iba de visita con mi madre, y ella y sus hermanas eran unas niñas pálidas que venían a besarme, y me llevaban de la mano para que jugásemos, unas veces en la torre, otras en la terraza, otras en el mirador que daba al camino y al jardín" (p. 100; "Poor Concha, obsessed with memories, insisted that we wander through the palace calling forth the memories of other times. Other times when I used to come with my mother to visit, she and her sisters were pale girls who would come forward to kiss me, and to lead me by the hand to play, sometimes in the tower, other times on the terrace, or in the bay window that looked out over the road and the garden"). Rather than simply narrating a nostalgic journey into childhood innocence, the speaker seems intent on portraying these "niñas pálidas" as manipulative; their frailty seems to have been a source of power over him. It would appear, then, that when Concha employs her waning strength to urge the marquis to relive the past, she does so with the motive of sustaining her domination over him. Her strategy of recapturing the past, reinforced by her current delicate state of health, seems to be crowned with success when the narrator recalls how, finally, "Yo, como un niño abandonado y sumiso, apoyé la frente sobre su pecho y entorné los párpados, respirando con anhelo delicioso y triste aquel perfume de flor que deshojaba" (p. 118; "Like an abandoned and submissive child I pressed my forehead to her chest, half closed my eyelids, breathing in passionately and sadly that perfume of a dying flower"). Yet if Concha apparently triumphs in these passages, the scenes the speaker presents are not successful in characterizing himself as victim. Whether by design or by accident, the speaker undermines his purpose of representing himself as an innocent victim in childhood and later as an adult.

The failure on the part of the speaker to convince the reader that he was seduced by, rather than the seducer of Concha, results from the tone and atmosphere he conveys. The concept of violator and violated is attenuated, if not negated, by the sensual ambience that permeates the entire narrative. If as a child the marquis was indeed seduced by Concha, either literally or figuratively, as the adult narrating these incidents he is obviously relishing the act of their verbal recreation. Whereas the apparent message concerns violated innocence, the more persuasive one glorifies sensuality as both a physical and narrative experience. As a result, the meanings, emanating from the same source, contradict one another. Yet they are not the only contradictory messages the speaker conveys.

In addition to what the narrator suggests concerning his childhood relationship with Concha, the same type of conflicting meanings arise in reference to the marquis's memories of the family histories. These histories, from both the Brandeso and Bradomín families, portray the power and dominance of the aristocracy and the lifestyle that went with that privileged social position:

> Yo recordaba nebulosamente aquel antiguo jardín donde los mirtos seculares dibujaban los cuatro escudos del fundador, en torno de una fuente abandonada. El jardín y el Palacio tenían esa vejez señorial y melancólica de los lugares por donde en otro tiempo pasó la vida amable de la galantería y del amor. Bajo la fronda de aquel laberinto, sobre las terrazas y en los salones, habían florecido las risas y los madrigales, cuando las manos blancas que en los viejos retratos sostienen apenas los pañolitos de encaje, iban deshojando las margaritas que guardan el cándido secreto de los corazones. ¡Hermosos y lejanos recuerdos! (p. 99)
>
> (I vaguely remembered that ancient garden where the secular myrtle formed the four coats of arms of the founders, around an abandoned fountain. The garden and the palace had that palatial and melancholy air that in the past served as a setting for the pleasant life of elegance and love. Below the foliage of that labyrinth, on the terraces and in the rooms, laughter and madrigals had flourished, when the white hands, which in the old portraits delicately hold lace handkerchiefs, slowly removed the petals from the daisies that held the secrets of a lover's heart. O those beautiful and distant memories!)

The nostalgic tone in this case responds to the passing of an era, to the loss of a past grandeur. Yet at the same time that the protagonist in the past seems to lament the decline of that aristocratic era and the power it represented, there is a hint of bitter irony in the form of another voice mocking the very values the protagonist seemed to champion. The key to this second voice is stylistic exaggeration. Especially in the second half of the passage, the imagery is overstated: "habían florecido las risas y los madrigales . . . las manos blancas . . . sostienen apenas los pañolitos de encaje, iban deshojando las margaritas que guardan el cándido secreto de los corazones." As a result of this exaggeration, the passage becomes double-voiced and conveys two conflicting attitudes, one of nostalgia, the other of mocking disdain—the latter culminating in the final exclamation: "¡Hermosos y lejanos recuerdos!"[62] One possible explanation for these conflicting messages involves the differences between the protagonist of the past and the narrator of the narrative present. That is to say, it is possible that the marquis in the distant past did feel nostalgia toward his aristocratic history, whereas in the narrative present he feels only disdain for the same heritage. In short, he is now a changed man. Rather than an accurate reflection of his present being, it is possible that the protagonist of the past is a distorted image of what the speaker now is.

The implication that the protagonist is a misshapen rather than an exact semblance of the speaker is reinforced as Concha leads the marquis on a tour of the palace. As they make their way from room to room, they see their own refracted images staring at them in the form of portraits of their ancestors, whose countenances are further deflected by mirrors:

> Los salones con antiguos cortinajes de damasco, espejos nebulosos y retratos familiares: Damas con basquiña, prelados de doctoral sonrisa, pálidas abadesas, torvos capitanes. En aquellas estancias nuestros pasos resonaban como en las iglesias desiertas, y al abrirse lentamente las puertas de floreados herrajes, exhalábase del fondo silencioso y oscuro, el perfume lejano de otras vidas. Solamente en un salón que tenía de corcho el estrado, nuestras pisadas no despertaron rumor alguno: Parecían pisadas de fantasmas, tácitas y sin eco. En el fondo de los espejos el salón se prolongaba hasta el ensueño como en un lago encantado, y los personajes de los retratos, aquellos obispos fundadores, aquellas tristes damiselas, aquellos avellanados mayorazgos parecían vivir olvidados en una paz secular. (p. 100)

> (The rooms with antique curtains, cloudy mirrors, and family portraits: skirted ladies, prelates with doctoral smiles, pale abbesses, stern captains. Our steps resonated in the rooms just as they do in deserted churches, and as the iron doors with their flower designs slowly opened, one inhaled in the silent and dark interior the distant perfume of other lives. Only in the salon that had a cork floor did our footsteps fail to awaken a murmur from the past: They seemed like the footsteps of phantoms, silent and without echo. In the mirrors the salon stretched as if in a fantasy into an enchanted lake, and the people in the portraits, those founding bishops, those sad damsels, those shriveled heirs, all seemed to exist forgotten in a secular peace.)

As the protagonist obediently followed Concha on that tour of their common family history, we receive no indication that he reacted in any way other than she intended: with nostalgic pride in their ancestry. The narrator in his narrative present, on the other hand, projects an ironic and censoring voice. Rather than nostalgia, the narrator makes the reader experience a Goyaesque decadence whose shadow extends from the distant past to encompass Concha and the marquis in their stroll through the rooms of the palace. This shadow with its comforting yet debilitating effect is suggested above all by the reference to the mirrors: "En el fondo de los espejos el salón se prolongaba hasta el ensueño como en un lago encantado." The reader should see the marquis and Concha as refracted images of their ancestors and of a social system based on the illusion of privilege and power—an illusion represented above all by Florisel, the obsequious and opportunistic servant assigned to the marquis by Concha.[63] The narrator's message, therefore, concerns decadence. As a result, Concha's illness and impending death form a metonymic link with the sociopolitical system of which she is a part.

But again the social meaning conveyed by the narrator's voice does not seem to correspond to the reading experience. In spite of signaling decadence, the narrative descriptions revel to such an extent in that decadence that sensual pleasure overshadows social concerns. Thus we see another conflict of meaning as the narrating self seems to oppose his past experiencing self.

Rather than a difference in attitude expressed by the protagonist on the one hand and the narrator on the other, another textual incompatibility paradoxically involves their similarity. In spite of the confessional mode implicit in the memoirs of a man described as "feo, católico y sentimental," the speaker conveys a glaring absence of remorse and repentance for any past sins. The protagonist of the past may be excused the display of blasphemous attitudes, but reader expectations dictate that the speaker in the present clearly and forcefully disavow those same attitudes. By failing to do so, the narrator contradicts his supposed mission in narrating.

As the theme of religious blasphemy emerges, our initial impression is that the narrator does indeed wish to separate himself from the protagonist. That desire is expressed by means of a temporal distance between the speaker in his narrative present and the protagonist of the past. For example, after receiving Concha's letter asking him to come be with her in her final hours, the marquis goes to visit her sisters, who are nuns living in a convent. When they confirm the gravity of Concha's illness, the protagonist enters a church, ostensibly to pray. Yet rather than concentrating on spiritual communion, he immediately focuses his attention on two women dressed in mourning who are praying at the various altars:

> En las manos pálidas de la que guiaba, distinguía el rosario: Era de nácar, y la cruz y las medallas de plata. Recordé que Concha rezaba con un rosario igual y que tenía escrúpulos de permitirme jugar con él. Era muy piadosa la pobre Concha, y sufría porque nuestros amores se le figuraban un pecado mortal. ¡Cuántas noches al entrar en su tocador, donde me daba cita, la hallé de rodillas! Sin hablar, levantaba los ojos hacia mí indicándome silencio. Yo me sentaba en un sillón y la veía rezar: Las cuentas del rosario pasaban con lentitud devota entre sus dedos pálidos. Algunas veces sin esperar a que concluyese, me acercaba y la sorprendía. Ella tornábase más blanca y se tapaba los ojos con las manos. ¡Yo amaba locamente aquella boca dolorosa, aquellos labios trémulos y contraídos, helados como los de una muerta! (p. 87)

> (In the pale hands of the one leading I could see the rosary; it was made of mother-of-

pearl, and the cross and medals were of silver. I remembered that Concha prayed with a similar rosary and she didn't like me to play with it. She was very pious, poor Concha; she suffered so, because she saw our love as a mortal sin. How many nights when I went to her boudoir where we had agreed to meet I found her kneeling! Without speaking she would raise her eyes towards me, signaling me to be silent. I would sit down on the sofa and watch her pray: The beads of the rosary passed with slow devotion through her pale fingers. Sometimes I would not wait for her to finish and would sneak up on her, surprising her while she prayed. She would turn even more pale and cover her eyes with her hands. Oh how I loved that painful mouth, those trembling clutching lips, as cold as death!)

The protagonist's sadistic irreverence is appalling; not only does he fail to respect Concha's devotion, but he takes special pleasure in violating it. And her anguished reaction to this sacrilege becomes an erotic stimulation for him with necrophilic connotations that presage their final meeting. In this initial scene Concha is violated, and although the subsequent narrative suggests that she felt more personal guilt than outrage from the violation, the episode seems designed to elicit shock and indignation from the reader. In other words, the speaker here seems to invite his reader to join him in severely censoring his past being, from which he separates himself temporally and emotionally by virtue of the past tenses of the verbs.

The elicitation of reader reaction is even more pronounced when the speaker describes the protagonist's arrival at the palace, where he is reunited with Concha. Again, erotic pleasure is expressed in religious terminology. Although bedridden, Concha insists on getting up and dressing when he arrives. He, in turn, insists on lending a helping hand:

Yo la vestía con el cuidado religioso y amante que visten las señoras devotas a las imágenes de que son camaristas. Cuando mis manos trémulas anudaron bajo su barbeta delicada, redonda y pálida, los cordones de aquella túnica blanca que parecía un hábito monacal, Concha se puso en pie, apoyándose en mis hombros. . . . La llama al surgir y levantarse, poní en la blancura eucarística de su tez, un rosado reflejo, como el sol en las estatuas antiguas labradas en mármol de Pharos. (pp. 92–93)

(I dressed her with the religious care and love with which devout women dress the images that they tend. When my trembling hands tied under her delicate, round, and pale barbette, the cords of that white tunic that looked like a monastic habit, Concha stood up, supporting herself with my shoulders. . . . The flame, rising and falling, cast upon her eucharistic pallor a pink reflection, like the sun in the ancient marble statues of the Pharaohs.)

The scene is described as though it were a religious ceremony celebrating communion, Concha's role being that of icon, or perhaps of the consecrated bread. The protagonist sees her as an inanimate object or as a symbol of sacrifice,[64] and that abstraction seems to inspire his emotion ("mis manos trémulas"). The emotion, moreover, is a sacrilege, for it conveys erotic passion rather than religious transcendence. In fact, throughout the novel the protagonist's attraction to Concha is expressed in religious terminology. For example, he notes that she had "la apariencia espiritual de una santa muy bella consumida por la penitencia y el ayuno" (p. 96; "the spiritual appearance of a saint consumed by penitence and fasting"); "Concha tenía la palidez delicada y enferma de una Dolorosa" (p. 97; "Concha had the delicate paleness and sickness of the Suffering Virgin"); "parecía una Madona soñada por un monje seráfico" (p. 99; "she looked like a Madonna dreamed up by a seraphic monk"). Such abuse of Christian terminology to communicate sexual attraction seems designed to alienate the reader from the protagonist. That process of alienation culminates when Concha comes to the marquis's room on the fateful night.

In the final scene between the two lovers, the blasphemous tone reaches a new height. Concha's explanation that she must go to confession the following morning and therefore cannot make love elicits the following reaction from the marquis: "Entonces, levantándome con helada y desdeñosa cortesía, le dije: —¿De manera que ya tengo un rival?" (p. 120; "Then, rising with cold and disdainful courtesy, I said: 'And so, I have a rival?' ") When he then threatens to leave the palace the next morning, Concha acquiesces. The dialogue of their love play, moreover, continues the sacrilegious tone as the Marquis complains when Concha strikes him with her unbraided hair: "—¡Es el azote de Dios! . . . —¡Azótame, Concha! . . . ¡Azótame como a un divino Nazareno! . . . ¡Azótame hasta morir! (p. 121; " 'It is the whip of God!' . . . 'Whip me, Concha! . . . Whip me like a divine Nazarene! . . . Whip me until I die!' ") Finally Concha responds to his heretical baiting: "—Me das miedo cuando dices esas impiedades . . . Sí, miedo, porque no eres tú quien habla: Es Satanás . . . Hasta tu voz parece otra . . . ¡Es Satanás!" (p. 121; "You frighten me when you say these impieties . . . Yes, I am afraid because you are not the one speaking: It is Satan . . . even your voice seems to be another . . . It is Satan's!") With the emphasis on an immediate scene or dialogue, the narrator seems to have all but removed himself from the narrative. Yet his presence is felt, even though his voice in this case is absent; superimposed on the characters' spoken words is the narrator's silent voice. This silent voice by now has lost any suggestion of censorship. By virtue of its repetition and especially of this climactic scene, the blasphemous vocabulary cannot be attributed solely to the protagonist's attitude; the narrator's silence, his failure to disavow explicitly any sympathy with the protagonist's attitude, constitutes his voice of complicity. If Concha heard Satan's voice when the protagonist spoke, the reader should hear that echo as the speaker narrates the episode. However, the similarity of attitude between protagonist and speaker is not limited to echoes. On occasion the narrator voices his attitude directly to his reader.

Perhaps the most significant direct statement by the narrator to his reader occurs early in the novel. As the two lovers recall the past, the marquis remembers when they parted two years ago. Because her mother was opposed to their relationship, Concha begged him at that time to leave her. This memory creates a hiatus in their conversation:

> Ninguno de nosotros quiso recordar el pasado y permanecimos silenciosos. Ella resignada. Yo con aquel gesto trágico y sombrío que ahora me hace sonreír. Un hermoso gesto que ya tengo un poco olvidado, porque las mujeres no se enamoran de los viejos, y sólo está bien en un Don Juan juvenil. ¡Ay, si todavía con los cabellos blancos, y las mejillas tristes, y la barba senatorial y augusta, puede quererme una niña, una hija espiritual llena de gracia y de candor, con ella me parece criminal otra actitud que la de un viejo prelado, confesor de princesas y teólogo de amor! (p. 94)
>
> (Neither of us wanted to remember the past and we remained in silence. She, resigned. I, with that tragic gesture that brings a smile to my face now. It was a beautiful gesture that now is a little rusty, because women don't fall in love with old men, and such a gesture only works for a young Don Juan. If only, in spite of my gray hair, my sad eyebrows, and my senatorial beard, a young girl could still love me, a spiritual child, graceful and innocent. With such a girl the only attitude that does not strike me as criminal is that of an elderly prelate, a confessor of princesses and a love theologian!)

With the switch to the present tense, "que ahora me hace sonreír," the narrator directly addresses his reader. His initial words, then, seem to indicate that he is ridiculing his past self and his former histrionic gestures. But then he conveys a different meaning when he calls it a beautiful gesture that, because of his age, is no longer effective. Finally, with an unmistakable touch of satanic irony, he yearns for the love of a young woman, "una hija espiritual," for whom he would play the role of a spiritual father who specializes in love theology. Rather than a repentant man disdaining his former ways, what emerges here is essentially the same marquis that we see in the past. Indeed, the ironic tone results precisely from the Christian terminology echoing the protagonist's attitude, which culminates with the narrator's fantasy of being a "teólogo de amor." If the protagonist was diabolical in his sacrilegious attitudes and words, the same must be said for the narrator. He therefore clearly rejects and even mocks Judeo-Christian values. As such, he directly challenges the projected reader, who has implicitly been indoctrinated in accordance with the values being ridiculed.[65]

Judeo-Christian values are further assaulted when, after narrating Concha's death immediately followed by the seduction of Isabel, the narrator asserts: "Yo soy un santo que ama siempre que está triste. La pobre Concha me lo habrá perdonado allá en el cielo. Ella, aquí en la tierra, ya sabía mi flaqueza" (p. 122; "I am a saint who is always in love, who is always sad. Poor Concha, there in heaven, probably has forgiven me. Here on earth, she already knew my weaknesses"). That outrage is followed by a grotesque description of how, when carrying Concha's body back to her own room, her hair became entangled in a hinge and he had to rip it loose. Finally, the narrator once again piously addresses the reader:

> Todavía hoy el recuerdo de la muerta es para mí de una tristeza depravada y sutil: Me araña el corazón como un gato tísico de ojos lucientes. El corazón sangra y se retuerce, y dentro de mí rie el Diablo que sabe convertir todos los dolores en placer. Mis recuerdos, glorias del alma perdidas, son como una música lívida y ardiente, triste y cruel, a cuyo extraño son danza el fantasma lloroso de mis amores. ¡Pobre y blanco fantasma, los gusanos le han comido los ojos, y las lágrimas ruedan de las cuencas! (p. 123)
>
> (Even today the memory of the dead woman has a depraved and subtle sadness for me: It tears at my heart like a consumptive cat with flashing eyes. My heart bleeds and twists, and inside me the Devil, who knows how to transform all pain into pleasure, laughs. My memories, lost glories of my soul, are like a livid and burning music, sad and cruel, to whose strange sound dances the weeping ghost of my loves. Poor white ghost, the worms have eaten your eyes, and tears flow in the sockets.)

This confession certainly eliminates any possibility of moral superiority on the part of the narrator vis-à-vis the protagonist. In addition, it betrays the motive behind his memoirs: "glorias del alma perdidas." That is, rather than repentance, his narration represents a glorification of his cult to pleasure. The only difference between narrator and protagonist is age and sexual prowess; the narrator is limited now to narratively reliving his past exploits, since he is beyond the age of achieving any new ones. He has played with his reader's expectations, hinting at his real motive but still leaving room for convention to prevail, until this final section of the novel, when the mask of piety is completely removed. Much in the manner in which the protagonist sadistically seduced Concha and Isabel, the narrator has seduced the reader.[66] Of course, the narrator uses the only power of seduction remaining to him, the act of sensually recreating his "glorias del alma perdidas."

If the narrator follows the picaresque formula of a *burlador* (seducer) toying with his own version of *vuestra merced* (your honor), what can be said about the posited author? We must first return to the contradiction concerning the protagonist's violated innocence and the speaker's glorification of sensuality. It is precisely this sensual dimension that conveys yet another level of double-voicing, in this case that of the posited author behind the narrator. The implied message of the posited author, however, is more difficult to decode than that of the narrator. Its focal point, nevertheless, must deal with pleasure in its various forms. That being the case, he would seem to reject the whole idea of victimization. Pleasure, whether in the guise of childhood fantasies, adult sexuality, or textual games, is its own justification. One is led to assume, therefore, that in the mind of the posited author the only victims are those who fail to join in the game, which in the case of his posited reader (as distinguished from the narrator's projected reader) would mean those who fail to appreciate the pleasure (irony) of the text.

The message concerning pleasure picks up further nuances in the contradiction concerning the protagonist's nostalgia for a particular glorious past and the narrator's criticism of the values represented by that past. The narrator's suggestion of decadence, in which Concha signals a moribund sociopolitical system, is also double-voiced. Again, the mood of sensuality tends to overshadow the social message, drawing the reader's attention to verbal artistry, to an impression of art for art's sake. The dominant message, therefore, is aesthetic rather than social: the textual creation of decadence is really an invitation to take a vicarious bite of the forbidden fruit.[67] Yet it is not a case of one reading in conflict with another, but of a fusion of the two. To render effective the message that society is decadent, art must transform that decadence into an aesthetic experience.[68] To do so, art must be privileged over all else in the text.

This emphasis on pure aesthetics implies a certain contradiction. In the final analysis, the excessive glorification of sensuality in *Sonata de otoño* undermines itself; the textual experience of sensuality as an end in itself paradoxically points at extratextual reality[69] and at a society devoid of any values capable of supplementing and enriching sensuality. In the very process of negating the narrator's social message, the posited author seems to be affirming it. In this sense, *Sonata de otoño* contradicts itself as an inevitable reflection, refracted of course, of a society characterized by contradiction.

The posited author's voice, however, is not limited to the doubled echo. In the epigraph mentioned earlier, he speaks without a refracting medium and in doing so distinguishes himself from the narrator: "Estas páginas son un fragmento de las 'Memorias Amables', que ya muy viejo empezó a escribir el Marqués de Bradomín. Un Don Juan admirable. ¡El más admirable tal vez! Era feo, católico y sentimental" (p. 2; "These pages are fragments of 'Fond Memories,' which, already at an advanced age, the marquis started to write. An admirable Don Juan. Maybe the most admirable! He was ugly, Catholic and sentimental"). In his very perceptive analysis of the *Sonatas*, Amado Alonso notes that Valle-Inclán's Don Juan is totally lacking in the spiritual dimension that characterizes the conventional Don Juan figure in literature.[70] That in this epigraph, therefore, the marquis is called an admirable Don Juan, "¡El más admirable tal vez!" implies a statement concerning the whole concept of confession, repentance, and salvation. Seen within the context of what happens in this novel and in the *Sonatas* in general, it is obvious that no Christian confession, no sign of Christian repentance, and no apparent justification for Christian salvation exists. These Christian terms, then, have been transformed—subverted—into textual signs; confession in this context equals a pretext for narrating, repentance is equated with the loss of physical sexual prowess, and salvation is provided by the pleasure of the text—in the act of writing for the posited author, and in the act of reading for his posited recipient.

As I have demonstrated, Valle-Inclán freely borrowed from other literary models, not to copy them but to transform if not subvert them.[71] In *Sonata de otoño* that process of subversion also includes a parody of the romantic conventions. For example, the narrator makes the following comment when recalling his departure from the palace for a short trip:

> Y nos besamos con el beso romántico de aquellos tiempos. Yo era el Cruzado que partía a Jerusalén, y Concha la Dama que le lloraba en su castillo al claro de la luna. Confieso que mientras llevé sobre los hombros la melena merovingia como Espronceda y como Zorrilla, nunca supe despedirme de otra manera. ¡Hoy los años me han impuesto la tonsura como a un diácono, y sólo me permiten murmurar un melancólico adiós! Felices tiempos los tiempos juveniles. (p. 109)
>
> (And we kissed with the romantic kiss of those times. I was the crusader leaving for Jerusalem, and Concha the lady crying in her castle in the moonlight. I confess that while I carried on my shoulders that long Merovingian-style hair like Zorrilla and Espronceda, I never knew any other way to take my leave. Now the years have imposed a deacon's bald crown on me, and I can only murmur a melancholy adiós! Happy are the times of youth.)

The narrator caricatures not only himself, but Concha as well. Both appear as comical distortions of the romantic hero/heroine tradition. As a result, the final words of the novel, which recreate the protagonist's anguish after the death of Concha, convey parodic implications: "¿Volvería a encontrar otra pálida princesa, de tristes ojos encantados, que me admirasen siempre magnífico? Ante esta duda lloré. ¡Lloré como un Dios antiguo al extinguirse su culto!" (p. 124; "Will I ever again find a pale princess, with sad and enchanted eyes, who will always admire me? Doubting this, I cried. I cried like an ancient God whose cult has just passed on"). As he strives to create a new cult, the posited author feels obliged to subvert a competing one from the past. Indeed, the *Sonatas* serve as a vehicle for deifying art, for expressing the literary experience in eucharistic terms. The posited author's blasphemy, therefore, far exceeds that expressed by the protagonist or the narrator. After all, they are mere refractions of his real voice. The message of the real voice is far too revolutionary for the likes of the "feo, católico y sentimental" Marqués de Bradomín.

In general, the *Sonatas* have been maligned more than praised. Critics, and I believe with justification, much prefer Valle-Inclán's later *esperpentos,* often citing their closer ties to social reality.[72] Yet the preceding critical focus based on Bakhtin's concept of double-voicing does reveal that *Sonata de otoño* has a closer tie to social reality than has generally been recognized.[73] The same would hold true for the other *Sonatas*. What distinguishes them from their precursors of the previous century is the degree to which that tie is refracted. Realism, of course, attempts to minimize the refraction and indeed to create the illusion that there is none, that the sign and what the sign stands for are one and the same. Of the four 1902 novels analyzed here,

Sonata de otoño represents the most radical rejection of the signifier-signified canon of the previous century. Consequently, it most presages what came to be labeled vanguard fiction in the 1920s and 1930s.

The conscious effort on the part of these four novelists to renovate Spanish fiction in 1902 left an imprint of change on that genre still visible today. Pío Baroja, in *Camino de perfección,* forged a trail away from mimetic renditions of reality, a trail that was eagerly followed by most of his own and the subsequent generation of novelists. José Martínez Ruiz, in *La voluntad,* also demonstrated subjective realism as a viable alternative for novelistic representation, along with new concepts of action and character that were to become distinguishing characteristics of the so-called new art. Miguel de Unamuno, in *Amor y pedagogía,* turned the spotlight on language itself as he began a personal trajectory that would redefine the author/character relationship and blur the boundary between fiction and reality, two more techniques whose traces we can detect in the generations that followed him. Finally, Ramón del Valle-Inclán, in *Sonata de otoño,* provided the formula for foregrounding art itself that would become the very motto for the new artists. Collectively, therefore, these four novels represent the point of departure for the renovating process of Spanish fiction in the twentieth century. The subsequent chapters demonstrate how some of the major techniques initiated in 1902 evolved as the century progressed.

2 1916

In the field of fiction, the second decade of the twentieth century represents something of a hiatus for the members of the Generation of '98. As noted in the Introduction, although Baroja was the most productive of the group, he chose a more traditional path after his early novels, and therefore his later works did not represent innovations to prevailing canons. Immediately after *La voluntad,* Martínez Ruiz wrote two novels, *Antonio Azorín* (1903) and *Confesiones de un pequeño filósofo* (1904), and then until the 1920s dedicated himself almost exclusively to writing nonfiction. Valle-Inclán, in addition to the other three *Sonatas* and some collections of stories, published, between 1902 and 1909, the trilogies *La guerra carlista* and *Comedias bárbaras* (although the final play of the latter, *Cara de plata,* did not appear until 1923). In the second decade his major works, other than drama, were the book of essays, *La lámpara maravillosa* (1916), and the account of his visit to the French trenches during the war, *La media noche: Visión estelar de un momento de guerra* (1917). Of the four novelists who initiated the revolution of 1902 in fictional modes, then, only Unamuno reached his artistic peak in the second decade of the century.

The pause in fictional innovations from 1910 until 1920 may reflect what many argue was the termination of the Generation of '98. Yet if one adheres to the technical definition of a literary generation, it is possible to argue that it does not end until its members die. Literary historians, nevertheless, tend to agree that the sociopolitical atmosphere that determined the nature of the Generation of '98 began to alter by mid-decade, and by 1919 the generation itself had definitively ended.

If the beginning of the sociopolitical change can be pinpointed to a single year, 1914 would seem to be the logical date. Not only did that year mark the beginning of World War I, but it also heralded the emergence of a new literary generation in Spain. The Generation of 1914, or "novecentismo" (nine-hundredism), headed by José Ortega y Gasset, included among its members Pérez de Ayala, Benjamín Jarnés, and Ramón Gómez de la Serna.[1] (Ortega, Jarnés, and Gómez de la Serna are generally identified with the vanguard movement, of course.) This new generation is popularly considered to have been more politically active, more European, more optimistic, and in the field of literature, more innovative than the generation it followed. Yet even in the first categories mentioned, the distinctions tend to be overstated. Especially in their early years, the members of the Generation of '98 were very political and often advocated radical social change.[2] As for their alleged provincialism, no less a figure than Rubén Darío referred to the literary contributions of the Generation of '98 as "la universalización del alma española" (universalizing the Spanish soul).[3] Whereas Ortega's group may have been more optimistic politically, that optimism does not manifest itself in the quality or quantity of fiction its members published in the second decade. Indeed, of the four mentioned above, only Ortega and Pérez de Ayala wrote works between 1910 and 1919 that are generally included among their major contributions. Finally, then, the novelistic innovations appearing in the second decade and credited to the new generation represent extensions and refinements of techniques already exhibited by the previous generation. In short, although a new group of important writers did emerge during the teens, with the exception of Ortega and Pérez de Ayala, that group did not assert itself until the following decade. Rather than marking the end of one generation and the beginning of a completely new one, in the field of fiction the years 1910 through 1919 represent a period of assimilation. The older novelists, again excepting Unamuno, tended to experiment with other genres, developing new techniques that they would eventually integrate into their earlier poetics. The new group, by way of contrast, was undergoing an apprenticeship in which imitation was more visible than innovation.

The two key figures of the second decade of the century, therefore, are Unamuno and Pérez de Ayala. They each produced works during the period that rank among their major contributions, and which demonstrate the common link between the old and new generations. We will now, therefore, examine two novelettes that appeared in 1916, one written by Unamuno, the charter member of the Generation of '98, and the other by Pérez de Ayala, a member of the so-called Generation of 1914 but sometimes also included with the Unamuno group. In the case of Unamuno we will trace a personal trajectory that extends from *Amor y pedagogía,* through *Niebla,* to "Nada menos que todo un hombre." With Pérez de Ayala, on the other hand, the line of contact is indirect. We will analyze how the textual strategies he applies to "La caída de los Limones" reveal the imprint of his immediate predecessors from the Generation of '98.

"Nada menos que todo un hombre"

As noted in the preceding chapter and according to Miguel de Unamuno's own statements, his approach to fiction changed radically after writing his first novel, *Paz en la guerra.* Whereas when he wrote that novel he was, in his own words, an "oviparous novelist"—he accumulated details over a period of time which in turn allowed him to "hatch" his characters—after *Paz en la guerra* he became a "viviparous novelist"—the characters were not hatched but born live; they became independent from the creative authority of the author.[4] The most dramatic example in which the reader participates in the process of a character becoming independent from his creator is *Niebla* (1914). In "Nada menos que todo un hombre," on the other hand—initially published just two years after *Niebla*—the reader participates in the result of such a process, that is, in the previously established freedom of the Unamunian character. It should be understood, moreover, that the character's freedom is really the illusion of autonomy. Yet since fiction by definition deals with illusion, that of character autonomy is no less valid than the one we commonly label *realism.*

If *Amor y pedagogía* represents Unamuno's apprenticeship in the process of freeing his characters from his own creative authority, he achieves the title of craftsman with the work that immediately follows. In the famous confrontation that occurs in Chapter 31 of *Niebla,* Augusto Pérez goes to Salamanca to inform Unamuno of his decision to kill himself. As everyone remembers, the fictional Unamuno denies Augusto permission, and Augusto's subsequent death leaves several unanswered questions concerning fictional authority. Augusto himself raises some of these questions in his reply to Unamuno after the latter points out to him that as a protagonist, he is a mere fictional being. Augusto then counters, "—No sea, mi querido don Miguel—añadió—, que sea usted y no yo el ente de ficción, ni vivo ni muerto" ("'It could be, my dear Don Miguel,' he added, 'that it is you and not I who is the fictional being, neither alive nor dead'").[5] Augusto may be stretching the point when he contends that Unamuno is more fictitious than he, but certainly the Unamuno appearing in Chapter 31 is *as* fictitious as Augusto. That being the case, creation and creator exist on the same narrative level, representing equal narrative authority. That is to say, one does not speak with any more hierarchical privilege than the other. As a result, when the fictitious Unamuno insists that Augusto's death was "por mi libérrimo albedrío y decisión" (p. 17; "by my own free will and decision"), we have no more reason to accept his word than we do that of Augusto's landlady, who insists, "Lo de mi señorito ha sido un suicidio y nada más que un suicidio. ¡Se salió con la suya!" (p. 160; "My young master's death was a suicide and only a suicide. He got what he wanted"). What is revolutionary about *Niebla,* then, is that because the source of fictional truth has been removed, the reader has no way of knowing what or who is responsible for Augusto's death. The issue of fictional truth becomes even more crucial in "Nada menos que todo un hombre," for here the protagonist himself determines the reality of the novel. Before examining how the protagonist assumes such authority over the text, a word is in order concerning the concept of fictional truth itself.

Briefly stated, fictional truth is that part of a work of fiction that we accept without challenge. For example, when the narrator tells us at the beginning of *Niebla* that Augusto put his hand out his door to see if it was raining, we accept the "reality" of that act even though we know that Augusto Pérez himself is a fiction. Yet we do not suspend our disbelief in the face of everything we read in a work of fiction. We only do so, according to Martínez Bonati, in the case of mimetic language, that is to say, in the case of what is commonly called narration—the basic narrator's discourses concerning the events of the novel. At times, again according to Martínez Bonati, the basic narrator can delegate his role as the source of veracity to a character by establishing the character as a spokesperson for the narrator's views; if the narrator ever reclaims his authority or contradicts his personage, however, he immediately achieves credibility over the character. In other words, when personages speak they do not automatically achieve reliability, whereas the narrator, when narrating, does.[6] As we just saw in *Niebla,* however, this source of fictional truth enjoyed by the narrator can be undermined, and the process of undermining it constitutes the essence in that novel of the assault on prevailing novelistic canons. In the case of "Nada menos que todo un hombre," the product rather than the process of undermining the narrator's authority makes the novel such an intriguing aesthetic experience. What for Augusto Pérez was the end of his search for an escape from the mist, for a means of authenticating his existence,[7] is the point of departure for Alejandro Gómez. Alejandro is intent primarily on authenticating others' existence.

The episode most dramatically demonstrating Alejandro's role as creator of others' reality concerns an alleged affair between Alejandro's wife Julia and the count of Bordaviella. The "facts" as determined by the narrator's mimetic language are skimpy at best. Julia is tormented by self-doubts because her husband refuses to tell her that he loves her. As a result, "La pobre mujer se obstinaba en provocar celos en su marido, como piedra de toque de su querer, mas no lo conseguía" ("The poor woman persisted in provoking her husband's jealousy, as a means of proving his love, but to no avail").[8]

With an eye to goading Alejandro into a display of jealousy, she begins to encourage the visits of the count to her home. For his part, the count, who is seeking solace from an unhappy and passionless marriage, declares in unequivocal terms his amorous intentions. Over a period of time Julia, out of frustration over Alejandro's lack of concern, begins to listen more intently to the count's overtures, and "sobre todo a hacer ostentación de la amistad ante su marido" (p. 125; "and above all to make a show of their friendship in front of her husband").

That is nearly all the factual information the narrator provides concerning the episode between Julia and the count. As to whether an affair occurred, the reader, essentially in the same position as the husband, is all but forced to depend on the equivocal nature of character dialogue for determining what really happened. Yet if the reader, in the face of a lack of factual evidence, looks for circumstantial evidence to determine the reality of the episode, Alejandro rejects that approach from the beginning: "¡Yo no vivo de apariencias, sino de realidades!" (p. 119; "I do not live by appearances, but by realities!") What follows in the novel serves to define his concept of reality and to demonstrate how he imposes that definition on others.

Alejandro's method for imposing his own ontological view begins in a totally implausible manner. According to the narrator, "Vino a aumentar la congoja de la pobre Julia el que llegó a descubrir que su marido andaba en torpes enredos con una criada zafia y nada bonita" (p. 123; "The discovery that her husband was involved with an uncouth and not very pretty maid increased Julia's anguish"). In spite of the narrator's factual statement, when Julia accuses Alejandro of being unfaithful, he adamantly denies it and in fact counters with his own accusation: "¡Bueno! ¡La neurastenia! ¡Y yo que te creía en camino de curación!" (p. 123; "Great! Neurasthenia! And I believed you were on the road to being cured"). Alejandro does not deny the affair—in fact, he admits it in claiming that it has no importance—but rather refuses to concede that he has been unfaithful to his wife. This type of rationalization, along with the exaggeratedly sexist justification he offers Julia—"Siempre gallina, amarga la cocina" (p. 123; "Chicken every day ruins the appetite")—completely undermines Alejandro's credibility with the reader. He is not the type of person one tends to trust. Yet this very lack of credibility, along with his male arrogance, constitutes textual strategies designed to underscore the authority he ultimately achieves. No matter how unacceptable his rationalization when he insists that Julia is crazy in accusing him of infidelity, or how offensive his male chauvinism when justifying his affair with the servant, his cognitive approach and his personality are destined to dominate the text as the episode of Julia and the count develops.

Julia's frustration intensifies in the face of the complete indifference with which Alejandro reacts to the count's daily visits to their home. Finally, when she suggests to her husband that he should no longer consent to the count's visits and he counters that she, not he, is consenting to them, Julia cannot contain herself and shouts: "¡Pues no he de consentirlo, si es mi amante! Ya lo has oído, mi amante. ¡El michino es mi amante!" (p. 125; "Well, why shouldn't I consent, if he is my lover! Now you have heard it, my lover. The little kitten is my lover!") This confession, which seems to affirm categorically a sexual affair between Julia and the count, is dismissed by Alejandro: "¡Llegarse a creer que tiene un amante! ¡Es decir, querer hacérmelo creer! ¡Como si mi mujer pudiese faltarme a mí! ¡A mí! Alejandro Gómez no es ningún michino; no conseguirás lo que buscas, no conseguirás que yo te regale los oídos con palabras de novela y de tes danzantes o condales. Mi casa no es un teatro" (p. 126; "To reach the point of believing that you have a lover! I mean, to try to make me believe it! As if my wife could be unfaithful to me! To me! Alejandro Gómez is no kitten; you will not get what you want, you will not get me to regale your ears with literary or tea-time or aristocratic dialogue. My house is not a theater"). If at the beginning the reader is inclined to agree with Alejandro that the confession is Julia's desperate stratagem to make her husband jealous, the incredibly egotistical explanation that he offers—that *his* wife could not be unfaithful to *him*—cancels the reader's initial response. In fact, if anything, the reader now wants to believe Julia; yet in view of what the narrator has indicated, trusting her word is difficult at best. As a result, the reader does not know what or whom to believe: a suspect confession or an absurdly egotistical apologia. In short, at this point in "Nada menos que todo un hombre," the only reality is the impossibility of knowing what is real and what is mere appearance.

In an obvious attempt to impose his own rendition of Julia's avowal of adultery, Alejandro gathers two psychiatrists and the count in his home and then brings Julia to testify before the group. When Alejandro begins by explaining that his wife is suffering from the hallucination that she is having an affair with the count, Julia offers an immediate response:

> —¡Sí, es mi amante!—le interrumpió ella—. Y si no que lo diga él.
> El conde miraba al suelo.
> —Ya ve usted, señor conde—dijo Alejandro al de Bordaviella—, cómo persiste en su locura. Porque usted no ha tenido, no ha podido tener ningún género de esas relaciones con mi mujer.
> —¡Claro que no!—exclamó el conde. (p. 127)

> ("Yes, he is my lover!" she interrupted. "And if you don't believe me, let him speak up."
> The count was looking at the floor.
> "Now you see, Count," said Alejandro to the man from Bordaviella, "how she persists in her insanity. Because you have not had, nor could you have had, any type of these relations with my wife."
> "Of course not!" exclaimed the count.)

Since this is obviously a climactic scene in the novel, the reader looks for a key in the dialogue to the real version of the story. In doing so, he is inclined to dismiss Alejandro, whether he could be right or not, just because his egotism is so exasperating. Attention is then directed to the discourses of other characters as a possible source of the truth.

Julia, of course, is the first one to consider, but given her obsession with making her husband jealous, the reader must continue to suspect her confession, which with its defiantly boastful tone is really not even a confession. In short, rather than serving as spokeswoman for the truth, she may well be a source of lies. If we have reason to suspect Julia of lying, we are virtually certain that the count is guilty of the same thing. If there is a key to the truth here, though, it seems to be the count. He is obviously so frightened of Alejandro that when he agrees with the latter's explanation that nothing could possibly have occurred between him and Julia, the reader assumes the opposite. Very likely his lie points at the truth, and corroborating the count are two other liars. The psychiatrists compromise their ethics by declaring Julia insane, even though they are persuaded that she is sane, so as to free her from her husband. In hypocritically confirming Alejandro's assertion, they pretend to be denying it. Accordingly, the reader is faced with the contradictory essence of language. Discourse refracts rather than reflects reality; the spoken word constitutes a medium of lies, a mere appearance of truth.[9]

There is yet another dimension to the contradiction. If on the one hand the count and the psychiatrists apparently reveal the truth by lying, they also abdicate their own reality by accepting, although hypocritically, Alejandro's. They transform themselves into nonbeings.[10] When, therefore, Alejandro says to the count earlier, "usted no ha tenido, no ha podido tener ningún género de esas relaciones con mi mujer," in effect he was right. Julia's affair was not with a man, but with a simulacrum of a man, a mere phantasm. In short, the affair was not real, but a fiction. After being deceived initially by the discourses of the count and the psychiatrists, or by the appearance of reality, the reader finally realizes that up to this point in "Nada menos que todo un hombre" only Alejandro speaks with the authority capable of defining the reality of the text.

Alejandro's authority is immediately corroborated by the only character in the text who could do so: Julia. After having been committed to an insane asylum by the psychiatrists, she begins to feel that she is really losing her mind. She calls Alejandro, declaring, "Sí, tienes razón, Alejandro, tienes razón; he estado loca, loca de remate. Y por darte celos, nada más que por darte celos, inventé aquellas cosas. Todo fue mentira. ¿Cómo iba a faltarte yo? ¿Yo? ¿A ti? ¿Me crees ahora?" (p. 130; "Yes, you are right, Alejandro, you're right; I have been crazy, totally crazy. And it was all to make you jealous, only to make you jealous, that I invented those things. Everything was a lie. How was I going to deceive you? I? Deceive you? Do you believe me now?") Although it still could be argued that Julia is lying in order to be released from the insane asylum, Alejandro soon persuades her and the reader that what she is now saying is the truth.

The evidence that Alejandro offers consists of reminding her of a conversation that occurred shortly after they were married. Julia asked him at that time if, as it was rumored, he had murdered his first wife. He recalls that he answered by asking her if that is what she believed, and she remembers replying, "Que no lo creía, que no podía creerlo" (p. 130; "I did not believe it, I could not believe it"). Alejandro in turn answers: "Pues ahora yo te digo que no creí nunca, que no pude creer que tú te hubieses entregado al michino ése. ¿Te basta?" (p. 131; "And now I'll tell you that I never believed you, I refused to believe that you could have been with that kitten. Now are you satisfied?"). The explanation is sufficient for Julia, and it should also be for the readers, especially if they take care to analyze the verb tenses. When Julia says, "no creía, que no podía creerlo," the imperfect tense of the verbs communicates her inability to believe such a thing. That is to say, perhaps because of her love for him she had no control over her reaction; she was simply unable to accept what people said. When, on the other hand, Alejandro says, "no creí, que no pude creer," the preterit tenses indicate that he refused to believe. In his case, then, it is a question of will power, of a conscious rejection. As a result, if he as the husband refuses to believe in the infidelity of his wife, in effect there is no infidelity. After all, who other than the offended person has a right to decide what is an offense? Reality, in short, responds to what one wills it to be, and everything else is mere appearance.

Julia's confession that her affair with the count was a lie may itself have been a lie when she said it, but if so, that lie is now the unequivocal truth, thanks to Alejandro. When later, therefore, the count recants his denial made before Alejandro and tries to force Julia to admit that they were lovers, she devastates his feeble attempt to reclaim his reality:

—Pero, Julia . . .
—¿Qué? ¿Vuelve usted a las andadas? ¿No le he dicho que estaba entonces loca?
—A quien le van a volver ustedes loco, entre su marido y usted, es a mí . . .
—¿A usted? ¿Loco a usted? No me parece fácil . . .
—¡Claro! ¡El michino!
Julia se echó a reir. Y el conde, corrido y abochornado, salió de aquella casa decidido a no volver más a ella." (pp. 136–37)

("But, Julia . . ."
"What? Are you starting on that business again? Didn't I tell you that I was crazy?"
"The person who is going crazy, thanks to you and your husband, is I . . . "
"You? Crazy? I don't think that is possible . . . "
"Of course! The kitten!"
Julia began to laugh. And the count, embarrassed and flushed, left the house knowing that he would never return to it.)

Julia now not only corroborates Alejandro's reality but also joins him in creating it. Together they have usurped the role of the posited author to offer their own definition of *realidad íntima* (intimate reality), one of Unamuno's favorite expressions. As a result, the reader has no alternative but to suspend his disbelief and accept their definition, for a failure to do so would constitute a rejection of the fictional truth of the novel.

Although originally published independently, "Nada menos que todo un hombre" was later added to the collection entitled, *Tres novelas ejemplares y un prólogo.* As the prologue to the collection makes clear, will power, or *querer ser,* is the central theme of each of the works. The preceding analysis has demonstrated that will power is more than a theme in "Nada menos que todo un hombre." Alejandro not only persuades Julia that one creates one's own reality and that of others through an act of will, but he also shows how a character can create the fictional truth for the work in which he or she appears. A worthy heir of Augusto Pérez, Alejandro preempts the posited author's authority and determines the fictional truth of the novel. And Alejandro does not need to resort to a dramatic confrontation with a fictitious author to do so. After all, he is no mere character in the conventional sense of the word; he is "nada menos que todo un hombre." Just as the two negatives affirm rather than negate—*nada* really signifies *algo,* and *menos* equals *más,* in this expression[11]—Alejandro is something more. He is "todo un hombre," one capable of creating his own, Julia's, the count's, the psychiatrists', and even the reader's reality. Alejandro Gómez thus redefines the concept of a fictional character and at least to some degree that of nonfictional beings.

Julia, by virtue of learning from Alejandro's lesson, also is transformed into a creator, and Alejandro is forced to confess: "Soy yo tuyo más que tú mía . . . ¡Julia! ¡Julia! ¡Mi Diosa! ¡Mi todo!" (p. 131; "I belong to you more than you belong to me . . . Julia! Julia! My Goddess! My everything!") Later he will identify himself as "¡Nada más que tu hombre . . . , el que tú me has hecho!" (p. 140; "Only your man . . . the one you have created!")[12] Whereas Alejandro seems to be surrendering his autonomy by admitting that he is Julia's creation, he merely culminates what Augusto Pérez began back in Salamanca; he definitively proclaims the Unamunian characters' freedom from their fictitious author. Certainly Augusto Pérez would be proud.[13]

But there is a contradiction inherent in the liberty of these fictional beings. After freeing themselves so that they can create one another, the two have no alternative but to destroy themselves, because if they do not destroy themselves, if they are alive when the novel ends, one would have to conclude that the posited author determined their destiny; only by killing themselves can they remain free of their creator—and so the contradiction. In the novel the characters achieve autonomy from their creator only to find themselves imprisoned by the textual reality that they themselves have created. They can will their own deaths, but they cannot transcend the fictional world in which they exist. Their "voluntad" is now limited to a "noluntad" (p. 17). Alejandro's body at the end is both "desangrado y ensangrentado" (p. 141; "bled and bloodied"). Creation begets destruction. Freedom leads to enslavement. Reality is fiction. The contradictions, moreover, do not end here.

Unamuno's novels are unquestionably highly subjective, and for that reason they have been severely criticized. Detractors complain that the author speaks every time a character should be speaking; Unamuno does not write novels, he writes essays awkwardly disguised as novels. As a result, the novelist most intent on freeing his characters from authorial control stands accused of totally subjugating them. His textual strategies turn against themselves. He cannot still the echo of his doubled voice; his strategies amplify the very authorial sound they are designed to silence. In his efforts to erase his structural presence in "Nada menos que todo un hombre," the posited author amplifies even more clearly his audio presence. He cannot escape the web of contradictions he has spun, perhaps because in the final analysis those contradictions are what define reality not only in the fictional text called "Nada menos que todo un hombre," but also in the other text we call existence.

The year after the publication of the story of Alejandro and Julia, Unamuno offered *Abel Sánchez,* followed by a whole series of other works in which characters struggle against each other and their creator in search of absolute autonomy. That trajectory toward character autonomy can be seen as culminating with *Cómo se hace una novela* (1925), a work that totally challenges generic classifications. Some consider it an essay, while others defend it as a novel about writing a novel.[14] If one accepts the latter definition, it tends to complete a circle leading back to *Amor y pedagogía* and the novelist as the protagonist of the novel. Yet the very polemic over the generic classification of *Cómo se hace una novela* reflects how Unamuno's trajectory led him to an extreme that could no longer serve as a model for himself or others. Indeed, he returned to a more conventional form with his *San Manuel Bueno, mártir* (1932). To find the pattern that he imprinted on Spanish fiction of the 1920s and 1930s and on his own works just prior to *Cómo se hace una novela,* one must look, therefore, to *Amor y pedagogía, Niebla,* and "Nada menos que todo un hombre." Those three works reveal the formula for his attempt to redefine the prevailing concept of a fictitious character. In the same year Pérez de Ayala, on the other hand, offers a totally different model for his contribution to the new fictional art.

"La caída de los Limones"

For some literary historians, Ramón Pérez de Ayala represents one of the cornerstones of the Generation of 1914, while others consider him more a building block of the Generation of '98. Whatever architectural metaphor one employs to classify him vis-à-vis the two literary generations, Pérez de Ayala ranks as one of the most important innovators of Spanish fiction in the early twentieth century. Although his first important contribution to a new concept of novelistic form, *Novelas poemáticas de la vida española,* was not published until 1916, the roots of that work can be traced to the rebellion of 1902 against the nineteenth-century paradigm.[15]

Pérez de Ayala's contribution to the renovation of Spanish fiction, moreover, is not limited to his *Novelas poemáticas. Belarmino y Apolonio* (1921), *Tigre Juan* (1924) and its sequel, *El curandero de su honra* (1926), and *El ombligo del mundo* (1924), all qualify as innovative works of fiction that contributed to a redefinition of that genre.[16] Yet the *Novelas poemáticas* represent not only his personal transition as a novelist, but also the development of a whole new subgenre.[17] Both chronologically and aesthetically, these novelettes take us one significant step closer to what is popularly labeled vanguard fiction.

The most obvious structural characteristic of the work is the use of a poem to introduce each chapter.[18] In general terms, the poems project a parodic atmosphere: mythic in "Prometeo," epic in "Luz de domingo," and fairy tale in "La caída de los Limones."[19] The function of the poems, however, is not limited to parodying literary genres. The juxtaposition of poems and narratives in these novelettes is yet another example of refraction. The introductory poem serves to present a theme and tone, sometimes serious but usually humorous, and the narrative offers a variation on that theme and tone; whatever is projected in the poem is mirrored in the narrative but in a deflected form. The posited author's voice, therefore, emerges from the relationship between the message of the poem and that of the narrative. It is really a case of double refraction; the narrative refracts the message of the poem, and the combination of the poem and the narrative refract the posited author's voice. Although the process applies to each novelette, it achieves its most complex effect in "La caída de los Limones."[20]

The anecdote of "La caída de los Limones" concerns a powerful provincial *cacique* family and its political and moral decline. The only male heir to the family name, Arias, with the help of his constant companion Bermudo, brutally rapes a young woman and then murders her and her mother.[21] When circumstantial evidence implicates the man to whom his sister Dominica is engaged, an ambitious young lawyer attracted by the Limón family's political power, the fiancé is arrested for the crime. After months of witnessing his sister's suffering, Arias finally confesses. He and his accomplice Bermudo, the mentally retarded son of Arias's own wet nurse, are condemned to death for the murder. Upon his release from prison, the fiancé promptly breaks his engagement to Dominica. The events surrounding the execution are told by a first-person narrator who is staying in the same boardinghouse where Dominica and Arias's other sister, Fernanda, come to witness the administration of the death penalty. That first-person narrative frames the body of the text, which in turn is narrated in the third person and recounts the past events leading up to the time of the execution.

The initial poem introduces the framing scene of the sisters' arrival at the boardinghouse:

Ayer eran dos rosas frescas,
blancas y bermejas,
como leche y fresas.
Hoy son dos pobres rosas secas,
de carne marchita y morena.
Ayer, espinas por defuera,
como adorno y para defensa.
Hoy, en el corazón las llevan
clavadas, como duras flechas.
Todos se humillaban a olerlas.
Ahora, todos las pisotean.
¡Ay, las dos pobres rosas secas
que ya todos las pisotean!
¡En qué paró tanta lindeza![22]

(Yesterday they were two fresh roses,
white and red,

like milk and strawberries,
Today they are two poor, dry roses,
stained and brown.
Yesterday, thorns around the outside,
adornment and defense.
Today, they wear them pierced in their heart,
like sharp arrows.
All humbled themselves to smell them.
Now, everyone tramples them.
Oh, those poor dried-up roses
that everyone now tramples!
Oh, how such beauty came to an end!)

The poem has a disconcerting effect because it does not fall into the conventional mode of what is considered good lyric poetry. First, the rhyme scheme of e-a for every verse creates a monotonous and simplistic effect. In addition, this could be considered a textbook example of forcing a central image, in this case the time-honored rose. The similes, "rosas frescas . . . leche y fresas" and "rosas secas . . . carne marchita y morena" have a prosaic, even cookbook ring to them. Equally "unpoetic" are the verses, "Todos se humillaban a olerlas. / Ahora, todos las pisotean." The concluding exclamatory verses, then, underscore the prosaic essence of the poem and thereby betray the reader's expectations built around the lyric tradition of the rose. Yet this betrayal is not an artistic flaw but rather an important textual strategy pointing at the narrative recreation of the theme in the subsequent chapter.[23]

In the narrative, the witness-narrator's attention is attracted by two mysterious women who appear in the boardinghouse. As he describes them, we cannot help but see superimposed on the description the verses, "rosas frescas . . . rosas secas":

Eran de edad indefinida. Estaban entrambas dentro de ese dilatado lapso de tiempo que abarca desde el punto en que la mujer comienza a perder juventud, lozanía e incentivo, hasta el acabamiento de toda gracia de femineidad y hermosura, edad que va de los treinta, y aun menos, a los cincuenta, y aun más, desenvolviéndose con tan sutiles y personales gradaciones que es punto menos que imposible calcularles los años entonces, y a eso suelen acogerse ellas para disimularlos y mermarlos. (p. 93)

(They were of an undefined age. Both were within that protracted lapse of time that begins at the point at which a woman begins to lose her youth, vigor, and incentive and extends until the end of all feminine grace and beauty, the age that ranges from thirty, even less, to fifty or more, unfolding with such subtle gradations that it is almost impossible to calculate it, a task made even more difficult by the fact that such women tend to hide and understate their true age.)

Not only is their resemblance to "rosas frescas" at best a faded image from the past, but even their present condition is depersonalized: "el punto en que la mujer comienza a perder juventud." These, then, are pure "rosas secas," an image that is transformed in the narrative to the much more colloquial, "como se dice en el duro lenguaje de cada día, tenían toda la traza de ser dos solteronas" (p. 93; "as they say in harsh everyday language, they showed every sign of being two old maids"). Finally, their loss of sociopolitical status, conveyed by the "oler/pisotear" contrast in the poem, in the narrative concerns the question of petty urban sophistication versus provincialism: "Era evidente que pertenecían a buena familia provinciana y que habían venido en contadas ocasiones a Madrid. Vestían sencillamente, de color nazareno, y mostraban, por ciertos detalles, ser personas de gusto poco educado" (p. 93; "It was evident that they came from a good provincial family and that they had come to Madrid only a few times. They dressed simply, in yellow, and showed, by certain details, to be people of unsophisticated taste").

As demonstrated by the preceding comparison, the awkward poetic expression of the initial poem of the novelette anticipates the narrative; the poem is a parody of the poetic convention of the rose, and the narrative is a cynical mockery of two women caught in tragic circumstances. By means of such a juxtaposition the posited author projects his voice, expressing the question of the compatibility of poetic ideals and tragic elements in the modern world. Each subsequent chapter serves to add nuances to that basic message, which is refracted in each chapter by a poem and a narrative, which in turn refract one another.

If in the first chapter the poem and the narrative combine to project the insidious influence of a prosaic world on human values, in the second chapter the projection is to more cosmic forces, with the tone correspondingly more serious:

> En la campal llanura de los cielos,
> dos campeones búscanse sin fin.
> Uno es el día, el blanco caballero.
> Otro es la noche, el negro paladín.
> Se persiguen, mas no se encuentran nunca.
> Sobre la tierra, cabalgan de paso.
> Y según pasan los anuncian
> las campanas en los campanarios.
> El *Angelus* del alba canta:
> "La noche huye. La noche ha huido".
> "El día se pierde en la distancia."
> Llora el *Angelus* vespertino.
> Talán, talán.
> Campana de plata.
> Ha nacido un nuevo cristiano.
> ¡Oh blanco misterio!
> Talán, talán.

Campana de bronce.
¡Oh negro arcano!
Llevan un hombre al cementerio. (p. 94)

(In the battlefields of the skies,
two champions pursue each other endlessly.
One is day, the white gentleman.
The other is night, the black paladin.
They chase each other, but never meet.
They ride casually over the earth.
And their passing is announced
by the bells in the campanile.
The *Angelus* of dawn sings:
"Night flees. Night has fled."
"Daytime is lost in the distance,"
cries the *Angelus* of twilight.
Dong, dong.
Silver bell.
A new Christian has been born.
Oh white mystery!
Dong, dong.
Bronze bell.
Oh black secret!
They are carrying a man to the cemetery.)

The image of day and night as two warriors in eternal pursuit of one another establishes a basic pattern of polarity. That opposition then extends to a religious level with the reference to the bells as they announce the morning and evening Angelus. The next phase in the poem unites all the previous images around the basic theme as the bells announce a birth ("Ha nacido un nuevo cristiano. / ¡Oh blanco misterio!") and a death ("¡Oh negro arcano! / Llevan un hombre al cementerio"). As opposed to the first poem of the novelette, this one is lyric rather than prosaic; the images are not cliches, and they expand in significance from one strophe to the next in an original and effective manner. The key to the message emerges in the last two strophes. There the contrast between the birth of a new "Christian" and the death of a man, with no qualifying adjectives to identify him, conveys a sense of bitter protest. In this case the protest seems not so much against a prosaic world as against Christianity and its failure, at least from the point of view of the speaker, to offer an adequate solution to the polarity between life and death around which the whole poem develops.

Although the poem is refracted in the subsequent narrative that describes how the two women are preparing their black mourning clothes in the same room where white baby clothes are being prepared for the birth of the landlady's daughter's first child, the refraction in this case is not as radical as in the previous chapter. In effect, this is probably the least distorted reflection in the novelette of one of the poems in a narrative. Here the poem does project a broader, more profound, and more universal significance to the anecdotal situation described in the narrative.[24]

Directly related to the poem and narrative of the second chapter are those of the concluding Chapter 11, which serves to complete the frame. This final chapter relates the birth of the child and the execution of the two murderers. The first event requires little commentary: "Margarita dio a luz un niño, feliz y trabajosamente, a las seis de la tarde" (p. 138; "Margarita gave birth to a child, happily and laboriously, at six in the afternoon"). The second, however, was not without incident, and the narrator claims to base his summary on newspaper accounts:

> Desde tiempo inmemorial no se habían verificado en Guadalfranco ejecuciones capitales. Hubieron de emplear para el caso un verdugo improvisado e ignorante de sus deberes, un mal aficionado de verdugo, que prolongó la agonía de los reos por espacio de una hora. La población entera cercaba la prisión, en tanto ajusticiaban a los dos reos. Como tardasen en arbolar la bandera negra, signo de que ya estaban muertos, la muchedumbre se amotinó y quiso tomar la cárcel por asalto. Al izar la bandera fúnebre, el motín se agravó. Temían los amotinados que se les hubiera engañado. Recelaban que se hubiera fingido la ejecución, para luego poner en salvo al hijo del aborrecido cacique, procurándole la huida a Portugal. Por cerciorarse, derribaron la puerta de la prisión, y, uno por uno, todos los habitantes de Guadalfranco fueron viendo con sus propios ojos a los dos ahorcados. Quienes los ultrajaban, quienes se mofaban, algunos les escupieron en el rostro. (pp. 138–39)

> (Since time immemorial capital punishment has not been witnessed in Guadalfranco. It happened that they hired to do the task a nonprofessional who was not attentive to his duties, a poor excuse of an executioner who prolonged the suffering of the two prisoners for an hour. The whole town surrounded the prison when the execution began. Since they delayed hoisting the black flag, the signal that the prisoners were dead, the crowd began to riot and tried to take possession of the jail. When they finally raised the funeral flag, the riot intensified. The crowd was afraid that they had been tricked. They suspected that the execution had been faked and that later the son of the hated political boss would be freed and provided passage to Portugal. To make sure that that didn't happen, they broke down the door of the prison, and one by one all the citizens of Guadalfranco examined with their own eyes the two hanged men. There were some who cursed them, some who made fun of them, and a few who spit in their faces.)

Prefacing this scene, in which the judges are as barbarous as the judged, is a poem repeating the images of the bells tolling alternately for a birth and a death, and the unresolvable "caballero blanco/caballero negro" conflict posited in the poem of Chapter 2. The narrative ends at a Sunday dinner in which a Republican politician, whose party is destined to replace the Limón family dominance, lauds the execution of Arias in the presence of the victim's sisters. The politician's insensitivity is but one more indication of justice being equivocally served, and as such, representing another echo from the poem of this final chapter: "Apuremos el vaso colmado / con el vino color de miel. / En el fondo del vaso hay guardado / sabor de cicuta y de hiel" (p. 136; "Let's drain the copious cup / with wine the color of honey. / In the bottom of the glass there remains / the flavor of hemlock and of bile"). And so the circle is complete. This final chapter links with the first two chapters to frame the novel; the action announced in the beginning is realized in the final section as the images of white/black and day/night point toward the concepts of birth/death and salvation/condemnation (and even *cacique/* republican), polar images that tend to fuse in the observer's eyes as a result of their vertiginous pursuit of one another. That effect, then, constitutes the posited author's message of eternal circularity, a message conveyed by the framing structure and its internal poem/narrative composition.

Chapter 3 represents the beginning of the framed construct and also a change from an intradiegetic witness narrator to an extradiegetic anonymous voice. The verse introducing Chapter 3 also reestablishes the parodic tone of the initial poem. It begins with a certain pomposity: "Vieja ciudad de piedra cincelada / y de barro el más deleznable. / Eternidad eternizada / y vanidad de lo mudable / . . . Nidal del arrojado romancero" (p. 97; "Old city of chiseled stone / and of the slipperiest mud. / Eternalized eternity / and vanity of the changeable / . . . home of the daring ballad"). The final verse quoted assures that the model being parodied is clear. In addition to the rhyme scheme, the ballad form is also evident in the middle section, which offers a dialogue, much more melodramatic than dramatic, between the speaker and a dying nobleman: "Apuré hasta las heces mi vino / en el cáliz de mi destino" ("I swallowed to the dregs my wine / in the chalice of my destiny"). Finally, the verses end with an image that in the sole context of the poem seems to leave little to the imagination: "Están posados en su cabeza / la mariposa del ensueño / y el escorpión de la pereza" (p. 97; "Resting on his head / the butterfly of dreams / and the scorpion of idleness").

The narrative refraction concerns the provincial city of Guadalfranco, and the history of how Enrique Limón, an outsider, married into the powerful Uceda family that ruled the province. The first words of the narrative, "Guadalfranco es una vieja ciudad española" (p. 98; "Guadalfranco is an old Spanish city"), are an almost direct echo of the first verse of the poem, "Vieja ciudad de piedra cincelada." The refracting process begins in earnest, however, when the now-extradiegetic narrator relates an anecdote in which a man claimed that Guadalfranco was a fictitious city invented by Sagasta (one of Alfonso XII's ministers) in order to justify budget cuts to certain constituents. At the conclusion of the anecdote the narrator interrupts his narrative to observe: "¡Son tantas las ciudades españolas que parecen inventadas por Sagasta! . . . Ciudades que un tiempo fueron heroicas, esforzadas, activas y abundantes, hoy sólo tienen una existencia imaginaria y soporífica" (p. 100; "There are so many Spanish cities that seem to have been invented by Sagasta! . . . Cities that once upon a time were heroic, aggressive, active, and in great quantity, today having only an imaginary and dreamy existence"). This editorial comment points back at the poem and its parody of the epic/ballad tradition. Whereas in Chapter 2 the lyric quality of the poem lends depth and universality to the anecdotal situation, here the opposite is true; the parodic poem seems somewhat frivolous and self-serving until we read the narrator's comment and realize that any attempt to recreate the epic/ballad tradition in a modern context perforce leads to parody. The narrative, in other words, rescues the poem from its apparent frivolity and allows us to see it in retrospect as a serious comment on modern Spanish reality.

A more complex effect results from the narrative explanation of the biological decline of the Uceda/Limón family. When Enrique Limón married Fernanda, the last marriageable member of the Uceda family, they produced sixteen offspring, of whom only three survived. The first born was Fernanda, and after the subsequent death of thirteen siblings, Dominica was born. Six years later the mother died giving birth to the only male, "al cual se le impuso el nombre de Arias, en recuerdo de un antepasado glorioso, conquistador de vastos reinos en las Indias occidentales" (p. 103; "to whom they gave the name Arias, in memory of a glorious ancestor, conqueror of vast kingdoms in the West Indies"). The later Arias, however, shows little resemblance to his namesake: "La criatura, aunque enclenque y enfermiza, se aferró a vivir" (p. 103; "The creature, although thin and sickly, held on to life"). This narrative account of the Uceda/Limón family, and specifically of Arias as the last surviving male heir to the family name, refracts the final image of the poem: "Están posados en su cabeza / la mariposa del ensueño / y el escorpión de la pereza." In this case, however, we are led simultaneously in two directions: the narrative takes us back to the poem, but then the poem projects us into the future of the next narrative. The posited author relies on this juxtaposing strategy to expand the significance of the poem; an image that within its context alone seemed excessively obvious suddenly achieves new complexity when viewed within the dual context of the poem and the narrative.

The first step into the future, Chapter 4, also involves a simultaneous return to the past. This dual projection is triggered by the introductory poem, which relies on the fairy tale as its literary model: "Albas nacaradas. País de las hadas" (p. 104; "Mother-of-pearl dawns. Land of fairies"). In this make-believe land strolls a prince with his entourage. He is reassured by the song of a finch: "El mundo es un vasto país encantado / y Tú eres del mundo Señor natural" ("The world is a vast enchanted country / and You are the natural Lord of this world"). Only the answering song of a grackle disturbs the idyllic mood: "Señor, / que nunca se rompa este encantamiento" (p. 104; "Sir / may this enchantment never be broken"). The image of the prince in the enchanted garden with the finch's soothing song reminds the reader of

Arias and his birth into the Uceda/Limón *cacique* (political machine) family. The grackle's song, on the other hand, takes the reader back to the image of the scorpion and to the narrative describing Arias as weak and sickly. The conflict projects us into the future, where we look to the narrative to resolve the contradiction.

Again the narrative recreates in refracted form the images from the poem. Arias's entourage is composed of his sister Dominica, "la reina madre; madre, a la par que niña, por gracioso milagro" (pp. 106–07; "the queen mother; mother, at the same time she is a child, by virtue of a miracle"); Bermudo, "al modo de mastín del príncipe" (p. 107; "like a mastiff to the prince"), and the family dog Delfín, "un gnomo, velludo y riente" (p. 107; "a gnome, hairy and smiling"). But this world of enchantment is threatened by an outside force: "Y más allá de aquel mundo quieto, el mundo de las disputas, de los tráfagos, presidido por la adusta Fernanda y el viejo papá, que muy de tarde en tarde caía por Guadalfranco a visitar los estados y dar un beso a los hijos" (p. 107; "And beyond that quiet world, the world of turmoil, of business deals, presided over by Fernanda and the old father, who from time to time would drop by Guadalfranco to visit his estates and to kiss his children"). Once again the posited author's voice emerges by virtue of his structuring role, and his ominous message in this case concerns self-deception. A fairy tale carried to extreme, he seems to suggest, has the potential to become a tale of horror.

The poem of Chapter 5 represents another radical change in style as it switches from the fairy tale of the previous chapter to didactic/philosophical poetry:

Todas las olas se deshacen
contra el muro de lo infinito.
En el mar infinito se caen
y se pierden todos los ríos.
Las hazañas y los desmanes
se derriten en el olvido.
En la barca de tus afanes
vas con la corriente del río;
vas aguas abajo, a ahogarte
en la sima de lo infinito.
¡Quiera Dios que no te remanses
sobre la presa del molino! (p. 108)

(All the waves dissolve
against the wall of infinity.
Into the infinite sea empty
and are lost all rivers.
The deeds and disgraces
melt into the forgotten.
In the vessel of your desires

you flow with the current of the river;
you flow downstream, to drown
in the abyss of infinity.
May God protect you from becoming grounded
on the millstream dam!)

The initial tone is ponderous and portentous with the repetition of the word "infinito," the archetypal image of the rivers emptying into the sea, and the *ubi sunt* theme. Even the switch to the familiar second person fails to alter the tone as the words "ahogarte," "sima," and "infinito" negate any soothing effect the familiar address might have. But then the final two verses make a mockery of the previous ones, with the speaker's absurd warning against the danger of grounding a boat on a millstream dam; he switches from the metaphysical to the trivial, from the archetypal to the mundane.

The narrative seems intent on a literal realization of the prosaic theme as Arias, acting out a child's dream of conquest, steals a boat and with Dominica, Bermudo, and Delfín as his crew, promptly grounds the craft on a millstream dam: "Esta fue la primera y última aventura en acción. Las demás fueron aventuras de fantasía, en la penumbra vespertina del huerto. Y, sobre todo, recitaciones de los versos de Arias" (p. 110; "This was the first and the last action-adventure. The rest were fantasy-adventures dreamed in the twilight of the garden. And, above all, recitations of Arias's verses"). Again there is a process of refracted echoes. Whereas the poem progresses from the sublime to the ridiculous, the narrative begins with an apparently innocuous childhood incident and develops it into a serious reflection of personality development; in the poem the serious is trivialized, while in the narrative the trivial assumes tragic implications. By virtue of this reverse mirror imaging, both the poem and the narrative transcend their own limitations; the poem becomes more than a mere parody of the Jorge Manrique tradition, and the narrative becomes more than a mere rendering of childhood pranks. Drawing on one another, therefore, they speak to a world in which philosophical preoccupations and childhood innocence are no longer viable. Such a double-voiced message emerges by virtue of the textual strategy of reverse reflections in Chapter 5.

The poem at the beginning of Chapter 6 reintroduces the fairy tale model: "Una vez, érase que se era . . ." (p. 111; "Once upon a time there was . . ."). This is not a fairy tale of love and happy endings, however, but one of cruelty and death. The princess in this case destroys her doll because it does not flatter her: "Y habla entonces por un milagro / antes de morir, la muñeca: / 'Yo te quería más que nadie, / aunque decirlo no pudiera'./ Una vez, érase que se era . . ." ("And the doll speaks by a miracle / before dying: / 'I loved you most of all, / even though I could not say it.' / Once upon a time there was . . ."). This is an unexpected fairy tale because the enchantment fails to lead to a solution. The miracle at the end by which the doll is inspirited, rather than righting the wrong, merely adds force to the act of cruelty. The fairy tale genre, as a result, projects an unexpectedly negative view of the world as it directs the reader to the narrative.

The narrative concerns Arias's jealousy of the attention that Dominica pays to their humanlike dog Delfín:

> Un día, el viejo gnomo cayó en el regazo de Dominica, al cabo de rauda y parabólica excursión aérea. Como no es privilegio perteneciente a la naturaleza canina el de volar, Dominica no pudo por menos de pasmarse viendo que Delfín acudía hasta ella por tan sutiles y no acostumbrados derroteros. Por otra parte, Delfín no celebraba con petulantes gañidos su triunfo momentáneo sobre las leyes de la gravitación; antes vení quejándose y doliéndose tristemente, rabo entre piernas. Delfín no había volado por propio esfuerzo o antojo. El motor había sido ajeno a su voluntad e industria. Residía en el pie de Arias. (p. 113)

> (One day the old gnome fell into Dominica's lap, at the end of a swift and allegoric aerial excursion. Since flying is not a privilege associated with canine nature, Dominica could not help but be astonished seeing Delfín approach her by such a subtle and unaccustomed course. On the other hand, Delfín did not celebrate, with petulant yelps, his momentary triumph over the laws of gravity; on the contrary, he was complaining sadly, with his tail between his legs. Delfín had not flown by his own force or desire. The driving force was separate from his own will power and resources. The driving force was Arias's foot.)

In the poem the cruelty of the princess inspires in the reader shock and sadness; in the narrative the cruelty of Arias comes across as humorous, even if it is a black humor. That farcical tone, moreover, must be seen in conjunction with the poem. The fairy tale form of the poem, with its magical power to animate inanimate objects, conveys a sense of good prevailing over evil. Reader expectations are betrayed, however, as the magic gives way to an all-too-worldly act of cruelty. In a somewhat reverse manner, the satirical way in which Delfín is reduced to an object and his flight equated with a phenomenon of physics conveys a callous attitude on the part of the speaker. Yet that attitude underscores even more Arias's pathological bent for violence. The posited author's message, therefore, concerns the pervasiveness of evil. The magic of the fairy tale no longer demonstrates the power of virtue, but rather the insidiousness of cruelty. This being the state of our modern world, the only defense seems to be to satirize magic itself by demythifying it: Delfín did not fly, he was kicked. We do not live in a fairyland where good prevails over evil, but in a real world in which evil is rewarded, at least to judge by Delfín's response to Arias's cruelty: "En los últimos meses de su vida fue casi más amigo de Arias que de Dominica" (p. 114; "In the final days of his life he was almost a better friend to Arias than to Dominica"). In a world where barbarity begets loyalty, a farcical tone may be the only one appropriate. That message again emerges by virtue of the juxtaposition of the two genres as they reflect and refract one another.

The element of farce continues in Chapter 7 with the introduction of a new character with the caricatural name Próspero Merlo. Próspero is a young, ambitious lawyer new in town (much the same as Enrique Limón was years earlier) who sets out to ingratiate himself with the Limón family. The father, realizing that Fernanda needs a male ally if she is to maintain effective control over their political machine, proposes to the family that Dominica marry Próspero. Arias, who knows nothing of the relationship between Próspero and Dominica, bitterly accuses his sister of hypocrisy, implying infidelity. When in response she promises to refuse an offer of marriage, Arias suddenly apologizes and insists that she marry the young lawyer. Preceding this story of amoral political expediency and incestuous jealousy is an excessively stylized and declamatory poem that speaks of the lust for power in cosmic terms: "¡Poder! ¡Poder! ¡Oh vino de divina / borrachera! El más alto de los bienes" (p. 115; "Power! Power! Oh the wine of a divine / drunken party! The most valued of gifts"). Contrasted with this lofty tone, we have Próspero Merlo, "joven abogado de altaneras miras, inteligencia despejada y lengua flúida" (p. 117; "a young lawyer with an arrogant gaze, confident intelligence and a fluid tongue"), the father's callous machinations, and of course the second manifestation of Arias's pathological devotion to his sister.

The focus centers more and more on Arias and his jealousy as the novel progresses, but the dramatic tension resulting from that conflict is again counterbalanced. Love is the theme of the poem introducing Chapter 8, and references to the tragic Ophelia and Hamlet precede the final strophe: "¡Amor! Alumbras, manso o furibundo, / antorcha roja o recogido foco, / la tragicomedia del mundo . . . / Pero estás en las manos de un loco" (p. 122; "Love! You illuminate softly and fiercely, / red torch or delicate point of light, / the tragicomedy of the world . . . / But you are in the hands of a madman"). The narrative projection of the poem concerns how Arias outwardly supports the marriage between Dominica and Próspero, "Pero, estando a solas, Arias sufre mortal angustia" (p. 125; "But when he is alone, Arias suffers mortal anguish"). He then falls in love with a woman he has seen only three times and to whom he has never spoken. When he confesses his anguish, Bermudo "se decide a hacer uso del don de la palabra, de que tan avaro es" (pp. 125–26; "decides to make use of the gift of speech, about which he is so miserly") and volunteers to bring her to his suffering friend. Arias's suppressed infatuation plus the suggestion of physical force implicit in Bermudo's offer portend tragic consequences.

Yet the poem does not project pure tragedy, but rather "la tragicomedia del mundo." Since tragicomedy also involves farcical elements, the narrative offers, along with its own examples of comedy, a totally nontragic tone. This second tone emerges from the narrator's rhetorical questions: "¿En dónde se meten Arias y su leal y hermético secuaz?" (p. 123; "What are Arias and his loyal and silent follower up to?"); "¿Qué podrá hacer el pobre Bermudo por aliviar a Arias? ¿Qué le sucede a Arias?" (p. 125; "What do you suppose poor Bermudo will do to help Arias? What is happening to Arias?"). Such questions, along with the satirical description of Próspero—"Por el descote de la camisa asoman negras, flamígeras y culebreantes hebras de cabello, porque el abogado es hombre de pelo en pecho" (p. 124; "Over the neckline of his shirt, black flame-like and serpentine threads of hair appear, because the lawyer is a man with hair on his chest")—mock the dramatic tension as it builds. The resulting clash of tones, therefore, is another example of a double voicing that echoes the poem by suggesting that the time of classical tragedy has indeed passed, and no modern tragedy is devoid of its farcical elements.

A type of farce comes across even in the poem of the next chapter, which deals with the brutal murder and rape. The speaker of the poem moralistically accuses nighttime of being an evil in itself: "Origen de todos los males, / porque, acogidos a su seno, / animales y hombres se ayuntan, / y, encendidos de un furor ciego, / perpetúan la vida en la tierra" (p. 127; "The origin of all evil / because, huddling in its bosom, / animals and men come together, / and, ignited with a blind fury, / they perpetuate life on earth"). Of course, sex is the real target of the speaker's censorship. The synecdochical relationship that he draws between it and nighttime comically reflects his need for a euphemistic expression. This *beato* (pious) attitude of the speaker toward sex suggests someone who leads an unnaturally sheltered existence, a suspicion corroborated in the next strophe: "Suena la esquila del convento. / Es hora de maitines. Pasan / los santos monjes a sus rezos. / 'De los pecados de la noche, / ¡Líbranos, Señor y Dios nuestro! / ¡Que cante el gallo matutino / y caiga Lucifer al infierno!' " ("The bell of the convent sounds. / It is the hour of matins. They pass by to pray / the sainted monks. / 'Free us! Our Lord and God / from the sins of the night! / May the morning rooster crow / and may Lucifer fall into hell' "). Apparently, the speaker is among those frightened monks who appeal to God to protect them from the evils of the night. Their plea, however, sounds amusingly childlike as it conveys a certain pleasure in the very danger threatening them. Indeed, the first verse of the final strophe, "Ki-ki-ri-kí," is a child's onomatopoetic rendition of a rooster's crowing, which reinforces the sensation of a puerile delight in horror. But then, in violent opposition, the poem concludes: "Amanece otro nuevo día. / Pero alguien ya no podrá verlo" ("Another day dawns. / But someone will no longer see it"). Suddenly the tone is transmogrified; playful farce becomes chilling understatement as the reader looks apprehensively to the narrative for a resolution of the conflicting tone.

Following Próspero's announcement that he must make a business visit that evening to the widow Candelero and her daughter, the latter being the woman who has so obsessed Arias, the narrator announces: "Al día siguiente la viuda de Candelero y su hija aparecieron en su casa asesinadas, cosidas a puñaladas. La hija tenía veintisiete heridas, y presentaba señales evidentes de haber sido forzada" (p. 129; "The next day the widow of Candelero and her daughter were discovered murdered in their house, stabbed to death. The daughter had twenty-seven wounds and showed clear signs that she had been raped"). Although Próspero is arrested when some of his personal items are found at the scene, the reader knows that Arias is responsible for this heinous crime. Arias, for his part, tries to comfort Dominica by assuring her that there must be a terrible error, and that in any case their influential connections in Madrid can take care of everything. But Don Enrique, who now is too weak to take on such a task, turns over to his son Arias the responsibility of arranging things in Madrid: "El tímido y perezoso Arias dilataba su viaje a Madrid. Pasaron así tres meses. En esto, don Enrique falleció" (p. 130; "The timid and lazy Arias delayed his trip to Madrid. Three months passed. During this period, Don Enrique died"). This narrative account of moral insensitivity, political corruption, and generational *abulia* (apathy) is once again informed by the preceding poem, and beyond that by all the preceding sets of poems and narratives. The playful, satirical presentation of the monks' fear points toward the underlying motives of this crime. They reveal their sexual suppression in their prayers of deliverance from the evils of the night; because of their monastic isolation and vows of chastity, sex is a totally alien and evil force that they cannot confront directly. The expression of sex as an evil spirit, therefore, forms the basis of the humor in the poem. Notwithstanding that humorous tone, the underlying problem is pathologically serious, as the final verses make clear.

In the narrative, Arias serves as a refracted image of the monks. His horrendous crime results from an inability to confront the sexual drive that obsesses him. And again in a reverse imaging process, he relies on political influences to shield him from moral responsibility for his act. *Caciquismo* (political bossism) is his monastery. Arias is a product and reflection of a society that treats sexual drives as if they were evil spirits. And since it is a question of evil spirits, the next logical step is to disregard individual moral responsibility. The posited author's message concerns the relationship between comically inconsistent attitudes, and a tragic loss of moral responsibility. The cast for this tragicomedy clearly is not limited to the characters in the novelette, but encompasses a whole society.[25]

The poem introducing Chapter 10 underscores the tragic rather than the comic elements as the tragicomedy continues:

En principio era la sombra;
la sombra letárgica y caótica;
un anonadamiento; la nada cóncava.
No había colores ni formas.
Surgió el verbo. Surgió la voz maravillosa.
Y con la voz se hizo la luz, aparecieron las cosas.
Se desplegó la acción, nació la historia.
Se hizo la luz, con dolientes congojas.
Todos los alumbramientos dejan las entrañas rotas.

Se hizo la luz. Se ve la sangre roja
sobre el cuerpo virginal que se desploma.
Y, no obstante, había noche tenebrosa.
Porque la luz era el verbo dentro de la sombra. (p. 131)

(In the beginning there was darkness;
lethargic and chaotic darkness;
an annihilation; concave nothingness.
There were no colors or forms.
Then came the word. The marvelous voice sprang forth.
And with the voice light was created, and objects appeared.
The action unfolded, history was born.
Light was created, with painful sorrows.
All the acts of giving forth light result in a shattered womb.
Light was created. You see the red blood
over the virginal body that lies in a heap.
And, nevertheless, there was gloomy night
Because the light was the word spoken in darkness.)

The Bible is the obvious referent for the first half of this poem. The initial verses project a logocentric view of the universe in which the Word is the source of all meaning; it creates matter and provides significance for human existence. Genesis, of course, is the source of that Judeo-Christian message. But the second half of the poem offers a new meaning for the concept of the Word, that new interpretation signaled by the verse, "Se desplegó la acción, nació la historia." As matter evolves into human beings, the act of creation takes on a new connotation: "Se hizo la luz, con dolientes congojas. / Todos los alumbramientos dejan las entrañas rotas." The creation of matter involves miraculous transformation; the creation of humans involves pain and suffering. The Word changed darkness into light, but in the process it also revealed acts of human destruction: "Se ve la sangre roja / sobre el cuerpo virginal que se desploma." In this new reading of Genesis we discover that the Word is not the source at all, but merely one more step along a path of infinite deferral, "Porque la luz era el verbo dentro de la sombra." The abyss—"un anonadamiento; la nada cóncava"—it is suggested, is waiting just beyond the area illuminated by the falsely reassuring light of Christianity.

In the narrative, Arias, shielded by the darkness in Dominica's bedroom, confesses his crime to her. He concludes by insisting: "En todo el tiempo no dijo una palabra. Jamás llegué a oír el sonido de su voz. Si hubiera hablado, creo que no la hubiera matado; se hubiera hecho la luz. Pero no habló, no habló" (p. 134; "In the whole time she did not say one word. I never heard the sound of her voice. If she had spoken, I believe I might not have killed her; light would have been created. But she did not speak; she did not speak"). It is difficult to accept Arias's claim. First, his conditional sentence in effect shifts the blame to his victim. We know, however, that he killed her because of flaws in his character that have been made clear in the preceding sets of poems and narratives. In addition, his confidence in the redeeming power of her voice, considered within the context of the poem introducing this chapter, seems to be illusory. If the young lady had spoken, she would have done so within a moral vacuum as far as Arias is concerned, and therefore the reader should draw the parallel between this situation and that described by the verse, "la luz era el verbo dentro de la sombra."

As each chapter has demonstrated, in order to understand Arias's actions we must first understand his character, and to understand his character we must trace the line leading from it to the socio-religious forces determining it. That tracing process, in turn, requires us to follow a refracted rather than a straight line from poem to narrative and then back again. Only by so doing can we hope to approach the posited author's polysemic message, one that involves the dark side of human nature, the role of society in fostering its destructive potential, the inability of Christianity to reconcile the basic contradiction of existence, and finally the question of literature responding to other literature as perhaps the only means of defining and confronting the human condition.

Apparently relying on Pérez de Ayala's own comments in the preface to the 1942 edition of *Troteras y danzaderas*,[26] critics have tended to summarize the content of the poems and then turn their attention to the narratives. As a result, their treatment of the poems in many cases contradicts the author's stated intentions. He speaks of "poesía de la verdad" (poetry of truth) and of the synthesizing rather than analytical function of the lyric mode as an indication of the subtlety and complexity that he intended for the poems in this collection. They cannot adequately be reduced to plot and theme summaries as so often has been the practice. Indeed, as the author suggested and as the preceding analysis has demonstrated, the poems and the narratives are in dialogic relationship with one another; each individual poem and narrative informs and is informed by the other, as each set informs and is informed by the preceding and the subsequent. In addition, the poems are in dialogic (sometimes parodic) relationship with a variety of lyric traditions, as the fictional work is in a dialogic relationship with Spanish society of 1916. Finally, there is the dialogic relationship between the posited author and his posited reader, a relationship in which "La caída de los Limones" serves as discursive medium. The *Novelas poemáticas*, therefore, can be seen as a classic example of Bakhtin's concept of "the dialogic imagination." This dialogic emphasis, in turn, represents the major contribution of this work to a renovation of Spanish fiction. The strategies initiated in 1902 to redefine novelistic canons evolved by 1916 into a new type of fiction. "Nada menos que todo un hombre" and "La caída de los Limones" are not mere youthful experiments; they are mature expressions of a new concept of novelistic art. As that concept evolves into the next decade, literary historians will label it vanguardism. The point is clear. That movement was the result of an evolution, not of an eruption.

3 1923–1926

From the point of view of literary history, the 1920s are all but synonymous with the Spanish vanguard movement. Not only were the bookstores flooded with examples of the new art, but the kiosks bulged with magazines that defined and propagated its poetics. In fact, perhaps no Spanish literary school has been so characterized by the number of journals and magazines dedicated exclusively to it.[1]

Whether because or in spite of the degree to which it was sponsored and defined by periodicals, vanguardism has fared no better than most other movements in reference to the arbitrary way in which works are or are not assigned to it. Indeed, it appears that the label *vanguard* was more a question of acceptance by one of the recognized journals than of the style and content of the works produced by a given writer.[2]

However arbitrarily the selection process was applied in Spain, the movement itself has defining ideological roots that can be traced perhaps to romanticism, or at least to the last part of the previous century. Renato Poggioli,[3] who without question has provided the most probing and comprehensive study of vanguardism, lists as its principal philosophical bases nihilism (the need to destroy previous models), dadaism (absurd repetition or the celebration of nothingness), agonism (pathos and the belief in a miracle of change), futurism (a primitivism or primordialism from which will emerge a new series), and decadentism (passive hostility toward contemporary civilization). To these categories one should add expressionism (parodic exaggeration), cubism (geometric dehumanization), and of course surrealism (an oneiric view of reality).[4] As the preceding summary reveals, the ideological bases are not totally compatible. And so, in spite of the insistence on orthodoxy by its Spanish high priests in the 1920s, the religion itself was marked by certain contradictions.

But the vanguard movement generally is identified with aesthetic, not philosophical preoccupations; it is popularly identified with an attempt to resurrect art for art's sake. And the primary credit for defining how that effort is expressed artistically must go to Gustavo Pérez Firmat.[5] A glance at several of his chapter titles conveys the essence of what he sees in the movement: "A Pneumatic Aesthetics," "Closed World," "Decharacterization," "From Palimpsest to Pastiche," and "The Novel as Matrass." In a word, Pérez Firmat stresses the textual strategies designed to undermine the realist tradition in reference to imagery, plot and reader reaction, characterization, narrative authority, and objectivity. Using a variety of texts to demonstrate, he defines the movement as quintessentially antimimetic. In addition, parody, satire, and sensuality have been advocated as stylistic constants of the movement,[6] along with a system of metaphorization inspired by technology and economic prosperity.[7]

There is one work, however, that not only defined the new art but actually determined how Spanish fiction was written from the second half of the 1920s up to the time of the Civil War. That work, of course, is *La deshumanización del arte* (1925) by José Ortega y Gasset. And if there is a single concept that can be considered a key to Ortega's treatise, it would have to be art as a game. Ortega argued that the new aesthetic rejected the conventional transcendent pretensions of art; he stated that this new approach defined true art as that which calls attention to its own artifices and does not aspire to being more than it is: a game. Although generally literary historians point to dehumanization as the culprit, the analyses that follow will demonstrate that the obsession with avoiding transcendent implications was much more decisive in the early demise of the vanguard movement. Martínez Ruiz (Azorín) and Valle-Inclán incorporated many of the fundamental textual strategies identified with vanguardism, but in *Doña Inés* (1925) and *Tirano Banderas* (1926), respectively, they managed to use those strategies to project messages that addressed universal human concerns. The result in each case was not only a personal masterpiece, but a work that stands as one of the benchmarks of twentieth-century Spanish fiction. Gómez de la Serna, on the other hand, seemed so intent in *El novelista* (1923) to avoid transcendent implications that one of his best efforts qualifies as merely an interesting but minor work. Less tied to the doctrine of pure game and more successful than Gómez de la Serna as a novelist, at least according to past and current tastes, is Jarnés in *El convidado de papel* (1924). Finally, Salinas, with *Víspera del gozo* (1926), wrote what is arguably the best example of vanguardism we have in Spanish prose fiction. But in each of his stories reality supplants the game; pure aesthetics is exposed as another type of escapism, no more or less so than that provided by the verboten melodrama.

The thread we have been tracing from 1902 forms a knot here around the years 1923–1926. This is the period in which the Spanish vanguard movement officially began, and of course it is also the time during which Martínez Ruiz and Valle-Inclán wrote their most important novels. They demonstrate most dramatically the culminating link, since they were also a part of the initial movement to renovate Spanish fiction, but the innovations of Gómez de la Serna, Jarnés, and Salinas also can better be appreciated when seen within the temporal context being projected. They, just as surely as the two members of the Generation of '98, are inexorably linked to the past, and specifically to 1902 and the rebellion initiated that year against the canons of realism.

Doña Inés

Martínez Ruiz in *Félix Vargas* (1928)—whose title was later changed to *El caballero inactual*—and in *Superrealismo* (1929)—later changed to *El libro de Levante*—became an even more blatant advocate of the new art. In fact, one can argue that his advocacy stance in these later novels undermined their success as an aesthetic experience; he was guilty in them of yet another kind of didacticism. It is not an exaggeration, nevertheless, to say that *Doña Inés* (1925), written by one of the original members of the Generation of '98, represents one of the most effective examples found anywhere of the *arte joven*. *Tirano Banderas,* appearing the very next year and also written by one of the "old group," is perhaps the only novel that surpasses *Doña Inés* as an artistic expression of the new aesthetic.

Doña Inés is justifiably entrenched in the canons of twentieth-century Spanish fiction. Many, in fact, consider it a fulfillment of the promise displayed in *La voluntad.* Although *Doña Inés* is both temporally and aesthetically contiguous with the vanguard movement, rarely if ever has the novel been identified with the new art. Critics have tended to stress serious philosophical implications of theme (time),[8] stylistics (descriptions),[9] and structure (interior duplication),[10] with only token reference to humorous elements. But the humor they tend to dismiss is more than just another thematic, stylistic, or structural element; humor in the form of parody is a strategy designed to bring to the foreground the conventions of previous novelistic movements with an eye toward furthering the renovation of Spanish fiction initiated in 1902 and significantly refined in the next decade. *Doña Inés,* in short, is a novel whose primary focus is on art itself; it is perhaps the most subtle example of its time of art for art's sake written by a charter member of the Generation of '98.

If parody is the basic strategy for shifting the focus from the object created to the art of creating it, the basic substrategy to that end is a subversion of reader expectations. That process of undermining what the reader anticipates begins with the title itself of the novel, a woman's name, reinforced by the subtitle, "*(Historia de amor)*."[11] The combination of title and subtitle predisposes reader expectations toward a conventional love story. In effect there are two such stories in the novel, and the first one concerns a day in which Doña Inés goes to an apartment for a rendezvous with her lover, Don Juan. After she waits anxiously for Don Juan to appear, a letter finally arrives with the apparent message that he is terminating their relationship. The first story ends with the somewhat aging Doña Inés alone in the room caressing some gold coins. On the surface it is the conventional love story of unrequited love; that convention is betrayed, however, by the way the story is told.

After being predisposed by the title and subtitle, the reader's expectations are further molded by the initial passage of the novel: "En 1840 y en Madrid. Son los primeros días de junio; media tarde. Por una callejuela avanza un transeúnte. La callejuela pertenece al barrio de Segovia. Las afueras del barrio de Segovia son extensas" (p. 69; "In 1840 and in Madrid. In the first days of June; mid-afternoon. A passer-by advances on the narrow street. The street belongs to the Segovia district. The outskirts of the Segovia district are extensive"). Then follows a list of the names of surrounding neighborhoods, businesses, private homes, religious sanctuaries, and finally this item of interest: "En las afueras del barrio de Segovia está enclavada la Fábrica del gas" (p. 69; "The Gas Factory is located on the outskirts of the Segovia district"). With the reader expecting to read a love story and, by virtue of the date indicated, 1840, one that corresponds to the model of romanticism, the list of names, and above all the notice of the location of the gas factory, humorously subvert those initial expectations.

The second paragraph continues the visitor's guide format as it lists the plazas and streets of the Segovia zone of Madrid. Included with the second list is a description of the houses in this area: "Las escaleras pronas y oscuras evocan viejas novelas de Balzac y de Víctor Hugo en primitivas traducciones" (p. 70; "The dark, steep stairs evoke images of old Balzac and Victor Hugo novels in primitive translation"). The direct reference to Balzac and Víctor Hugo reinforces the connotation of the 1840 date of the first sentence in the novel. The combination of that date and this reference to the French novelists, therefore, serves to foreground the two dominant literary styles of the previous century and thus represents a strategy for further influencing reader expectations. A love story in the style of either author suggests social issues, melodrama, and tragedy. Yet up to this point digressions have skirted social issues and totally negated any hint of melodrama and tragedy. What is more, it is difficult to take seriously any works with the modifier, "en primitivas traducciones." That adjective clause, along with the notation on the gas factory, serve as signs pointing not at a tragic love story, but at an apparent parody of that genre. In short, from the very beginning of the novel we detect the sound of the posited author's ironic voice that emerges as literary conventions are violated and reader expectations are subverted.

The suggestion of parody becomes more pronounced with the initial sentence of Chapter 2: "El transeúnte que avanza por la callejuela es una mujer" (p. 72; "The advancing passer-by is a woman"). Although the definite article alerts the reader to her previous introduction, he is almost obliged to look back at the third sentence of the novel as a reminder that she was indeed mentioned before ("Por una callejuela avanza un transeúnte"). Not only was she anonymous in that initial introduction, but she was also genderless. Now that she has achieved a degree of visibility and above all gender, the reader anticipates her role, perhaps even that of romantic heroine, in the prominently announced love story.

With the reader's attention now focused on the anonymous woman walking along the street, the narrator seems ready to fulfill expectations as he begins a detailed description of this character:

Va trajeada la desconocida con una falda de color malva; el corpiño es del mismo color. En falda y corpiño irisa la joyante seda. Tres amplios volantes rodean la falda; la adorna una trepa de sutiles encajes. Del talle, angosto y apretado, baja ensanchándose el vestido hasta formar cerca del tobillo un ancho círculo. El pie aparece breve.

Asciende tersa la media de seda color de rosa. El arranque de las piernas se muestra sólido y limpiamente torneado. Y, sobre el empeine gordezuelo del pie, y sobre el arranque de la pierna, los listones de seda negra, que parten del chapín y se alejan hacia arriba, dando vueltas, marcan en la carne muelle ligeros surcos. La desconocida es alta y esbelta. El seno, lleno y firme, retiembla ligeramente con el caminar presuroso. Cuando la dama se inclina, el ancho círculo de la falda—sostenido por ligero tontillo—se levanta en su parte de atrás y deja ver la pierna de una línea perfecta. (p. 72)

(The anonymous woman is well dressed in a mauve skirt with a bodice of the same color. The silk of the skirt and bodice glow with a jewel-like iridescence. Three ample ruffles surround the skirt, and it is trimmed with subtle inlay of lace. From the waist, narrow and tightly bound, the dress becomes wider as it falls until it forms a wide circle near the ankle. Her foot barely is visible. The rose-colored stocking smoothly ascends. The legs are solid and nicely shaped. And, over the fatty instep of her foot, past the outline of her legs, the black silk ribbons that are fastened at the shoe and climb upwards, leave slight imprints on her spongy flesh. The mysterious woman is tall and slender. Her bosom, full and firm, shudders slightly with her quick steps. When the woman leans over, the wide circle of her skirt—sustained by the delicate petticoat—rises up to reveal a perfectly proportioned leg.)

The initial lines seem to confirm that this woman belongs to the social class appropriate for a romantic heroine. In fact, the reader can almost see Balzac's realist canons imprinted on the description: outward appearances mirror a character's personality and social status, since humans are the product of their environment (in addition to their heredity). Yet rather than echoing realist/naturalist principles, this description seems designed to satirize the heroine by probing beneath her outward layer of clothing. As the narrator scrutinizes the anonymous woman, the emphasis changes from the social status inherent in the type of clothing she is wearing (a realist approach), to an unflattering peek beneath that clothing. And what is revealed beneath the elegant attire violates the conventions of the idealized romantic heroine: "talle, angosto y apretado . . . el empeine gordezuelo del pie . . . en la carne muelle ligeros surcos." Then, as a humorous climax to the visual image, the narrator notes: "Cuando la dama se inclina, el ancho círculo de la falda—sostenido por ligero tontillo—se levanta en su parte de atrás y deja ver la pierna de una línea perfecta." There is an unmistakably mischievous wink inherent in the presentation of the woman in such an awkward and revealing posture. A true gentleman, after all, should look the other way. By choosing to scrutinize the apparent heroine in such an ungentlemanly fashion, the narrator ridicules the very concept of the idealized female protagonist and seriously undermines this character's potential to play the conventional love-story role in which she is cast.

Since this is supposed to be a classic tale of romance, the reader should anticipate a tragic turn of events, and the speaker again indicates that he is cognizant of his addressee as he turns his attention to the woman's facial expression: "De pronto, un pensamiento triste conturba a la desconocida: la mirada se eleva y un instante resalta en lo trigueño de la faz lo blanco de los ojos. En la boca angosta, los labios gruesos y como cortados a bisel—y ésta es una de las particularidades de la fisonomía—, cuando están juntos, apretados, diseñando un mohín infantil, dan a la cara una suave expresión de melancolía" (p. 73; "Suddenly, a sad thought troubles the woman: her gaze rises and in an instant the whites of her eyes glare against her olive colored skin. On her narrow mouth, her thick lips give the appearance of having been cut to a beveled edge—and this is one of the peculiarities of her physiognomy—when they are pressed together, tightened, forming a baby's pout, they give her face a gentle expression of melancholy"). A melancholy expression dissected in this way becomes a parody of itself. The character cannot be taken seriously; rather than potentially tragic she is puerilely comical. Even her gestures betray her as a miscast Thespian: "Cuando la dama camina, lentamente, con majestad, de rato en rato enarca el busto como si fuera a respirar. Otras veces, con movimiento presto y nervioso, Doña Inés de Silva—que éste es el nombre de la bella desconocida—hace ademán de aupar y recoger en el seno el amplio y fino encaje de la mantilla" (p. 74; "When the woman walks, slowly, with majesty, from time to time she arches her breast as if to breathe. Other times, with a quick and nervous movement, Doña Inés de Silva—which is the name of the beautiful woman—makes a gesture to hoist up and catch in her bosom the fine lace of her shawl"). Finally the narrator reluctantly confirms the reader's suspicion that the anonymous pedestrian is indeed the principal character. Yet the studied effect of her motions—"hace ademán de aupar"—transforms the would-be drama into a farce; Doña Inés is cast as slapstick comedienne rather than tragic heroine. As a result of this violation of the nineteenth-century paradigm, the reader's attention shifts from the character's trials and tribulations to the conventions of characterization and plot typical of the previous century. In short, the story in this novel is not about love, but about art.

The intention to reveal the simulacrum for what it is, to lay bare the conventions of the love story, becomes even clearer when the narrator intrudes with his own voice. One example of such an illusion-shattering narrative interruption occurs as Doña Inés is awaiting the arrival of her lover Don Juan:[12]

> Doña Inés está en el cuartito de la costanilla. No sucede nada; todo está tranquilo. Ha salido la dama por la puerta de la derecha y traía en la mano un plato con un vaso de agua. Al llegar frente al balcón, se ha detenido. Ha levantado el vaso y lo ha mirado a trasluz. Ha dudado un momento y ha vuelto a entrar por donde había salido. Al cabo de un instante, ha tornado a salir con otro vaso de agua—o el mismo con otra agua—y ha desaparecido por una de las puertas de la izquierda. No sucede nada; Doña Inés está tranquila. ¿Está tranquila del todo? Se ha sentado la dama en el canapé y ha puesto su mano derecha extendida sobre el muslo; en la mano reluce la piedra azul de un zafiro. Miraba fijamente el zafiro Doña Inés; luego, pasaba suave-

mente la mano izquierda sobre la mano derecha. ¿Está tranquila del todo la señora? (p. 77)

(Doña Inés is in the small room off a narrow street. Nothing is happening; all is tranquil. The woman has exited by the door to the right and was carrying in her hand a plate with a glass of water. Arriving in front of the balcony she has paused. She has lifted the glass to the light. She has hesitated a moment and has reentered the door from which she exited. After an instant she has appeared with another glass of water—or maybe the same glass with different water—and has disappeared through the door to the left. Nothing is happening; Doña Inés is calm. Is she totally calm? She has sat down under the canopy and has extended her right hand over her thigh; on her hand sparkles the blue of a sapphire stone. She looks at the sapphire. Later she gently passes her left hand over her right. Is the woman totally calm?)

The narrator first calls attention to his presence with the parenthetical clarification, "ha tornado a salir con otro vaso de agua—o el mismo con otra agua." By so doing, he not only mocks the supposed invisibility of the narrator so often cited in reference to realism/naturalism, but he also mocks their pseudoscientific exactness to detail. Then, his rhetorical questions completely ridicule dramatic tension; Doña Inés's anxiety is comically melodramatic, a complete parody not only of the romantic tradition, but also of its twentieth-century clone, the *novela rosa* (sentimental or romantic novel).[13]

After the previous example of mock dramatic tension, the emphasis begins to shift more pronouncedly from the convention of characterization to that of action. The tension of Doña Inés's vigil, for example, is resolved by a comic version of the theatrical event: "Y ahora sí que ha sucedido algo, repentinamente: en el silencio de la estancia ha sonado con furia y ha vuelto a sonar la campanilla de la puerta" (p. 78; "And now, something has really happened, unexpectedly: in the silence of the room the doorbell has rung with a fury"). This announcement of the arrival of a letter, an obvious parody of the cliffhanger tradition, is followed by another narrative intrusion:

Considerad cómo la señora trae la carta: el brazo derecho cae lacio a lo largo del cuerpo; la mano tiene cogida la carta por un ángulo. Una carta puede traer la dicha y puede traer el infortunio. No será nada lo que signifique la carta que Doña Inés acaba de recibir; otras cartas como ésta, en este cuartito, ha recibido ya. Avanza lentamente hacia el velador que hay en un rincón y deja allí pausadamente la carta. Una actriz no lo haría mejor. (p. 79)

(Consider how the woman is carrying the letter: her right arm limply falls over the length of her body; her hand grasps the letter at an angle. A letter can bring happiness and it can bring misfortune. The letter that she has just received probably doesn't mean anything; she has already received other letters just like this one in this little room. She slowly approaches the table in the corner and hesitantly leaves the letter there. An actress could not have done it better.)

This direct appeal to the reader completely defuses any dramatic tension inherent in the arrival of the letter. Instead of creating tension, the narrator directs the reader's attention to the formulas designed to produce drama by mocking Doña Inés's reaction. We must remember, moreover, that just as the narrator is a fictitious creation, so are the readers he addresses here; in the same way that the posited author's voice is refracted through the narrator, so our role as recipients is refracted through the narrator's fictitious readers. In other words, we are not being asked merely to observe Doña Inés, but also to observe the narrator asking his readers to observe her. Our role is to see the projected image, while at the same time observing the process of projecting it.

The emphasis falls even more on the reader's role in fiction when the narrator shifts to first-person plural verb form. Such a shift occurs after Doña Inés has read the letter and offered a display of anguish "como lo haría una consumada actriz" (p. 81; "just as an accomplished actress would do it"), which then inspires the narrator to comment:

> Nos hemos resignado ya al dolor. Hemos entrado ya en la región de la enfermedad. El pavor de antes del tránsito y en el tránsito, ha pasado ya. Desde esta luctuosa ribera, nuestros ojos contemplan la otra ribera apacible y deleitosa de la salud, allá enfrente. ¿Cuándo volveremos a ella? Y, ¿es seguro que volveremos? ¡Adiós, adiós, amigos! (p. 81)
>
> (We have now resigned ourselves to the pain. We have entered into the region of illness. The dread before the transit and in the transit has already passed. From this mournful shore our eyes contemplate the other pleasant and delightful shore of health, there in front. When will we return to it? And, can we be sure we will return? Goodbye, goodbye, friends!)

At first glance the use of the first-person plural is designed to elicit the active participation of the readers; the speaker has projected himself into the role of the protagonist and invites his readers to do the same. Yet because of the exaggerated mode of expression, no empathy results from this projection. On the contrary, the identification is a mockery. And it is not merely a case of the narrator encouraging his readers to laugh at Doña Inés, but of the posited author humorously inviting us to recognize the literary convention involved. If we limit our role to that of the narrator's readers, we merely see irony directed at certain character types;[14] if we play the role elicited by the posited author's strategy, we see the parodic treatment of a whole literary tradition. As is always the case, the discourses are double-voiced, and the posited author's message (parody) comes to us refracted through that of the narrator (irony).

The first segment of this "love story" ends with Doña Inés left waiting alone in her room. Anecdotally, it is the eternal story of unrequited love. Yet that story is but a pretext. It is not the tale of romance but the formulas on which the tale depends that draw our attention. Beginning with Chapter 8, the locale changes, and with it occurs another variation of the eternal love story.

Not only is there a switch of scene and a modification of basic love anecdote in the eighth chapter, but also a new set of literary codes are foregrounded. As the action switches to the provincial city of Segovia, the pastoral rather than the romantic tradition becomes the primary target of literary parody.

Accompanying the changes already noted, there is also a new status for Doña Inés in the novel. Although she still plays the principal role in the romance situation, she now does so as a real character rather than a mere caricature. And the strategy of binary oppositions keys her development into the role of authentic protagonist. That strategy first emerges in a description of her Segovian house: "La casa—medio rústica, medio ciudadana—se levanta entre la ciudad y el campo" (p. 94; "The house—half rustic, and half cosmopolitan—rises between the city and the countryside"). The house is further divided into a downstairs and an upstairs, and the narrator tells us that as a child Doña Inés used to sit in the stairway landing between the two floors listening to the adults talk. That midpoint hiding place where she felt both near to and removed from the others also points to an essential aspect of her personality:

> Y esta extraña sensación de cercanidad y distanciamiento del mundo, a un tiempo mismo, debía repercutir a lo largo de toda la vida de la niña y constituir el núcleo de su personalidad. La esquividad, el apartamiento, la enconada aversión hacia una sociedad estúpida y gazmoña habían de impulsarla poderosamente por un lado; y por otro había de sentirse llevada hacia el efusivo y múltiple trato humano, con calor, con cordialidad, con emoción. (pp. 96–97)

> (And this strange sensation of the nearness to and distance from the world, at the same time, must have reverberated throughout the life of the girl and must have constituted the nucleus of her personality. The shyness, the isolation, the angry aversion toward a stupid and hypocritical society were to push her powerfully to one side; and on the other hand she was to feel herself attracted to the warmth of multiple human relationships, with their passion, with their cordiality, with their emotion.)

Such binary oppositions in this case serve to reveal a conflict within Doña Inés that provides depth to her character and therefore marks a change in her role in the novel. Whereas in the first segment of the love story she is the direct target of the narrator's mocking tone, in the second segment the supporting cast ("una sociedad estúpida y gazmoña") becomes the object of ridicule. With this switch in emphasis, the posited author's message expands to include society as well as literary styles. The new love story, therefore, is yet another pretext, in this case for demonstrating the symbiosis between societal and literary traditions.

The love story of the second part of the novel is a triangle involving Diego (a young poet), Plácida, (a childhood friend of Doña Inés), and of course Doña Inés. Plácida is in love with Diego but keeps their romance a secret from Doña Inés, who fortuitously meets Diego and is attracted to him. One day Doña Inés and Diego meet in the cathedral, and they exchange a passionate kiss. That kiss becomes the motive for public scandal involving the bishop, the mayor, and most of the population of Segovia. In addition and most significantly for Doña Inés, it is the source of Plácida's display of utter desolation. As a result of the latter, Doña Inés abandons Segovia and emigrates to Argentina, leaving part of her estate to Plácida so that she and Diego can marry.

The makeup of the supporting cast reveals the shift in literary model: an idyllic setting, a protective shepherd, the fair maiden to whom he is a devoted vassal, a young poet who is the object of affection for the two female protagonists, and finally a wise consul for the rival female protagonist, Doña Inés. The triangle is also duplicated by the tragic history of Doña Beatriz, a distant relative of Doña Inés, as narrated by the latter's uncle, Don Pablo. In short, from romanticism the model has shifted to the epic/pastoral tradition, which in turn forms a direct link with Spanish provincial society in 1925.

Serving as a base for the parody in the second segment are the descriptions of nature. Since the setting is a provincial capital, the narrator offers what one expects to be an appropriately bucolic description of the arrival of dawn: "La inmensa y menuda orquesta de los grillos, terminado ya el concierto diario, ha bajado sus élitros como se baja la tapa de un piano" (p. 118; "The immense and tiny orchestra of crickets, already having finished the daily concert, has lowered its wings as if they were the top of a piano"). It has been suggested that this passage echoes some of Ramón Gómez de la Serna's *greguerías*[15] (aphorisms). The analogy seems appropriate, since like Don Ramón's word-plays, the passage cited begins as if it were going to repeat a common literary conceit but then offers a new and unsuspected twist at the end. In short, it subverts reader expectations and therefore parodies the whole Ovidian tradition of the idyllic setting, or *lugar ameno* in Spanish literature.

The parody of bucolic settings becomes even more obvious in the description of the poplar grove near the castle where Doña Inés often goes to reflect:

> Llenan los senderos plantas silvestres: la caléndula con su botón y pétalos amarillos: la matricaria con sus pétalos blancos y botón de oro; el simpático gordolobo—*verbascum thapsus*—con su pináculo de florecitas de un amarillo claro y sus hojas vestidas de sedosa borra blanca; la clemátides— *clamatis vitalba*—o hierba del pordiosero, con sus flores blancas o violáceas, dignas de ser secadas entre las páginas del *Buscón*. (p. 136)
>
> (The wild plants fill the paths: the marigold with its yellow button and petals; the daisy with its white petals and the button of gold; the nice mullein—*verbascum thap-*

sus—with its pinnacle of clear yellow, tiny flowers and leaves of silky white; the clematis—*clamatis vitalba*—or beggars' weed, with its white and violet flowers, worthy to be dried between the pages of the *Buscón*.)

The combination of folk names—"gordolobo, hierba del pordiosero"—and their technical Latin terms creates a humorous contrast. In addition, when the narrator says that the flowers of the *clamatis vitalba* are worthy to be pressed between the pages of the *Buscón,* he cites the title of a work that represents an antithesis of pastoral idealism and the *lugar ameno* tradition. Finally, he draws the passage to a humorous conclusion by describing the sound of a fountain: "en lo hondo, en un subterráneo, el son pausado, intercadente, del agua que se entrederrama, que se derrama despacio, con lentitud" (p. 136; "in the depths of a cave, the halting, intercadent sound of the water that slowly spills out, sluggishly"). The humorous contrasts, apparently inappropriate literary reference, and rhetorical excesses serve to parody the literary tradition echoed by the passage. And when Doña Inés and Diego first cast eyes on one another, we see yet other methods for parodying idyllic nature: "El aire es más resplandeciente ahora. Los pájaros trinan con más alegría. Canta la calandria y contesta el ruiseñor. Las flores tienen sus matices más vivos. Las montañas son más azules. El agua es más cristalina. El cielo es más brillante" (p. 142; "The air is more radiant now. The birds chirp with more happiness. The lark sings and the nightingale answers. The hues of the flowers are alive. The mountains are even more blue. The water is more crystalline. The sky is more brilliant"). In addition to the excessive repetition of the adverb "más," the lines "Canta la calandria / y responde el ruiseñor" are lifted directly from a popular Spanish ballad.[16] Whereas such foregrounding of literary codes as demonstrated in the examples above reveals an obvious parodic intent, the parody also offers the first hint of a message from the posited author that is not merely concerned with literature itself: an unmasking of the myth associating pastoral ideals to provincial cities such as Segovia.

The parody of a pastoral setting is not limited to descriptions of nature, however, for it even includes a shepherd devoted to serving his mistress Plácida: "Matías el pastor estaba en la majada. Cuando ha venido a Segovia la señora, le han mandado un recado. Ha venido Matías a la ciudad y ha traído sus dos perros. A uno le llaman Barcino y a otro le dicen Luciente. El uno es de color bermejo y el otro es de color blanco" (p. 121; "Matías, the shepherd, was with his flock. When her ladyship came to Segovia, they sent him the message. Matías has come to the city and has brought his two dogs. One they call Barcino and the other Luciente. One is red and the other white"). Matías, in mock pastoral tradition, also feels obliged to prove his status as Plácida's protector through physical exploits: "El pastor ha jurado coger con la mano una raposa. Ha trabajado mucho Matías para cogerla y no lo ha conseguido. Una vez puso la mano en el cerro a una raposita, y la raposita le encentó un dedo de un mordisco, y salió escapada . . . El pastor se ha marchado a Segovia. Con Matías se han ido sus dos mastines. A uno le llaman Barcino; a otro le dicen Luciente. El uno es de color bermejo; el otro es de color blanco" (p. 122; "The shepherd has sworn to catch a fox with his hands. Matías has worked hard to catch it, and he hasn't succeeded. Once he put his hand in the den of a fox, and the fox nipped his finger and got away . . . The shepherd has left Segovia. His two mastiffs have gone with Matías . . . One they call Barcino; the other Luciente. One is red; the other white"). Not only is his goal of catching a fox with his hands ridiculous in itself, but the use of the diminutive—"raposita"—along with the infelicitous results that left him disgraced in the eyes of his colleagues makes a farce of the whole literary tradition of faithful vassals and tests of skill and courage. And so the ballad tradition with its tag-line repetition serves as a device for criticizing a society that, by implication, continues to espouse such values. More and more the posited author's message seems directed not at literature itself, but at the society that certain types of literature reflect.

Most representative of the society are two of the points in the love triangle, Diego and Plácida. Diego is very similar to the pastoral model. In addition to being a poet, he is young, handsome, and given to solitude and contemplation. His role, in the final analysis, is basically passive, and by virtue of his propensity to conform, he survives the effects of the scandal. Diego is presented as a pastoral stereotype, more of an icon than a character; such a presentation also projects a social message.

Plácida, by way of contrast, offers some significant new dimensions to the pastoral model from which she is drawn. The first variation occurs with her introduction into the novel and results from a second message voiced over the literary model that Plácida represents: "A primera hora de la mañana baja Plácida de su cuarto. Plácida es hija de unos labradores de Garcillán; los padres de Doña Inés los favorecieron en su tiempo; Plácida vivió cuando niña en la casa de Segovia con Doña Inés. No ha querido vivir de asiento en Madrid. Ha venido ahora a la ciudad para asistir a Doña Inés" (p. 119; "At early morning Plácida comes down from her room. Plácida is the daughter of some workers from Garcillán; Doña Inés's parents took care of them in their time; when she was a child Plácida lived in Doña Inés's house, in Segovia. She did not want to live in Madrid. She has come to the city now to assist Doña Inés"). This example of parataxis (semicolons rather than linking words and short, simple sentences) constitutes a stylistic anachronism; it is an epic style out of place in a modern context. As a result of such a disparity between style and context, Plácida strikes the reader as herself an anachronism; she conveys the sensation of leading a formulaic existence, which in turn may be designed to reflect the role of provincial women in general.

The implication that Plácida reflects an anachronistic social type gains added credibility when the narrator elects to scrutinize her physical appearance:

Plácida sonreía. Plácida es alta y cenceña. En la tez tersa y brillante—al igual que en las exculturas sagradas— brillan los dientes blancos. En la blancura de la piel se enciende el rosicler de las mejillas. Los labios y las mejillas de la moza son—usando de una imagen de que gustaba usar Lope—pétalos de rosa caídos en naterones cándidos. El cuerpo fino y duro se mueve ondulando. Viste la moza una falda de indiana azul celeste con un ribete blanco y el busto va ceñido por un pañuelo de fondo punzó y ramos también blancos. (p. 127)

(Plácida was smiling. Plácida is tall and thin. In her smooth and shiny complexion—equal to that of the sacred statues—her white teeth shine. The rosy pink of her cheeks gives a glow to the whiteness of her skin. Her maiden lips and cheeks are—borrowing an image that Lope liked to use— rose petals piled up like cottage cheese. Her fine, hard body moves in waves. She wears a skirt of Indian sky blue with a white border, and the bodice is anchored by a white scarf with white designs of branches.)

We are offered, of course, not the description of a believable character, but an idealization, a literary cliche. And as if the description itself were not enough with the pure whites, rosy reds, and celestial blues, the parenthetical reference to Lope is clearly designed to label this description as a parodic literary conceit. From the exterior, Plácida with her perpetual smile seems born to play the sacrificial role of loyal servant; she seems to represent the ideal of the provincial woman, but an ideal based on a literary model totally out of date.

The first indication that the idealized exterior hides another dimension occurs when Doña Inés touches a packet of papers in Plácida's room, and at her friend's look of alarm, Doña Inés begins to make allusion to Diego:

Plácida ya no sonreía. Si Doña Inés hubiera escudriñado el paquete oculto en el armario, debajo del blanco paño, hubiera visto que muchos de esos papeles están llenos de versos. Las ventanas dan al campo y a la ciudad. La Sierra se columbra en la lejanía. Cuatro o seis álamos, cerca de la casa, ponen sus cimas agudas—a causa de la perspectiva—junto a las últimas pinceladas blancas de la nieve de la montaña. (p. 128)

(Plácida was no longer smiling. If Doña Inés had searched the secret package in the cupboard, underneath the white cloth, she would have seen that many of the papers are full of verses. The windows look out over the countryside and the city. You can make out the range of mountains in the distance. Four or six poplars, near the house, stick their dagger-like points—a result of the viewing perspective—very near the last white patches of snow on the mountain.)

Suddenly the exterior image of absolute congeniality and purity of thought is replaced by the suggestion of piercing jealousy. That impression emerges primarily from a subtle change in focalization in the last sentence of the passage. Rather than viewing her from the outside, the parenthetical notice, "a causa de la perspectiva," signals that now we are sharing the same view she observes. Thus the dagger-like "cimas agudas" and the cold and distant "últimas pinceladas blancas de la nieve de la montaña" tell us more about the state of mind of the viewer than they do about the view. Behind her façade of happiness and virtue, Plácida apparently hides some emotions glossed over by the muses of the past.

Near the end of the novel and as a result of the kiss and the public scandal it creates, Plácida appears to be disconsolate. On a gray and rainy winter day with fog lending an ashen color to the countryside, Doña Inés goes to her friend's room in an attempt to soothe the poor girl's suffering: "La cara de Plácida está tercamente vuelta hacia el muro. Y la voz de Inés, susurrante, dice, mientras las manos se crispan y el corazón siente suprema angustia: '¡No le quiero, no le quiero!' De lo ceniciento de la niebla comienzan a emerger en el campo los finos álamos verdes" (p. 203; "Plácida's face is stubbornly turned toward the wall. And Inés's voice, whispering, says, while her hands twitch and her heart feels supreme anguish: 'I do not love him, I do not love him!' From the ashen snow the fine green poplars begin to emerge"). In a masterful stoke of understatement, the narrator informs us that Plácida's strategy has worked. The display of total bereftness has allowed the apparently simple provincial girl to extract the declaration of surrender she has been seeking from her sophisticated urban rival. Doña Inés does not succumb to pressures from the bishop, or the mayor, or popular opinion; she is done in by the bewitching allure of a literary convention, a simulacrum of innocence, devotion, and sacrifice. Plácida, the voice of the posited author seems to be saying, represents the corrupted pastoral model in the Spain of 1925. Although the façade of the same ideals remains intact, behind the archetypal image we find perhaps the most striking example in the novel of the essence of a "sociedad estúpida y gazmoña" (p. 97) from which Doña Inés was repelled even as a child.

Whereas Plácida represents the corruption of pastoral values in the modern world, the interpolated story of Doña Beatriz demonstrates what happens to heroic tragedy when repeated in a modern context. This tragedy, narrated by Don Pablo, concerns a woman who falls in love with a young troubadour. When they are discovered by her jealous husband, he avenges himself by sending the troubadour's head on a platter to his wife. Doña Inés, a descendent of Doña Beatriz, mirrors her ancestor's story in an example of what has come to be labeled interior duplication.[17] Yet the image reflected by the mirrored situation is refracted in such a way that it also forms a parody, although a sad one, of the tragic source.

The parodic relationship between the two stories becomes apparent when Don Pablo begins to tell Doña Inés the tragic climax to Doña Beatriz's love tale. Throughout Chapter 33 Doña Inés is a type of foil in her role as the reluctant but captivated recipient of a horror tale:

> Tengo miedo de oír esa historia. ¿Qué sucedió después? . . . No quisiera escuchar más de esa historia. ¿Qué es lo que pasó luego? . . . No quisiera oír más. ¿Qué suce-

dió el día de la fiesta? . . . No puedo escuchar más ¿Qué sucedió luego? . . . No, no quiero escuchar más. ¿Qué sucedió después? (pp. 160–62)

(I am afraid to hear this story. What happened after? . . . I wouldn't want to listen to any more of this story. What happened then? . . . I would not want to hear more. What happened the day of the party? . . . No, I do not want to hear any more. What happened afterwards?)

It is difficult to imagine a more ideal listener for a tragic story. In fact, she is so perfect in her role that she parodies the effect elicited by the horror genre. This type of comic exaggeration, then, sets the stage for the refraction that occurs as Doña Beatriz's heroic tragedy is duplicated by the decidedly unheroic fiasco of Doña Inés and Diego.

As opposed to the Doña Beatriz classic tragedy, there is no aggrieved husband, or even parent, to lend dramatic and tragic dimensions to the kiss between Doña Inés and Diego. The only individual perhaps wronged is Plácida, who resorts to deceit as a means to a very pragmatic vindication. Since both Doña Inés and Diego are unmarried, the profanation is limited to the place where the kiss took place: the cathedral. The injured party, therefore, is an institution, and society is the protector of its honor.

The comic potential of an institution cast into the role of the avenger of tainted honor is not lost on the narrator, who begins the chapter following the kiss with the following notice:

Las nubes, redondas y blancas, corren veloces sobre el fondo de añil. Las veletas, mudables y locas—son veletas—, giran y tornan a girar de Norte a Sur, de Este a Oeste. No saben lo que hacen . . . Una lechuza ha salido de un campanario en pleno día; un avariento ha dado dos cuartos de limosna. Todo está revuelto y trastornado. El beso ha removido los posos sensuales de la ciudad . . . Las veletas—son veletas—giran alocadas. (pp. 178–79)

(The clouds, round and white, move quickly over the blue background. The weather vanes, changeable and crazy—they are weather vanes—turn and spin to the north, to the south, from east to west. They don't know what they are doing . . . An owl has flown from the bell tower in broad daylight; a miser has given two small coins to charity. Everything is out of joint and turned around. The kiss has removed the sensual dregs from the city . . . The weather vanes—they are weather vanes—are spinning wildly.)

The mocking tone to the supposed earth-shattering impact of the kiss is underscored by the repetition of the parenthetical explanation, "Las veletas—son veletas." By pretending to reassure his reader that these events are not really the result of cosmic interference, in effect the narrator raises a possibility that, given the mundane nature of the occurrences (the wind blowing, an owl flying during the day, and a miser giving a small amount of money to a beggar), is comical. But of course a society intent on seeing cosmic forces at work will find them one way or another.

The title to the following chapter, "Aquelarre en Segovia," announces that supernatural elements are indeed at work. The exaggeratedly ominous beginning of the chapter, however, assures us that these forces are not to be taken too seriously: "Nubes pardas. Ruido de cedazos. Araña en espejo. Salero derribado" (p. 180; "Brown clouds. Noise from sieves. Spider in mirror. An overturned salt shaker"). The narrator completely undermines any remaining magical connotations when he parenthetically clarifies that the four would-be witches, "salen por el portal—no por la chimenea—a la calle" (p. 181; "leave by the door—not by the chimney—to get to the street"). In effect, the witches in question are four gossipers who, residing in the four corners of the city, gather at a fifth lady's home in the center to discuss the scandal. Again the mundane is underscored by virtue of its mock supernatural presentation. Of course the target of the mockery is society itself, a society perhaps so bored by its daily existence that it feels compelled to put an exaggerated importance on a trivial event.

But no honor drama would be complete without a challenge to a duel, and in this case the challenger is Don Herminio Larrea, a man who lives in the same boardinghouse with Diego. Don Herminio summons to combat a newspaper writer who wrote some satiric verses directed at Doña Inés. Don Herminio reads his message in the square in the noonday sun, but only a small boy, a pigeon, and a stray dog brave the elements to listen to it. When a woman looking out her window at the strange group asks a neighbor also observing the scene what is going on, the second lady answers, "¡Pregón de pescado!" (He's selling fish!), and soon the whole city is talking about Don Herminio reading his "pregón de pescado" in the city square—a fittingly comic epitaph for the death of heroic deeds in our modern world. Doña Inés, as a result, suffers tragic consequences but without virtue of having participated in an event of heroic proportions. Her story is simultaneously a comic and a tragic refraction of that of Doña Beatriz and the anachronistic literary tradition it represents.

In the final chapters of the novel there is an increasing tendency to satirize social types rather than to parody literary styles. As the scandal of the kiss spreads to the highest levels, the bishop and an archpriest speak like politicians, while the civil governor attempts to play the fraternal role with Diego that is normally associated with the clergy. Doña Inés finally departs for the New World aboard the newly invented steamship, and Don Pablo laments the end of European civilization. Yet literary parody is not completely abandoned and appears most noticeably in the titles to Chapter 49, "¿Epílogo? No; todavía no"; Chapter 51, "Tampoco es esto epílogo"; and Chapter 52, "Epílogo," with the initial sentence of the chapter: "Sí; esto sí es epílogo" (p. 219; "Yes, this indeed is the epilogue"). This final parody of nineteenth-century novelistic form seems designed to remind the reader that one of the fundamental messages of the novel concerns the nature of literature itself.[18]

Given the emphasis placed on parody in the preceding analysis, there is a danger of appearing to trivialize the novel. After all, over the years critics have discussed in very serious terms the absence of dramatic tension, the plight of Doña Inés and the fickle Don Juan, the duplication involved in the two love triangles, the insensitivity of the populace, the harshness of the secular and ecclesiastical authorities, and the philosophical discourses of Don Pablo. Yet our analysis demonstrates that parody forms a part of the presentation of each of these aspects, and to ignore that comic device is to do the novel an injustice. Recognizing the parodic element, moreover, does not trivialize the thematic implications of the novel; it does make these implications less ponderously "transcendent" in tone.

The term *transcendent,* one will have guessed, is borrowed from Ortega's essay, the "Dehumanization of Art," which appeared in the same year as *Doña Inés*.[19] Noting the coincidence of dates does not mean to suggest that Martínez Ruiz was directly influenced by Ortega's treatise, but rather that both writers expressed in the same year, one as a novelist and the other as an essayist, a similar and obviously spreading aesthetic attitude. Stated in another way, to understand more clearly the implications of Ortega's thesis one can profitably read *Doña Inés* with it in mind; to appreciate more fully the role of parody in that novel one can profitably read it with Ortega's concept of the "intranscendencia del arte nuevo" (lack of transcendence of the new art) in mind. That concept, as defined by Ortega, involves presenting art as a game so as to diminish its transcendent pretensions but without trivializing it in the process. In fact, Ortega allows that the game can have serious implications. *Doña Inés* can be seen, then, as an example of Ortega's thesis put into practice. Parody serves to underscore art as art, as a game, and therefore the "serious" messages one finds in the novel are more palatable; they are conclusions drawn from an aesthetic experience rather than from a didactic sermon. Furthermore, that experience results not merely from parody, but also from a structural principle perhaps best explained by reference to Emil Staiger's concept of "lo épico" (the epic dimension).

The essence of "lo épico," according to Staiger, is the paratactic construction and its effect of arresting temporal progression. Staiger equates a movement toward "lo dramático" (the dramatic dimension)—syntactic constructions of linking words that produce progression, tension, and ultimate resolution—with the advent of Christianity. He argues that the structuring principle of the conventional novel is "lo dramático." As we entered the twentieth century, however, Staiger feels that existentialism replaced Christianity as the primary spiritual doctrine, and he ends his book with the speculation that as a reflection of the new philosophical trend, we may well anticipate the novel turning to "lo épico" as its structuring principle.[20]

Doña Inés can be seen, therefore, not only as a reflection of the aesthetic dogma espoused by Ortega, but also as a fulfillment of Staiger's prophesy. The lack of dramatic tension, the eternal repetition of types and *topos*, the temporally frozen image of hypocrisy and intolerance, and the response of literature to literature, are all parodic expressions of "lo épico." Although written by a member of the "old group," *Doña Inés* incarnates the "new art." What is new in the novel, what links it directly with the vanguard movement in fiction, is its playful resurrection of an ancient structural principle. *Tirano Banderas*, appearing the year after and also written by one of the original members of the old generation, offers yet another expression of that structural principle.

Tirano Banderas

At the beginning of Part 4 of *Tirano Banderas*, one of the protagonists, the Indian Zacarías, is presented in the following manner: "El alfarero movía los pinceles con lenta minucia, cautivo en un dual contradictorio de acciones y pensamientos"[21] ("The potter moved the brushes with slow deliberation, captive of a dual contradiction of actions and thoughts"). This image, projected in the center section of the novel, reflects in capsule form the underlying structural principle of Valle-Inclán's modern masterpiece.

Whereas *Doña Inés* features a revival of "lo épico" in a parodic mode, *Tirano Banderas* revives and combines it with the *esperpento*, a literary style created and named by Valle-Inclán himself.[22] In fact, for years that novel has been considered as something of an oddity, a unique experiment in novelistic expression that resists classification in the general categories created for early twentieth-century Spanish literature.[23] Recently, however, the Generation of '98 label assigned to its author has been overcome, and the novel has been recognized as bona fide vanguard and even postmodernist fiction.[24]

Yet *Tirano Banderas* is also an example of an *engagé* novel, a label generally considered the antithesis of the vanguard movement. In large degree the greatness of the novel, then, can be attributed to its ability to represent avant-garde techniques and sociopolitical concerns simultaneously; it can be read as art for art's sake, or as a political statement on a historical event. Of course, to limit the reading to novelistic experimentation or ideological message is to do the novel a great injustice, for the two are inseparable. Together they enable the work to transcend the temporal limits inherent in a mere technical tour de force or historical documentation and to project a new and dynamic view of the process inherent in dictatorships and revolutions. The referent is not the Porfirio Díaz dictatorship and the Mexican Revolution per se, nor even Hispanic American despots and coups per se, but the process itself of oppression and rebellion. In short, Valle-Inclán relies on a complex and contradictory plan of composition in *Tirano Banderas* to transform the particular into the universal.

Given the contradictory complexity of the novel, it is not surprising that a polemic has developed concerning its final message. On one side are those who argue that the novel signifies the futility of revolutionary change, and the advocates of such a reading inevitably underscore its circular structure to support their thesis.[25] Those who challenge the failed rebellion interpretation insist that there is a linear movement, and therefore revolutionary change is realized.[26] Since both sides of the polemic support their arguments with convincing textual (and even extratextual) evidence, it seems clear that the novel somehow points at both the failure and the success of political revolt; in short, and referring again to the image quoted at the beginning of this essay, the projected message involves contradiction itself.

If the novel seems to work against itself, the roots of that conflict can be traced to the relationship between the story *(histoire),* and how that story is presented to the reader *(récit).* The *histoire,* which the reader has to reconstruct, concerns approximately twenty-four hours in which the oppressed people of Tierra Caliente rise in rebellion against their dictator, Tirano Banderas. In an epilogue the action shifts first to the morning after the rebel attack when the tyrant meets his death, and then to three days later when his body is quartered and displayed in four parts of the country. Within this story of military strategy, internal politics, diplomatic posturing, opportunism, idealism, sadism, and human sacrifice, there is another personal story of an Indian whose son is killed, and who then wreaks vengeance on the person indirectly responsible for the child's death.

The preceding reconstruction of the *histoire,* however, is deceptively simple. The *récit* presents in a fragmented, nonchronological order the events summarized. To begin with, the novel has an exterior frame consisting of a prologue and the epilogue already mentioned. Most of the action of the prologue involves the climactic attack against the dictator and therefore corresponds chronologically to the final events in the *histoire.* Yet there is an apparent exception to the chronology of events within the prologue, and that deviation and its implications, to be examined in detail later, is the ultimate key to the contradictory message projected by the novel. Aside from that very significant exception, the *récit* offers the reader the same event in process at the beginning as at the end of the novel, thus creating the sensation of at least partial circularity.

Enclosed by the prologue and epilogue are seven "partes." Parts 1–3 and 5–7 are subdivided into three "libros," which in turn are subdivided into numbered units. Part 4, the structural center of the novel, is composed of seven books. Visually, the relationship between part and book is:

Prologue	1	2	3	4	5	6	7	Epilogue
	3	3	3	7	3	3	3	

If the symmetry revealed by this scheme suggests a carefully constructed novel, its structural exactness becomes even more apparent with the pattern formed by charting the appearances of the main character, Tirano Banderas, in the part/book relationship:[27]

Prologue	1	2	3	4	5	6	7	Epilogue
no	yes	no	no	no	no	yes	yes	yes
	no	no	no	no	no	no	no	
	yes	yes	no	no	no	no	yes	
				no				
				no				
				no				
				no				

An analysis of the pattern formed above reveals not merely symmetry, but also a mirror effect; the prologue and the epilogue on the one hand, and Parts 1–3 and 5–7 on the other, reflect one another in reverse order (since all the books in the second horizontal column have the same pattern, the left- and right-hand sides do not appear to be reversed). In fact, it has been astutely observed that the fourth book of Part 4, the precise middle of the novel, serves as a pivotal point from which the action reverses itself. In the first half of the novel (in this case excluding the prologue), all the action leads away from Tirano as the key characters try to escape from his reign of terror; in the second half all the action leads toward him as the revolutionary forces mobilize their opposition.[28] This reversal is reflected in the activities presented in each book. For example, in the third book of Part 2, Tirano receives a report from his police inspector that his order to arrest Don Roque, the leader of the opposition party, has been carried out. Tirano appears here with all his dictatorial power intact as he congratulates his inspector and suggests that Don Roque should not be handled too gently.

The reverse image of this action comes in the first book of Part 6 (see the schematic breakdown above). Now, with political pressures mounting against him, Tirano decides as a conciliatory gesture to go to the prison to talk to Don Roque and inform him that he is to be set free. When he arrives, Tirano, in another reversal of Part 2, inquires first of the jailer: "—¿Han sido tratados con toda la consideración que merecen tan ilustres patricios y sus compañeros?" (p. 189; "Have such illustrious patricians and their friends been treated with all the consideration due them?"). The mirror effect of reversed images created by the *récit*, therefore, responds to the *histoire* itself: the political collapse of a dictator.[29]

Separating the structural symmetry of the prologue and Parts 1–3 versus the epilogue and Parts 5–7 is the middle section, Part 4, in which the Indian Zacarías's son is killed and the father avenges his son's death before joining the revolutionary forces. The extremely individual nature of much of the action narrated here distinguishes it from the other sections of the novel and allows it to stand as an almost independent story. This is the point where the national and international issues of oppression and rebellion yield to personal commitment. In this middle section, Zacarías's acts are dictated by elementary concepts of love and honor, crime and punishment, with no concern for political ideology, public image, or legal nuances. Beyond the desire for immediate personal vengeance, only superstition influences him. What he does, in short, is determined by a primitive and extremely idiosyncratic moral code that forms a marked contrast not only to the amoral expediency of the dictatorship, but also to the idealistic philosophies championed by the revolutionaries.

Yet the apparent autonomy of Part 4 is totally misleading. It is not only the physical center of the novel, but also the structural hub around which revolve many of the events presented in fragmented and nonchronological order. In Part 1, for example, Doña Lupita, a fortune-teller, confidante of the dictator, and street vendor, complains to Tirano that one of his colonels broke four of her serving glasses and refused to pay for the damage. Influenced by his superstition that Lupita possesses magical powers to see into the future, the dictator orders the arrest of Domiciano Gándara, the impudent officer. Later that night, in Part 3, Domiciano is warned by a prostitute, also named Lupita and also with clairvoyant powers, that the police are coming to arrest him. Domiciano escapes in the early hours of the morning before Tirano's henchmen arrive and, remembering that the Indian Zacarías owes him a favor, goes to seek his assistance.

The action is continued in Part 4 just at sunrise, as Domiciano arrives at Zacarías's hut and persuades the Indian to take him to the ranch of Filomeno, a man who at this time is organizing an attack for that very night against the tyrant. Domiciano leaves his ring with the Indian's wife as payment for the special favor. She then takes the ring to the pawnshop of Don Quintín. Quintín argues with her over the price, finally giving her a fraction of the value, and their wrangling is overheard by a blind minstrel and his daughter, also recent victims of Quintín's usurious tactics. Shortly after Quintín learns of Domiciano's escape, knowing all along that the ring belonged to the colonel, he decides to take it to the police for fear of being implicated. Quintín tells them that Zacarías's wife pawned the ring, and they go to her hut around noontime and arrest her. When they do so, her toddler son is left unattended in front of the hut. Zacarías, upon returning from taking Domiciano to Filomeno's ranch, finds what remains of his son after the hogs and vultures have devoured him. Zacarías puts the remains in a sack, discovers the pawn ticket from Quintín's shop and the money for the ring, and with the sack as an amulet, the Indian goes in search of the person guilty of his son's death. He wagers the money from the pawned ring and wins enough to buy a horse, attributing his gambling luck to the amulet. He then happens upon the blind man and his daughter, overhears them talking about the argument between his wife and Quintín, and learns from them that Quintín reported her to the police. Knowing now that Quintín is the one responsible for the death of his son, Zacarías goes to the pawn shop, ties Quintín to his horse and, galloping through the streets, "con las espuelas en los ijares del caballo, sentía en la tensa reata el tirón del cuerpo que rebota en los guijarros" (p. 156; "with his spurs in the flanks of his horse, he felt, in the tense rope, the jerk of the body that bounced on the rocks"). Only when his need for personal vengeance is thus satisfied does Zacarías join Filomeno's army, just before the insurrection is to begin.

As the preceding summary demonstrates, Part 4 links the action of the novel in the very process of separating it. Rather than progressing from beginning to end, the events narrated on either side tend to flow toward this center. As a result of that process, Part 4 is the point of contact between the opposing forces of opportunism and idealism, passion and stoicism, civic commitment and personal honor. Although these opposing forces converge in Part 4, their differences are not resolved there; on the contrary, the function of this central section is to create for the reader an aesthetic confrontation with contradiction. Part 4 of *Tirano Banderas* is a novelistic "black hole," the point where the carefully constructed rational patterns converge and disintegrate, leading the reader into the irrational realms of existence, and specifically into the contradiction inherent in the revolutionary process itself.

The most obvious contradiction of political rebellion involves a circular concept: tyranny leads to revolution, but as history so often demonstrates, revolution leads to further tyranny. Yet history does not conform to a perfect circular pattern. Contradicting the circle are all the cases of successful coups, of rebellions that put an end to tyranny. In short, the revolutionary process sometimes follows a linear course; any attempt to create a totally symmetrical pattern reflecting armed political change is contradicted by the inevitable exceptions. That process of a disrupted pattern, therefore, provides the key to the structural function of Part 4 of *Tirano Banderas.* As we now examine first the principal characters, and then the framing action of the prologue, we will be led inexorably not to the end, but to the center of the novel; the pattern is neither circular nor linear, but helical.

Although he is conspicuously absent from the structural center of the novel, it is impossible to talk about this work without discussing the title character, Tirano Banderas. The narrator's portrayal of the protagonist is probably the most-often cited example from this novel of Valle-Inclán's *esperpento* technique. The essence of that novelistic approach involves distortion, one example of which in *Tirano Banderas* involves the use of similes that equate the tyrant with carrion-eating crows and other birds of prey and frequent repetitions of his favorite expression, "¡chac, chac!" Also, Tirano is generally viewed from an exterior angle, and in profile. The combination of point of focalization and pose conveys the impression of someone totally lacking in depth and contour; the reader feels as though he were looking at a shadow. These types of dehumanizing descriptive techniques relegate the character to a nonanthropoid category. He is not even a simulacrum of a human type.

But there is a contradiction even to this character. He is not always viewed only from the exterior, and when the narrator does penetrate his surface, the reader is offered a glance into the disturbingly human origin of a dehumanized type:

Tirano Banderas caminó taciturno. Los compadres, callados como en un entierro, formaban la escolta detrás. Se detuvo en la sombra del convento, bajo el alerta del guaita, que en el campanario sin campanas clavaba la luna con la bayoneta. Tirano Banderas estúvose mirando el cielo de estrellas. Amaba la noche y los astros: El arcano de bellos enigmas recogía el dolor de su alma tétrica: Sabía numerar el tiempo por las constelaciones: Con la matemática luminosa de las estrellas se maravillaba: La eternidad de las leyes siderales abría una coma religiosa en su estoica crueldad indiana. Atravesó la puerta del convento bajo el grito nocturno del guaita en la torre, y el retén, abriendo filas, presentó armas. Tirano Banderas, receloso, al pasar, escudriñaba el rostro oscuro de los soldados. (p. 62)

(Tirano Banderas walked silently. His companions, silent as if they were at a burial, formed an escort behind. He paused in the shadow of the convent, below the watchful sentry in the belfry without bells who stabbed the moon with his bayonet. Tirano Banderas was looking at the sky filled with stars. He loved the night and the stars. The mystery of those beautiful enigmas captured the pain of his gloomy soul. He knew how to tell time by the constellations. He marveled at the luminous mathematics of the stars. The eternity of the sidereal laws opened a religious vein in his stoic Indian cruelty. He passed through the door of the convent, below the nocturnal scream of the sentry in the tower, and the reserve corps, opening ranks, presented arms. Tirano Banderas, suspicious, scrutinized the dark faces of the soldiers as he passed.)

As opposed to the general method of presentation, this conveys a certain depth of character. The preponderance of preterit verb tenses underscores Tirano's temporality in the face of the atemporality of the astral universe. And although the scene takes place in a convent and with the tone of a religious ceremony, the setting and the tone are ironic. The convent has been converted into a fortress, and the bells that summoned the faithful to worship have been replaced by a sentry who "clavaba la luna con la bayoneta." Finally, the spiritual communion that Tirano experiences is inspired by mathematics, or the infinity of numbers, which again underscores his finite existence. He clearly senses the threat of eternal damnation, but he fails or refuses to recognize Christian morality as a possible counterforce.[30] Thus this penetration into Tirano provides a contradictory human depth to the predominantly nonhuman existence usually attributed to him. Such a contradiction, then, seems to provide the key to the posited author's voice and message: Tirano represents the true dictator. He has human qualities that he has allowed to become dehumanized by ignoring any moral responsibility for his actions. Tirano is, in short, simultaneously and contradictorily non-human and human, and perhaps by virtue of such a conflicting character, his presence is felt everywhere.

As demonstrated earlier, by plotting the appearances of the protagonist in the various books we achieve a very revealing insight into his function in the overall structure of the novel. In fact, he is prominent even in his absence; he calls attention to the center, to Part 4, by not appearing there at all. Again in accord with his contradictory essence, he directs the flow of the action to the very point from which he is excluded.

Most obviously juxtaposed to Tirano is Don Roque Cepeda, the leader of the opposing political party, and a character also physically absent from Part 4. Jailed by Tirano's police during a political rally, the focus in the second book of Part 5 is directed to Don Roque in his jail cell as he affirms his faith in the revolution to another prisoner:

> Hablaba con esa luz fervorosa de los agonizantes, confortados por la fe de una vida futura, cuando reciben la Eucaristía. Su cabeza tostada de santo campesino erguíase sobre la almohada como en una resurrección, y todo el bulto de su figura exprimíase bajo el sabanil como bajo un sudario. El otro prisionero le miró con amistosa expresión de burla y duda. (p. 171)

> (He spoke with the feverish glow of a dying person who, comforted by his faith in a future life, receives communion. His tanned face of a country saint raised from the pillow as in a resurrection, and all the bulk of his figure was wrung beneath the shroud-like sheet. The other prisoner looked at him with a friendly expression of mockery and doubt.)

As the binary opposite to Tirano, Don Roque is totally committed to humanitarianism. Yet there is an unmistakably mocking tone to this initial description of him, and the key to the reader's reaction to him is the point of focalization. The reader observes Don Roque through the eyes of his cellmate, who looks and listens "con amistosa expresión de burla y duda." Like the anonymous prisoner, the reader sees the evangelical zeal of Don Roque's patriotism as laughably suspect.[31] Although not dehumanized, he is certainly larger than life in the fervor of his convictions.

The extraterrestrial air of Don Roque becomes humorously evident when in the first book of Part 7, having just been released from prison, he pays a visit to Tirano:

> Don Roque, con una escolta de cuatro indios caballerangos, se detenía al otro lado del seto, sobre el camino, al pie de la talanquera. La frente tostada, el áureo sombrero en la mano, el potro cubierto de platas, daban a la figura del jinete, en las luces del ocaso, un prestigio de santoral románico. Tirano Banderas, con cuáquera mesura, hacía la farsa del acogimiento. (p. 216)

(Don Roque, with an escort of four Indian stablemen, paused on the other side of the partition, on the road, at the foot of the parapet. His tanned forehead, his gilded sombrero in his hand, his platinized pony, aided by the light of dusk— all this created the illusion that the horseman was a Roman saint. Tirano Banderas, with Quaker-like dignity, made a total farce of his welcome scene.)

Now the viewing point is through Tirano's eyes, and the same benevolent attitude displayed by the cellmate is not evident here. Indeed, there can be little question concerning the reverence that Tirano feels in the face of a "santoral románico," and the reader cannot help but share the tyrant's mocking disdain at the sight of this gilded and platinized politician. In their meeting Tirano persuades Don Roque to observe a truce until the present crisis has passed, at which time the dictator promises that there will be free and honest elections. Don Roque apparently accepts the offer, for as he leaves we again observe him through Tirano's eyes: "Don Roque, trotando por el camino, saludaba de lejos con el pañuelo. Niño Santos, asomado a la talanquera, respondía con la castora. Caballo y jinete ya iban ocultos por los altos maizales, y aun sobresalía el brazo con el blanco saludo del pañuelo: —¡Chac! ¡Chac! ¡Una paloma!" (p. 219; "Don Roque, trotting along the road, waved from afar with his handkerchief. Niño Santos, peering over the parapet, responded with his beaver cap. The horse and rider were already hidden by the high cornstalks, and his arm still appeared waving the white handkerchief: 'Chac! Chac! What a pigeon!'"). From Tirano's perspective Don Roque is indeed a pigeon that he has just plucked. And by virtue of using Tirano as the focalizing point, the posited author refracts his voice to such a degree that he criticizes Don Roque without appearing to do so. Don Roque contradicts his own role as revolutionary leader; he is too ingenuous to have any effect in a world with the likes of Tirano Banderas. And that message, a product of this example of double-voicing through focalization, is driven home forcefully by virtue of presenting him first through the eyes of one of Tirano's victims, and then from the tyrant's own cynical view. Don Roque and Tirano thus form binary opposites, and as such they project a circular image of the eternal conflict between tyranny and rebellion.[32] There will always be a Don Roque in response to a Tirano Banderas, and of course vice versa. Both are conspicuous by their absence in the middle section.

With the exception of Zacarías, the most prominent figure in Part 4 is Filomeno. As a Creole, he represents what many would consider the only solution to the sociopolitical problems of South America: a blending of Indian and Spanish blood and heritage. In fact, the initial description of him suggests that he represents just such a felicitous fusion: "Filomeno Cuevas sonreía. Era endrino y aguileño. Los dientes alobados, retinto de mostacho y entrecejo: En la figura prócer, acerado y bien dispuesto" (p. 131; "Filomeno Cuevas was smiling. He was dark-skinned and aquiline. His teeth were like a wolf's, and his mustache and brow were very dark. His build was imposing, steel-like, and well proportioned"). Although typically succinct, this description of Filomeno conveys the image of a true child of nature, and as a result he forms a dramatic contrast to the members of particularly the Spanish colony, but also to the cherub-like Don Roque, and the vulture-like Tirano Banderas. Filomeno is the hunter wolf, and like that animal he is cautious and astute. But significantly, the narrator does not provide access to Filomeno's inner self. Filomeno, certainly to a greater extent than any of the other major characters in the novel, is characterized solely by his appearance, words, and above all, his actions.

Perhaps the most obvious self-characterization of Filomeno comes in his discussion with Domiciano; Filomeno's candor and democratic motives are juxtaposed with Domiciano's duplicity and self-interests. But it is in a conversation with his wife explaining his decision to lead the armed rebellion that Filomeno provides the most intriguing insight into his character:

> —¡Por ti y los chamacos no cumplo mis deberes de ciudadano, Laurita! El último cholo que carga un fusil en el campo insurrecto aventaja en patriotismo a Filomeno Cuevas. ¡Yo he debido romper los lazos de la familia y no satisfacerme con ser un mero simpatizante! Laurita, por evitaros lloros, hoy el más último que milita en las filas revolucionarias me hace pendejo a mis propios ojos. Laurita, yo comercio y gano la plata, mientras otros se juegan vida y hacienda por defender las libertades públicas. Esta noche he visto conducir entre bayonetas a Don Roquito. Si ahora me rajo y no cargo un fusil, será que no tengo sangre ni vergüenza. ¡He tomado mi resolución y no quiero lágrimas, Laurita! (p. 133)
>
> (Because of you and the children I am not fulfilling my obligations as a citizen, my little Laura! The lowest mestizo who carries a gun in the revolutionary camp surpasses Filomeno Cuevas in patriotism. I should have broken my family ties and not have been satisfied with merely being sympathetic to the cause! My little Laurita, to protect you and the children from tears, today the lowest peon serving in the revolutionary forces makes me feel like an asshole. My little Laura, I make deals and earn money, while others risk their lives and property in order to defend public liberties. Tonight I saw them arrest little Don Roque at bayonet point. If I crack now and don't take up a gun, it will mean that I have no blood in my veins and no shame. I have made up my mind and I don't want any tears, my little Laura!)

Certainly this passage can and has been read as a noble declaration of revolutionary commitment—even if it may sound a bit too oratorical for a private conversation between husband and wife. And the reference to Don Roque, or more precisely "Roquito," emphasizes the difference between the two revolutionaries. Roque is an idealist, while Filomeno is an activist. Roque can inspire others, but he is ineffective—the diminutive—when it comes to actual leadership. Filomeno does not debate the issues; he reacts decisively to them. Filomeno, as a result, seems to represent a solution to the vicious circle implicit in the Tirano/Roque opposition. Yet, when Filomeno's words and actions are viewed in juxtaposition to those of Zacarías, who is the principal character of this same Part 4, that conclusion becomes somewhat equivocal. Filomeno's revolutionary commitment, noble as it may be, is at the expense of another kind of commitment. He also incarnates a type of self-contradiction.

While crediting Zacarías with playing a key structural role in Part 4, critics tend to overlook him when they discuss methods of characterization in the novel.[33] It seems to be sufficient to note that he is an enigmatic Indian. Yet he enjoys a relationship to the narrator that is unique among all the characters, and that relationship is tied directly to his structural role. The narrative introduction to him signals his fundamental and contradictory role in the novel:

> Zacarías San José, a causa de un chirlo que le rajaba la cara, era más conocido por Zacarías el Cruzado Tenía el chozo en un vasto charcal de juncos y médanos, allí donde dicen Campo del Perulero: En los bordes cenagosos picoteaban grandes cuervos, auras en los llanos andinos y zopilotes en el Seno de México. Algunos caballos mordían la hierba a lo largo de las acequias. Zacarías trabaja el barro, estilizando las fúnebres bichas de chiromayos y chiromecas. La vastedad de juncos y médanos flotaba en nieblas de amanecida. Hozaban los marranos en el cenagal, a espaldas del chozo, y el alfarero, sentado, sobre los talones, la chupalla en la cabeza, por todo vestido un camisote, decoraba con prolijas pinturas jícaras y guejas. Taciturno bajo una nube de moscas, miraba de largo en largo al bejucal donde había un caballo muerto. El Cruzado no estaba libre de recelos: Aquel zopilote que se había metido en el techado, azotándole con negro aleteo, era un mal presagio. Otro signo funesto, las pinturas vertidas. El amarillo, que presupone hieles, y el negro, que es cárcel, cuando no llama muerte, juntaban sus regueros. Y recordó súbitamente que la chinita, la noche pasada, al apagar la lumbre, tenía descubierta una salamandra bajo el metate de las tortillas. . . . El alfarero movía los pinceles con lenta minucia, cautivo en un dual contradictorio de acciones y pensamientos. (pp. 111–12)

> (Zacarías San José, because of a scar that crossed his face, was known as Zacarías the Crossed Man. He had a shack in the vast swamp of reeds and sand that was known as Perulero Country. In the muddy borders huge crows scavenged for food, while vultures did the same in the Andean plains and buzzards in the Bosom of Mexico. Some horses chewed the grass along the length of the irrigation ditches. Zacarías was working with mud, molding the mournful ornamental potteries of half-man, half-beast. The vast reeds and sand floated in the mists of dawn. The hogs rooted in the bog, behind the hut, and the potter was sitting on his heels, his straw hat on his head, dressed only in a large shirt, decorated with meticulous paintings of chinaware. Silently under a cloud of insects, he stared into the vines where a dead horse was lying. The Crossed Man was not free of premonitions: That buzzard that had landed on the roof, whipping it with his black wings, was an evil omen. The other sinister sign, the spilled paints: yellow, which signifies bile, and black, which is prison, if not death, flowed together. And he remembered suddenly that the night before the little woman had discovered a salamander underneath the tortillas. . . . The potter moved his brushes with slow deliberation, captive in the dual contradiction of actions and thoughts.)

The passage begins in typical fashion for the novel with the narrator providing a brief explanation for a physical feature, the scar, the source of the nickname. In short, the message at this point suggests once more that what is observable from the outside of a character is an accurate reflection of the inner self. But then begins a description of the area surrounding the hut where Zacarías lives, and what is projected initially lacks any focalizing point. As the adjectives connoting impending doom begin to accumulate—"grandes cuevos, auras, zopilotes, fúnebres bichas, nieblas de amanecida"—the reader is suddenly told that the scene is being viewed through Zacarías's eyes: "Taciturno bajo una nube de moscas, miraba de largo en largo al bejucal donde había un caballo muerto." Then, in one of the most extended summaries of internal thought processes in the entire novel, the narrator explains the series of evil omens that preoccupy the mind of Zacarías. By first allowing the reader to share the character's vision of an ominous landscape, and then by offering an explanation of his state of mind on this particular day, Zacarías emerges as the most "human" of all the characters in the novel. At the same time, the passage ends with the observation that points not only at his character, but also at the very structural key to the novel noted earlier: "cautivo en un dual contradictorio de acciones y pensamientos." As the action of this central part continues, it becomes clear that Zacarías serves to express on a personal, human level the contradictory essence of the novel.

By virtue of the narrative introduction, which explains Zacarías's obsession with presages on this day, the reader is as apprehensive as the character when Zacarías returns home after having delivered Domiciano to Filomeno's ranch:

> Zacarías el Cruzado, luego de atracar el esquife en una maraña de bejucos, se alzó sobre la barca, avizorando el chozo. La llanura de esteros y médanos, cruzada de acequias y aleteos de aves acuáticas, delatábase con encendidas manchas de toros y caballadas, entre prados y cañerlas. La cúpula del cielo recogía los ecos de la vida campañera en su vasto y sonoro silencio. En la turquesa del día orfeonaban su gruñido los marranos. Lloraba un perro muy lastimero. Zacarías, sobresaltado, le llamó con un silbido. (pp. 145–46)
>
> (Zacarías the Crossed Man, after tying the skiff to a clump of branches, stood up in the boat, spying on the shack. The plain of swamps and reeds, crossed by irrigation ditches and the fluttering of aquatic birds, became blurred by the glowing stains of bulls and horses, between meadows and cane fields. The cupola of the sky caught the echoes of country life in its vast and sonorous silence. In the turquoise of the day the hogs chanted their chorus of grunts. A dog howled very mournfully. Zacarías, alarmed, called him with a whistle.)

Again the passage begins with an exterior view of the Indian's arrival, but with the second sentence a shift emerges and the reader shares the character's view, and of course his premonitions. The sights and the accompanying sounds, the eerie chorus of rummaging hogs, and the mournful howling of the dog, are, therefore, far from neutral. The reader cannot help but share the Indian's anxiety as he sets out to investigate the reason for the ominous atmosphere:

El Cruzado monta el pistolón y camina con sombrío recelo: Pasa ante el chozo abierto y mudo. Penetra en la ciénaga: El perro le insta, sacudidas las orejas, el hocico al viento, con desolado tumulto, estremecida la pelambre, lastimero el resuello. Zacarías le va en seguimiento. Gruñen los marranos en el cenegal. Se asustan las gallinas al amparo del maguey culebrón. El negro vuelo de zopilotes que abate las alas sobre la pecina se remonta, asaltado del perro. Zacarías llega: Horrorizado y torvo, levanta un despojo sangriento. ¡Era cuanto encontraba de su chamaco! Los cerdos habían devorado la cara y las manos del niño: Los zopilotes le habían sacado el corazón del pecho. El indio se volvió al chozo: Encerró en su saco aquellos restos, y con ellos a los pies, sentado a la puerta se puso a cavilar. De tan quieto, las moscas le cubrían y los lagartos tomaban el sol a su vera. (p. 146)

(The Crossed Man loads his gun and walks with gloomy caution. He passes in front of the open, silent shack. He goes into the swamp. The dog presses against him, his ears pricked, his nose to the wind, confused, his hair on end, his breathing bated. Zacarías follows him. The hogs grunt in the quagmire. The hens become frightened and flee to the protection of the maguey tree. Having been assaulted by the dog, the buzzards beat their wings in black flight over the mud, fading in the distance. Zacarías arrives. Horrified and grim, he picks up the bloody remains. It was all that remained of his child! The hogs had devoured the face and hands of the child; the buzzards had pecked the heart from his chest. The Indian returned to his shack. He put the remains in a sack, and with them at his feet, he sat down in the doorway and began to think. He was so quiet that insects covered him and lizards sunned themselves at his side.)

The switch from the past tense to the historical present is a time-honored strategy to encourage reader identification, and that is its function here. The reader advances with Zacarías, pistol drawn, as he passes the empty hut and follows the dog into the swamp. And as the character and reader advance together, the sound of the hogs changes from a haunting chant to the discordant grunts of their insatiable, and by now ominous, hunger. With the sudden retreating flight of the vultures, Zacarías and the reader know that they have reached the object of their search. The initial placement of the adjectives "horrorizado y torvo" underscores the bond between character and reader; the emotional reaction precedes true comprehension as the remains of what was once Zacarías's son appear. With the switch then to the preterit tense, the reader paradoxically is drawn even closer to the character as he experiences Zacarías's shock and defensive retreat into himself, as he becomes one with the very nature that mutilated his son.

From this point Zacarías becomes a hermetic personage, with only the grotesque sack containing the remains of his son as a visual sign of grief. In fact, only at the moment when Zacarías realizes his vengeance is the seal on his inner self momentarily removed as the narrator notes: "Y consuela su estoica tristeza indiana Zacarías el Cruzado" (p. 156; "And Zacarías the Crossed Man consoles his stoic Indian sadness"). In spite of the violent and primitive nature of the vengeance against Quintín, the reader cannot help but share Zacarías's sense of at least partial consolation. The vengeance was not taken against the hogs and vultures, for although they were the immediate perpetrators, they possess no moral responsibility for their actions. Humans, on the other hand, are morally accountable for what they do, even if they do not violate conventional legal codes. In fact, one might argue that although the punishment administered may offend modern sensitivities, this is the only point in the novel where justice is served directly. There can be little question but that if the guilty party were brought before the most enlightened legal system in the Western world, he would be judged innocent. By all nonlegal standards of morality, however, Quintín is guilty. Zacarías naturally responds only to his own moral code, which, in spite of its primitive idiosyncrasy, in one sense is more "human" than Filomeno's. Unlike Filomeno, then, Zacarías places personal morality above civic responsibility. And where one might argue with a personal morality satisfied by murderous vengeance, it is no more barbarous than a civil morality that results in Tirano's bullet-riddled body being quartered and its parts displayed in four different border cities.

The preceding analysis demonstrates that although they ultimately fight for the same cause, Filomeno and Zacarías also form a type of binary opposition. One renounces family commitment for the sake of a revolutionary cause, and the other in effect jeopardizes the revolution for the sake of avenging a family member. Filomeno is certainly civilized, but to the point of being somewhat dehumanized; Zacarías, with his bloody amulet and primitive revenge, is uncivilized, but surprisingly humanized. Of course the posited author's voice emerges from such an opposition, but the message of that voice vis-à-vis tyranny and revolution is ambiguous at best. The presence of Zacarías and Filomeno on the same side could point to the necessary blending not only of Indian and Creole interests, but above all of personal and civic commitments to assure the success of revolutionary change. Yet in the action presented in the prologue just prior to the attack, Filomeno orders Zacarías: "—Y pasada esta noche sepulta esos restos. En la guerra el ánimo y la inventiva son los mejores amuletos. Dame la mano" (p. 33; "And when this night is over, bury those remains. In war courage and cunning are the best amulets. Shake on it"). It would appear, therefore, that the union being sealed with the handshake is to be strictly on Filomeno's terms; rather than a blending, it appears that one of the forces is asserting its values at the expense of the other's. In that case the underlying opposition concerning values still exists and raises the question concerning when it will surface again and lead to its own conflict. The answer to that question is not clearly provided by the novel, which is content to lead readers to the central Part 4, where they must confront the contradictory essence of the people who oppose and lead revolutionary change.

The flow toward the center, the twisting of the circle and of the straight line into a coil, is most dramatically demonstrated by the frame. As noted earlier, those who argue for the circular structure generally point to the prologue, where the action represented corresponds to the end of the *histoire,* or the epilogue. Interestingly, the straight-line advocates also cite the frame, emphasizing the chronological sequence of events that lead directly from the prologue to the epilogue; the frame "straightens" the framed body. The point of agreement for both schools of thought is the chronological sequence existing within the prologue/epilogue unit. Yet a careful analysis of the prologue casts doubt on its sequential development, and that doubt in turn undermines any attempt to reduce the structure of the novel to a perfect symmetry.

As noted at the beginning of this analysis, the action of one chapter or unit of the prologue seems to deviate from the order of events involved in all the others which deal with the final moments before the attack on Tirano. The first unit, for example, consists of the following narrative explanation: "Filomeno Cuevas, criollo ranchero, había dispuesto para aquella noche armar a sus peonadas con los fusiles ocultos en un manigual, y las glebas de indios, en difusas líneas, avanzaban por los esteros de Ticomaipu. Luna clara, nocturnos horizontes profundos de susurros y ecos" (p. 31; "Filomeno Cuevas, a creole rancher, had arranged to arm his workers that night with guns hidden in a swamp, and the Indians, in uneven lines, advanced through the Ticomaipu swamp. Clear moon, deep night horizons of rustles and echoes"). The action of the next unit apparently pertains to the same chronological sequence, as it begins with the following explanation: "Saliendo a Jarote Quemado con una tropilla de mayorales, arendó su montura el patrón, y a la luz de una linterna pasó lista" (p. 31; "Leaving Jarote Quemado with a troop of farmers, the boss tethered his mount, and he called the roster by the light of a lantern"). The roster call that follows consists almost entirely of dialogue as Filomeno reminds each volunteer of his responsibility in the attack. The last unit in the prologue finds them aboard a boat sailing toward Punta Serpientes, the initial point of attack: "Navegó la luna sobre la obra muerta de babor, bella la mar, el barco marinero" (p. 36; "The sailing boat navigated with the moon over the motionless work port, and the beauty of the sea"). The action represented in these sections is sequential, and in each there is a reference to nighttime.

The third unit, in contrast to the activities indicated in the other three, concerns an argument between Filomeno and Domiciano Gándara regarding the latter's role in the rebellion. Domiciano claims that he can provide the scientific expertise necessary for winning the battle: "¡Te improvisas general y no puedes entender un plano de batallas! Yo soy un científico, un diplomado en la Escuela Militar" (p. 33; "You are an improvising general and you can't understand a battle plan! I am a scientist, I have a degree from the Military School"). Filomeno, apparently somewhat swayed by the colonel's argument, answers: "—Domiciano, convénceme con un plan de campaña que aventaje al discurrido por mí, y te cedo el mando" (p. 34; "Domiciano, convince me with a campaign plan that is superior to the one I outlined and I will give you the command"). Domiciano then advocates postponing the uprising until more people from the mountain villages can be recruited. He also says that the war should be waged from the mountains, not on the plains of Punta Serpientes and Santa Fe where Tirano has his army. When he has heard enough of Domiciano's alternative strategy, Filomeno responds:

> Pero yo no soy científico, ni tratadista, ni pasé por la Academia de Cadetes. Tu plan de campaña no me satisface, Domiciano. Yo, como has visto, intento para esta noche un golpe sobre Santa Fe. De tiempo atrás vengo meditándolo, y casualmente en la ría, atracado al muelle, hay un pailebote en descarga. Trasbordo mi gente, y la desembarco en la playa de Punta Serpientes. Sorprendo a la guardia del castillo, armo a los presos, sublevo a las tropas de la Ciudadela. Ya están ganados los sargentos. Ese es mi plan Domiciano. (pp. 34–35)
>
> (But I am not a scientist, nor an essayist, nor did I pass through the Academy of Cadets. Your campaign plan does not satisfy me, Domiciano. As you have seen, I am planning an attack against Santa Fe for tonight. I have been considering it for a long time, and it just so happens that there is a pilot boat tied to the dock that is unloading at the pier. I will board my people and disembark them at the beach of Serpent Point. I will surprise the castle guard, arm the prisoners, and incite to rebellion the troops of the city. The sergeants are already won over. This is my plan, Domiciano.)

Although no specific time frame is provided other than the ambiguous "esta noche" for the attack, there is not the same sense of immediacy here as in the other units of the prologue and no reference as in each of the others to darkness. In addition, Filomeno's willingness even to engage in an argument such as this over leadership and basic strategy, and to offer to turn over the command if Domiciano can persuade him of the superiority of his plan, strongly suggests that this discussion occurs sometime before the final roll is called, assignments are reviewed, and the troops head for their objective.

This section draws to a close when Domiciano, realizing that his scientific plea is not effective, changes tactics and resorts to accusing Filomeno of advocating a foolish and impossible plan merely to serve his own political ambitions, and then makes a bitter and damning accusation to which Filomeno surprisingly offers no reply: "—Haz lo que te parezca. Sacrifica a tus peonadas. Después del sudor, les pides la sangre" (p. 36; "Do it how you want. Sacrifice your men. In addition to their sweat, you ask them for their blood"). When even this baiting fails to sway his host, Domiciano concludes by saying: "—En fin, tanto hablar seca la boca. Pásame tu cantimplora" ("Well, so much talk dries your mouth. Pass me your canteen"), to which the narrator notes, "Tras del trago, batió la yesca y encendió el chicote apagado, esparciéndose la ceniza por el vientre rotundo de ídolo tibetano" (p. 36; "After the drink, he hit the flint and lit his cigar, dropping ashes over his stomach, round as a Tibetan idol").

Although the action of this unit does not seem to follow the sequence of the others, a quick review of Domiciano's activities confirms that the discussion has to occur during the same day as the attack. He escaped in the early hours of the morning of day two, arriving at Zacarías's hut shortly after dawn, and in Part 4 Zacarías delivered him to Filomeno when it was still early morning: "—Mi viejo, he venido para desayunar en tu compañía. ¡Madrugas, mi viejo!" (p. 129; "Old buddy, I have come to eat breakfast in your company. You're up early, old buddy!"). And so the clue to just when on this second day the two argue over military tactics leads again to Part 4, the middle point toward which all action tends to flow.

The third book of Part 4 concerns the initial meeting between Domiciano and Filomeno, and therefore it is the logical place to look for clarification of the chronological moment of the scene in the prologue between the two men. That connection is provided by a series of echoes that in musical terminology might be called resonances.

Domiciano, transported by Zacarías in a canoe, arrives at Filomeno's ranch when "alegrábase la mañana" (p. 128; "morning was really in full swing"). After falsely claiming that Tirano discovered he was a revolutionary and for that reason tried to arrest him, Domiciano volunteers his expertise: "—¡Mi viejo, vamos a pelearle juntos el gallo al Generalito Banderas! ¡Filomeno, mi viejo, tú de milicias estás pelón, y te aprovecharán los consejos de un científico! Te nombro mi ayudante" (p. 131; "Old buddy, let's fight together against our little General Banderas! Filomeno, old buddy, you don't know anything about military strategy and the advice of a scientist will really help you! I will appoint you as my assistant"). When Filomeno tells Domiciano that he can lead the army if the men vote to have him as their general, and at any rate he will accompany them at least up to the time of the attack, Domiciano, realizing he is really being held prisoner, launches his own attack: "—Manís, harto me favoreces para que te dispute una bola de indios: A ti pertenece conducirlos a la matanza, pues eres el patrón y los pagas con tu plata" (p. 132; "You're crazy. You're doing me enough of a favor without my fighting with you over a bunch of Indians. It's up to you to lead them to the massacre, since you are their boss and you pay them with your money"). Finally he seems to resign himself to his fate when he says: "—Eso quiere decir que se puede echar otro trago" (p. 132; "That means that it's time for another drink"). Then, in the most dramatic echo of the prologue, the narrator notes: "Hablaba con el gollete de la cantimplora en la boca, tendido a la bartola en el jinocal, rotunda de panza de dios tibetano" (p. 132; "He spoke with the throat of the canteen in his mouth, stretched out in the seat with belly, round as a Tibetan god").

The resonances indicated above between the third unit of the prologue and the third book of Part 4 represent the loose ends unraveling any attempt to tie a perfectly geometrical ribbon around the structure of the novel.[34] Rather than a straight chronological progression within the prologue and then continued in the epilogue, the similarities indicate a twist; they suggest that the action of this third section of the prologue may be simultaneous with that of the center of the novel (that is to say, the morning after Domiciano's escape and Don Roque's arrest, and hours before the attack itself, which is the subject of the rest of the prologue). Yet a categorical claim that the action of the third section of the prologue and the third book of Part 4 is simultaneous would not be justified, any more than there is justification for categorically insisting that all the action of the frame is sequential.[35] The similarities of these sections from the prologue and Part 4, nevertheless, are sufficient for encouraging the reader to draw a connection between them and at least to entertain the possibility that they represent the same discussion. That possibility is as meaningful as any attempt at a definitive conclusion, for with that mere suggestion the frame opens up, and as it does so, there is an inevitable twist in any proposed circle or line explanation of the structure.[36]

The manner in which the frame flows to the center, thereby opening rather than closing the novel, constitutes a textual strategy of repetition with variation. And if repetition with variation is in itself something of a contradiction, even more contradictory are the implications of this technique on the reading experience. By repeating the essence but changing the details of the argument between Filomeno and Domiciano, the argument itself is simultaneously time-bound and timeless. The argument being waged between scientific strategy on the one hand, and passion and intuition on the other, is as timeless as the revolutionary process itself.[37] Yet the argument also pertains to the specific revolution being planned against an equally specific dictator named Tirano Banderas; abstract timelessness does not adequately define the plight of those individuals caught under Tirano's reign of terror. The situation represented in the novel inextricably draws into conflict synchronic and diachronic processes; the circular theme of tyranny and revolution is undermined by the linear development of a specific rebellion, and each in turn is subverted by a twist that turns the novel back to its own epicenter.[38]

Valle-Inclán confessed to changing his mind during the process of writing *Tirano Banderas* as to how he should portray the revolution.[39] Perhaps because of his own misgivings about the Mexican revolution, inspired by Alfonso Reyes's reports, he ended up writing a novel that conveys his own ambivalence; rather than offering a judgment as to the ultimate success or failure of the revolutionary process, perhaps he chose—consciously or not—to confront the reader with the contradiction inherent in tyranny and revolutionary change. Part 4 would seem to be the artistic response to that conscious or unconscious decision; it, in conjunction with the overall structure of the novel, projects the posited author's message.

Virtually every critic who has commented on *Tirano Banderas* has called attention to the lack of a clearly stated narrative attitude. The novel is not objective in the conventional sense of the word, however, for certainly the term *esperpento* itself connotes anything but objective representation. The key to how the novel can be simultaneously objective in narrative attitude and totally nonobjective in method of representation may be understood best by the concept of double-voicing. Rather than refracting his attitude primarily through a narrator, the posited author in this novel refracts his voice essentially through the structure itself of the novel. The resulting message, therefore, is the most ambiguous of any of the novels we have dealt with up to this point. It is precisely this new concept of objectivity, in which the posited authorial attitude must be decoded primarily from the structure rather than from a narrator's discourses, that links *Tirano Banderas* to the vanguard and postmodernist movement. Of course, this link leads to the crowning sets of contradictions: Valle-Inclán's most self-consciously contrived, most antirealistic novel is also his most socially committed, and this most socially committed novel represents his closest link to the vanguard movement that supposedly eschews socially committed art. Little wonder that this complex novel has so firmly entrenched itself in our canons, and that it has inspired polemics. The present essay will have served its purpose if it manages to sustain those polemics in any small way.

Finally, as opposed to the parodic mode of *Doña Inés*, the *esperpento* technique of distortion in *Tirano Banderas* links this novel with Ortega's exposition of dehumanization and "arte intranscendente." What is more, no other novel officially assigned to the vanguard movement approaches the avant-garde brilliance displayed in Valle-Inclán's *engagé* treatment of tyranny and revolution. He did not merely blend technique with a universal social message; he made them one and the same. In so doing, Valle-Inclán plotted the course for a level of artistic achievement perhaps unsurpassed by any literary movement to date; indeed, his own *Ruedo ibérico* may well be the only viable rival. Unfortunately, the charter members of vanguard fiction failed to respond to that message, and as a result many of their technical innovations have the ring of pure solipsism. That charge can be and has been leveled against Ramón Gómez de la Serna's works, and to a degree it applies to one of his best efforts, *El novelista* (1923). Yet this novel reflects Don Ramón's attempt to fuse mode of expression with a statement about the human social condition. If that fusion of technique and message is somewhat lacking when compared to what Valle-Inclán achieves in *Tirano Banderas*, the same can be said for perhaps every other Spanish novel written so far this century.

El novelista

"Turning from Valle-Inclán to Ramón Gómez de la Serna is like going from the theater to the circus: one leaves a demanding and significant experience for an idle and formless spectacle."[40] Although this analogy may be a bit harsh, it certainly contains more than a grain of truth, and to some extent it captures the difference between the works of the Generation of '98 and those of Spanish vanguardism.

After having examined vanguard elements in *Doña Inés* (1925) and *Tirano Banderas* (1926), we now take a short step back to 1923 to look at a novelist and a novel that have been clearly identified with the new movement. Ramón Gómez de la Serna's *El novelista* can be seen as the immediate precursor to Ortega's dehumanization exposition. This novel could well have served as the model for what Ortega defined as the new art. As such, *El novelista* also reveals what turns out to be an inherent danger in what Ortega defined and later championed. In the process of advocating a new concept of genre, this novel reflects an awareness of its immediate Generation of '98 predecessors that constitutes a debilitating anxiety of influence.[41] In his efforts in *El novelista* to separate himself from the likes of Unamuno, Valle-Inclán, Martínez Ruiz (Azorín), Pérez de Ayala, and Baroja, Gómez de la Serna apparently feels forced to negate by means of parody many of their textual strategies (especially those of Unamuno initiated in *Amor y pedagogía*). That effort generally fails to negate the models, undermining instead the effectiveness of the proposed substitute. In fact, one can argue that *El novelista,* in many senses the standard-bearer of vanguard fiction,[42] reveals the very limitations inherent in the movement that, at least in part, explain its short-lived existence.

The basic strategy of *El novelista* for redefining the genre is to switch the focus from the simulacrum to the act of simulating by making writing the subject of the novel.[43] The story concerns the efforts of a novelist, Andrés Castilla, to write several novels. These novels, in turn, appear in partial and fragmented form as the product of Andrés's efforts. By foregrounding in this way the fiction of the writing instance, the posited author provides himself with a forum from which he can comment on the nature itself of novels.

To demonstrate how the message concerning novelistic art is conveyed, it is necessary to outline in more detail the narrative structure of *El novelista.* First there is the enunciating instance of the posited author of the novel, whose act of writing is omnipresent but never expressly revealed. This is the generating force behind all the discourses of the novel. After the posited author, the extradiegetic narrator is next in the hierarchy. He is removed from the story of Andrés and his novels, but his voice dominates from the beginning to the end of the novel. At the first intradiegetic level is the protagonist/novelist Andrés, who is an author within the fiction. He is the focalizing point for most of the action as he grapples with the problem of how to write his various novels. The second intradiegetic level is composed of what Andrés writes.[44] These novels within the novel are display texts designed to demonstrate the problems in writing encountered by Andrés and the strategies he devises in an attempt to solve them. In summary, then, first we have the posited author, whose voice is always refracted by one of the other speakers in the novel. At the extradiegetic level is the narrator, whose voice we hear but whose act of narrating is not defined in time and space; contained within that narrative is Andrés, whose fictitious act of writing is specified in time and in space; contained within his narrative are the novel fragments that represent his creative efforts. Such a narrative structure is designed, once again, to foreground the strategies and conventions themselves of fiction. The novel, in other words, flaunts the fictionality of fiction.

In switching the focus from the story to the conventions involved in telling stories, Gómez de la Serna takes special pains to undermine any transcendent implications arising from that process. Indeed, *El novelista* seems designed especially to disavow the metaphysical traces of Unamuno. To that end, Gómez de la Serna employs a series of strategies, some involving parody, with the aim of stressing art as pure diversion, as a game.[45] Stated in another way, in *El novelista* he contrives to convey triviality where his predecessors labored to project transcendency.

Perhaps nowhere is the concept of literature as a game more striking than in the ending to the key interpolated novel fragment entitled "Pueblo de Adobes." Among the episodes narrated in this novel within the novel is that of an elderly rich and domineering woman, Doña Prepedigna, and her abused younger lover Clemente. Clemente is attracted by Engracia, a very large and voluptuous young woman known as "la giganta del pueblo" ("the town giant"). When Clemente can no longer contain his passion for Engracia, he takes advantage of one of her father's business trips to seduce her. After the father is safely on his way, Clemente heads for the shop where he knows he will find Engracia alone: "Tanto le apretó la sorda desesperación, la ciega tropelía, que salió corriendo con dirección al río seco y lleno de renacuajos"[46] ("He was so desperate, so blindly outraged, that he ran towards the dry river full of tadpoles"). Yet in this supposedly climactic moment of passion and eroticism, the second intradiegetic level narrative is interrupted: "El novelista pintó con colores mullidos y con sollamación el acto de recogimiento del hombre emparrillado sobre la giganta basta, retumbante, elefantina" (p. 164; "The novelist painted with soft colors and with passion the act of recognition of the man draped over the giant, rumbling, elephantine woman"). Such a switch in narrative levels, along with a vocabulary that mocks the passion being spent, eliminates any erotic effect—already attenuated by the gratuitous explanation that the river is filled with tadpoles. What is more, this sudden switch from the second intradiegetic level of an immediate scene to the extradiegetic level of narrative summary calls attention to the omnipresence of the posited author; the episode is double-voiced, and the message of the second voice seems to parody the contrived eroticism of the then-popular *novela rosa*.[47]

The implication of parody is reinforced with yet another switch in narrative level, a return to the second intradiegetic level of the immediate scene of the seduction: "Había unas cebollas que comía de pequeño en las eras y de las que le había quedado el vicio. Cuando Clemente desnudó los senos blancos de la giganta, se arrojó sobre ellos como si fueran de aquellas cebollas pulposas, jugosas, refrescantes" (p. 165; "When he was a child he used to eat onions in the garden, and that vice stayed with him. When Clemente uncovered the white breasts of the giant woman, he hurled himself on them as if they were those juicy, pulpy, refreshing onions"). Granted that certain fruit is often associated with passion and erotic symbolism, onions, at least in modern usage, do not typically fall into that category. As a result, and by virtue of the change in narrative levels, the mocking tone of the posited author overshadows the action being narrated; the emphasis has been shifted from the story to the game-playing involved in telling a story. The effect of such a switch is to create the kind of emotional distance between the reader and the action that Ortega would later define as an essential characteristic of the new art.

If the *novela rosa* was the primary target for the posited author's mockery in the examples above, he expands his objective in the next section to include aesthetics and social institutions. For example, he belittles the esoteric solemnity of art while criticizing capitalistic ideology with the following explanation of how Andrés searched for character models: "Cuando su producción era escandalosa por su caudal, tenía que recurrir a sistemas extraordinarios. Quizá era el primer novelista que había recurrido a los anuncios de periódicos" (p. 61; "When his production became scandalously inadequate, he had to resort to extraordinary means. Maybe he was the first novelist who had to resort to the want ads in newspapers"). The vocabulary with its Adam Smith textbook phrasing—"cuando su producción era escandalosa por su caudal"—plus the pragmatic and very businessman-like solution of a newspaper advertisement, convey a mocking tone directed at the two targets noted above. Moreover, the posited author seems to be poking fun at himself and his own artistic pretensions; he deprecates the very notion of pure art by creating this capitalistic solution for Andrés's problems.

The playfulness in the previous examples is also evident in the stories that Andrés fictitiously creates, which, more than novels within the novel, are games within the game. The anecdotes of the display texts virtually run the gamut of generic variations. There are melodramatic crimes of passion, marital infidelities, social protest stories (the most effective one concerns the fate of maids in Spanish society), an absurdist detective tale, character studies, and numerous examples of the *cuadro de costumbres* (slice of life) genre. Yet since all these anecdotes are not only embedded within the first narrative level of Andrés as novelist but are often fragmented and interrupted by shifts in narrative level, we are constantly reminded of their role as creations within a creation. Our tendency to identify emotionally with the action, therefore, is all but negated. Rather than being seduced by the illusion of real people in real situations, we are playfully made aware of the process behind the illusion.

The emphasis on process extends to a reliance on visual markers. For example, in the section of "La novela de la calle del Arbol" that appears in Chapter 6, there are several lines of dots suggesting deleted material:

> Quizá en alguno hay de esos árboles que surgen de pronto. Indudablemente ese palacio tiene un jardín que se ve desde las buhardillas. Ese jardín de los palacios por el que nadie pasea.
>
> . . . .
>
> Cuando se pusieron de luto subieron sus moños y así parecía que llevaban peinetas que engallaban sus mantos.
>
> . . . .
>
> ¡Cómo conocen los estancos los ciegos!
>
> . . . .
>
> De pronto se nos vuelven mujeres y vuelven a pasar por la misma calle. (p. 40)
>
> (Perhaps there is a residue in those trees that suddenly sprouts forth. Undoubtedly that palace has a garden that you can see from the attic. That palace garden through which no one wanders.
>
> . . . .
>
> When they went into mourning they put their hair in buns in such a way that it looked like they were wearing combs that fastened their shawls.
>
> . . . .
>
> How well the blind know the tobacco stands!
>
> . . . .
>
> Suddenly they turn into women and once again walk along the same street.)

On the one hand, this slice of life from a neighborhood of poor people struggling to survive qualifies as social protest; on the other, the extreme fragmentation and the prominence of the dots control any tendency to empathize with the characters. In fact, the dots serve as a strategy to jolt us again from the level of the story to the level of the fictitious writing of the story. Our attention keeps shifting from the verbal image of the victims to the image implicit in the dots of Andrés writing about these victims, and beyond him to the extradiegetic narrator, and finally to the posited author, creating in this way a Chinese box effect.

A similar effect results from the ellipses announced as "Pueblo de Adobes" is being narrated: "Ya estaba en el XIV" (p. 151; "He was already in the fourteenth chapter"); "Andrés Castilla iba ya por el capítulo XIX de la novela" (p. 156; "Andrés Castilla already was passing through chapter nineteen of the novel"); "Ya en su capítulo final, el XXI y definitivo" (p. 162; "He was already in his final chapter, the twenty-first and definitive one"). Of the same nature is the explanation of an analepsis in the midst of the anecdote concerning Siamese twins who meet a tragic end: "El novelista, en capítulos anteriores, donde aún era un secreto para Gracia aquella pasión de Dorotea, había trascrito las cartas apasionadas del pretendiente" (p. 232; "The novelist, in previous chapters where Dorotea's passion was still unknown to Gracia, had transcribed the passionate letters of her suitor"). Such announcements draw attention to literature as a contrivance, a game based on arbitrary conventions before which the players (readers) willingly suspend their disbelief. By unmasking the devices involved, the posited author encourages disbelief rather than its suspension. In fact, *El novelista* mocks the very concept of realistic sequences of action by rendering transparent the screen behind which the events are ordered. Realism redefines verisimilitude so as to equate it with real-seeming, and so evolves the convention of hiding the process of art; *El novelista* is intent on restoring the Aristotelian meaning of the term, not only by unmasking the way the game is played but also by championing the believability of the implausible.

Nowhere is a celebration of the implausible more apparent than when Andrés expresses one of his most cherished artistic aspirations: "¡Si yo pudiera hacer una novela con un farol sería un gran novelista!" (p. 66; "If I could only write a novel about a streetlight I would be a great novelist"). When Andrés then writes a novel with streetlights as protagonists, the posited author not only defies the realist version of verisimilitude but also parodies the very concept of characterization.[48] He signals us, in effect, that characterization is also a convention, perhaps the most sacred in fiction, but still a convention.

For fictitious characters to seem real they need a setting that also projects the illusion of reality. The extradiegetic narrator, therefore, feels compelled to peel away the façade that lends an illusory familiarity to creations like "Pueblo de Adobes": "En el recorrido del pueblo el novelista enamorado del detalle que hace verdad todo lo que es mentira escribía al pasar frente al edificio de la escuela" (p. 145; "In his excursions around the town the novelist, fond of details that turn lies into truth, would write as he passed by the front of the school"). As a result of this extradiegetic comment, the display text that follows, which offers a detailed description of the village, becomes a self-parody. Rather than being seduced by the illusion that he is viewing a real place, the reader sees the description as a mockery of realistic tenets. By virtue of this emphasis on the game and the rules involved in playing it, the characters never appear to be real, and as a result the reader is aware that their fates respond to artistic exigencies rather than to the whims of fortune.

As the novel draws to an end, therefore, the posited author cannot just let his characters die as though they were real people; he has to retire them from novelistic service: "El novelista había llegado al final deseado, a aquella tregua en que siempre volvía de un entierro, de una despedida, de una ausencia en que sus personajes se iban a la Isla de los Personajes de Novela ya explotados" (p. 251; "The novelist had arrived at the desired end, at that state of respite that he always experienced as he returned from a funeral, from a farewell, from an absence in which his characters went off to the Island of already exploited Novel Characters"). There is no room for confusion here between reality and fiction. The narrator has ensured that these simulacra are totally transparent verbal constructs. The process of fictionalizing has replaced the illusion of reality in this new version of novelistic form.

Not content to redefine his genre strictly in terms of how it departs from the realistic mode, the posited author also attempts to separate himself and his work from his immediate Generation of '98 predecessors, most prominent among whom is Unamuno. To accomplish this redefinition he turns to parody.

The first parodic intertextual reference to Unamuno again concerns the key interpolated story, "Pueblo de Adobes."[49] As that tale draws to what should be its climactic ending, the reader has been prepared to anticipate a switch to the narrating instance, and, indeed, he is not disappointed. While the young Clemente is in the process of seducing Engracia, suddenly the spotlight changes again to the fictitious act of writing, leaving the scene in darkness, as it were:

> Era el penúltimo capítulo, y en su desenlace daba a dos capítulos posibles, a cual más violentos pero contradictorios: ¿La monstruosa mente de la giganta veía factible con su cerebro de las cavernas, el vivir afortunada con Clemente después que éste hubiera matado a la vieja de la que se sabía heredero universal, o era ella la vieja implacable, la que sabiendo lo que perdía con el mozo cabalísimo, esperaba sorprenderlos en la noche crateriana del tejar y allí los mataba?
>
> El novelista estaba en ese momento de creador de destinos en que podía elegir entre vidas distintas.
>
> Era más sórdido matar a la vieja recalentada que el que la vieja, azuzada por su instinto a medio apagar, encendiese en el rescoldo del crimen la última pasión, el último goce en triduo espantoso. (p. 165)
>
> (It was the penultimate chapter, and the denouement offered two possible chapters, each as violent but contradictory as the other: Would the monstrous mind of the giant woman with her cavernous brain see fit to live happily with Clemente after he had killed the old woman who was known to have left her estate to him, or would the old woman be implacable and, realizing what she was losing in such a fine young man, wait to surprise them one crater-like night in the brickyard and murder them there?
>
> The novelist was in that creative moment of fate in which he could choose between different lives.
>
> It was a little more sordid to kill off the passion-torn old lady than to have her, spurred on by an instinct that was on the wane, try to rekindle it in the boiling pot of that ultimate passion, the final joy of a frightening triduum.)

The story is no longer what happens between and to Clemente and Engracia, but rather how to make the decision as to what happens to them. Product has been preempted by process; dramatic action is sacrificed for the sake of staging considerations. When the decision is finally made, Andrés opts for Doña Prepedigna murdering the two young lovers, a vengeance summarized from the first extradiegetic narrative level rather than presented as an immediate scene. Then, in total mockery of melodramatic tragedy, Andrés immediately launches into a discourse on the virtues of pure drinking water.

The ploy of discussing alternate endings within the text without question echoes Unamuno. In *Amor y pedagogía* the author was powerless to change the ending, in *Niebla* there is an unresolved dispute between the protagonist and the author as to the responsibility for Augusto's suicide, and in "Nada menos que todo un hombre" the protagonists decide their own fate. In the case of *El novelista* Andrés arbitrarily decides the characters' fate, even though he informs the reader as to the options and the reason for the final decision. Rather than repeating Unamuno's attempts to erase the boundary between fiction and reality, Gómez de la Serna seems much more intent on embossing it. In fact he subverts the Unamuno technique of alternate endings so as to create a totally different effect. Instead of the existential issue concerning the nature of reality, Gómez de la Serna limits himself to the aesthetic issue of shuffling plot options.

Another trademark of Unamuno that is subversively imitated is the author/character confrontation. Not only does the primary story of *El novelista* concern the act of writing the embedded novels, but the characters from those interpolated works also violate the world of their fictitious creator.[50] For example, *El novelista* begins with the protagonist Andrés's attempting to revise the second edition of another novel entitled "La apasionada." He feels he must change the heroine because he now realizes that her passion was false. His task of revising her, however, presents complications: "—El caso es—pensaba—que el público espera ya mi personaje, tal como fue concebido, y que nadie me perdonaría la modificación de su carácter. . . . Tal vez entonces perdiese todo lo que he ganado como novelista a través del tiempo" (p. 12; "The fact is—he thought—that the public expects my character to be just as he was conceived, and no one would forgive me for the modification of his personality. . . . Maybe then I would lose all I have gained over the years as a novelist"). The fictitious author claims to be a prisoner not only of his character but also of his own readers, again echoing *Amor y pedagogía* and *Niebla*. Yet his protests ring false. By virtue of the presence of the extradiegetic narrator, the character has in fact been altered already; the focus of our attention is not on the female protagonist of the embedded story but on the fictitious creator of that woman. Consequently, when the extradiegetic narrator reports that Andrés had discovered that her passion was false, she is so characterized.[51] Andrés is indeed a prisoner, but of the posited author, not of his readers' expectations. Contrary to the Unamunian efforts to transform the characters and readers into authors, in the case of *El novelista* the strategy is again designed to underscore fiction as fiction, to affirm rather than to challenge the authority of the posited author.

Authorial control of the fictional world is even more dramatically underscored by his decisions that determine the life and death of his characters. For example, one day Andrés confuses the address he is looking for and calls at a hotel where an unfamiliar woman comes to greet him: "Era, sin duda, un protagonista de novela en el traje de la verdad. Andrés habló con ella, pero cuando la dijo que era novelista ella se echó a llorar, rogándole que no dijera nada y, sobre todo, que no la matase al final de la novela" (p. 64; "She was, no doubt, a fictitious protagonist dressed in reality. Andrés spoke with her, but when he told her that he was a novelist she began to cry, begging him not to say anything and, above all, not to kill her at the end of the novel"). An even more striking example of the power of authors over their characters occurs when, at the end of yet another novel in which Siamese twins die, each one in effect sacrificing herself for the other, the narrator notes: "Veía su doble muñeca rota y sentía mayor pena que cuando mató a otros personajes" (p. 235; "He saw their two wrists slashed and felt more sorrow than when he killed other characters"). Although his sorrow seems to suggest a correspondence between reality and fiction, that experience is not shared by the reader. The shift to the first narrative level diverts the reader's focus from the fate of the twins to Andrés's writing about their deaths. Contrary to what Unamuno projects in his novels, Gómez de la Serna makes it clear that authors decide the fate of their creations. In doing so, he again, wittingly or not, affirms the arbitrary nature of this convention so entrenched in our tradition of fictional texts. Although the goal of *El novelista* may be to advocate a new genre, the techniques employed in this case actually tend to champion the essence of *deus ex machina.*

The strategy of foregrounding the conventions of fiction does not end with Andrés's merely talking about his characters. In what seems to be the most obvious parodic imitation of Unamuno, the characters challenge the fictitious novelist. One day, for example, Andrés's work is interrupted by a visitor to his house who insists on seeing him. When Andrés acquiesces and the man enters the house, the fictitious author stares at the intruder in an effort to recognize him: "—No me conoce, aunque me debería conocer. . . . Yo soy Alfredo, el personaje de su novela *La resina*" (p. 26; "You don't know me, even though you should. . . . I am Alfredo, the character of your novel *The Resin*"). He then quickly explains the motive for the visit: "—Esa obra le ha dado a usted, según sé, mucho dinero; justo es que se acuerde de mí, y o me dé algo de ese dinero, o me coloque en algún destino" (p. 27; "That work has earned you a great deal of money, according to what I understand; it's only fair that you remember me and give me some of that money, or find me a decent job"). In spite of this example of a character from the second intradiegetic narrative level's invading the first, the violation creates a humorous rather than a transcendent effect. The metaphysical question is eclipsed by a materialistic one: This fellow doesn't care who is real and who is merely a fictional being; he just wants his share of the action. The scene seems clearly to echo the Augusto Pérez/Miguel de Unamuno face-off. If indeed the intent was parody, and given the notoriety of Unamuno and his novel it seems logical that it was, the parodying version does not fare all that well in the comparison. In *Niebla,* the violation involved a character from the intradiegetic level's invading not just the extradiegetic level of the narrating instance, but also the sacred zone of the creating instance. Here it is merely the case of a violation from one intradiegetic level to the other; the conventional sanctity of the extradiegetic narrator and of the posited author are respected. In his apparent effort to eliminate the transcendent implications of the Unamuno technique, to expose art as mere game-playing, Gómez de la Serna simplifies the game itself. In doing that, he makes himself vulnerable to the charge that his new art is devoid not only of metaphysical implications but also of aesthetic complexity. Frivolity would seem to be a high price to pay for purifying art.

Perhaps in anticipation of negative reaction to his new form for the novel, the posited author incorporates his inevitable detractors within the work. They appear in the form of fictionalized critics who attack Andrés:

> Cada vez desconfiaban más de que fuese un novelista. Su visión sin pesadez, arbitraria como la vida y aferrada en vez de a una realidad simbólica y resabiada, a todas las realidades que pululan alrededor de un suceso, no satisfacía a los críticos que necesitaban la coordinación cortés, la fórmula urbana.
>
> El novelista era discutido frente a sus últimas novelas como frente a las primeras. Esta increación de la fama le hacía más el mismo.
>
> Los armaschismes vivían en derredor de su corazón impenitente, siempre mozo, siempre creyendo que la literatura es la ciencia mayor. (p. 128)

> (More and more they doubted that he was a novelist. His unpresumptuous vision, arbitrary as life itself and rather than anchored to a symbolic and clever reality, anchored to all the realities that swarmed around an event, didn't satisfy the critics who required polished structures, urbane plot formulas.
>
> The novelist was controversial for his last novels as well as for his first ones. This lack of fame made him be even more as he was.
>
> His impertinent heart was filled with jokes; he was eternally young, always believing that literature is the great science.)

In what is perhaps the most dramatic example in the novel of double-voicing, the posited author defines and defends his new genre by means of the criticisms leveled against the novels of Andrés. When these fictitious critics attack his unpresumptuous vision, his spontaneity, and his lack of a formulated plot structure, they define the new concept of realism projected by *El novelista*: "arbitraria como la vida y aferrada . . . a todas las realidades que pululan alrededor de un suceso." Above all the new novelist must write "siempre creyendo que la literatura es la ciencia mayor." This is apparently Don Ramón's way of expressing what Ortega would call "un arte intranscendente" and what others would call art for art's sake as alternatives to the recent symbolic metaphysics of Unamuno and his generation. The new art defined here does not project a supposed cosmic concern with existence, but rather an artistic concern with genre. In short, the posited author is championing an art that does not aspire beyond its own creative process.[52]

Yet it can be argued that an art form that does not aspire to transcend its own temporality projects a cosmic view of its own, even as it disdains such a view. On the last page of *El novelista* the extradiegetic narrator feels compelled to offer his own analysis of what Andrés has accomplished: "Ha cumplido un deber, ha hecho todo el destrozo posible en la hipocresía del mundo y ha evidenciado a su manera la intrascendencia del hombre" (p. 287; "He has paid a debt; he has attacked as much as possible the world's hypocrisy and he has proven in his own way Man's lack of transcendence"). Once again we see one of Ortega's buzzwords a year before he was to appropriate it. And it is a key word, for as used here it reveals its own contradiction. Rather than responding only to the goal of pure art, *intranscendencia* also reflects a philosophical view of existence. Behind his mask of frivolous play, the posited author of *El novelista* expresses his own tragic sense of life: "Hay que decir todas las frases, hay que fantasear todas las fantasías, hay que apuntar todas las realidades, hay que cruzar cuantas veces se pueda la carta del vano mundo, el mundo que morirá de un apagón" (p. 287; "It is necessary to speak all the sentences, it is necessary to dream all the fantasies, it is necessary to note every reality, it is necessary to cross as many times as possible the map of this vain world that will go out with the flick of a switch").[53]

Ramón Gómez de la Serna's new novel is certainly a radical departure from the realistic canons of the previous century and even of their more modern version as represented by Pío Baroja. Yet when compared to the works of the other members of the Generation of '98, *El novelista* is in many ways less new, more essentially conventional than its outward form would suggest. For example, as we already saw, Gómez de la Serna's novel is much less radical than that of Unamuno in its metafictional manipulations.[54] In addition, the fragmentation of anecdote in the display texts does not approach the complexity we find, for example, in *Tirano Banderas*. And the parody of previous novelistic styles, again evident primarily in the novels within the novel, never attains the subtlety of *Doña Inés* or "La caída de los Limones." Whereas apparently Gómez de la Serna was attempting to avoid the weighty tone of the works of Unamuno, Valle-Inclán, Azorín, Pérez de Ayala, and Baroja, his own expressions of inner anguish, especially in the passage cited at the end of the novel, belie his exterior jocularity.[55]

El novelista deserves recognition as one of the first self-conscious expressions of vanguard canons. Gómez de la Serna offers a new kind of novel, displaying most of the key points that Ortega would define one year later with such impact. Yet for all its virtues, *El novelista* reflects many of the inherent limitations that ultimately relegated the works of fiction of the vanguard movement to a secondary position in Spanish literary history. Literature that pretends to deny any meaning beyond its linguistic presence ultimately undermines its own reason for existence. In fact, we would not be considering the novel in this study if it had not achieved at least some degree of historical transcendence. In a sense, the saving grace of this novel and those of its persuasion that have escaped archival status is precisely a failure to realize the vanguard program of pure art for art's sake. Although a truism, it may be worth stating that art is written not only by but also for humans, and never just for itself.

El convidado de papel

Perhaps after José Ortega y Gasset, Benjamín Jarnés is the name most associated with the concept of dehumanized art. As a collaborator on the *Revista de Occidente,* Jarnés wrote essays, reviews, and fiction that helped define and propagate the *arte joven*.[56] As a result, one tends to read his novels as prototypes of the so-called dehumanized art described by Ortega.[57] Somewhat challenging to a dehumanized reading, however, is one that stresses the sensual and erotic aspects of Jarnés's novels.[58] Also, more recently, the focus has turned to self-consciousness or metafiction as these two concepts apply to various of his works.[59] The diversity of approaches outlined above attests to the complexity of this novelist, who is so often dismissed as frivolous. Next to Pedro Salinas, Benjamín Jarnés comes closest to realizing a felicitous blend of the old and new art,[60] as *El convidado de papel* demonstrates.

El convidado de papel, although dated 1924, was not published until 1928.[61] The author then offered a revised edition that appeared in 1934, and virtually every change reflects an effort to attenuate what might be considered some of the excesses of the new art.[62] In addition, then, to representing the only modern edition to date of a Jarnés novel, *El convidado de papel* offers a very interesting commentary on the length and nature of the vanguard movement itself.

Compared to *El novelista,* Jarnés's novel reflects an almost conventional respect for anecdote. The novel, presented by an extradiegetic narrator, concerns Julio, first at age ten and then as an adolescent seminary student (one supposes in his mid-teens, although his age in this period is not specified). In the prologue the ten-year-old Julio befriends a sensuous schoolteacher, Eulalia, who makes him aware of the potential force of his own innate sensuality. Eventually Eulalia is forced to resign from the school for flaunting her sexuality, and as she says good-bye to Julio, she warns him to abandon the town from which she is being exiled. Julio next appears as an advanced seminary student returning from summer vacation. As he observes various of his classmates routinely checking back into the seminary, he sees that one, Adolfo, discreetly hides from view of the others as he engages in an emotional departure from a mysterious woman. Then one day, during an excursion to the local park, Adolfo introduces Julio to his sister Lucía, who conveniently appears with the woman seen earlier with Adolfo and who turns out to be the Eulalia of the prologue. For Julio the Adolfo/Eulalia relationship becomes inspiration for his literary imagination. In spite of the ever-watchful eyes of the priests, Julio has been spending most of his study time writing erotic fictions based on literary models, and now he has real referents for his works. Finally Eulalia's visits to the seminary raise suspicions, there is a search of the students' rooms, her letters to Adolfo are discovered, he is expelled, and Julio leaves the seminary of his own volition.

The central conflict of *El convidado de papel* concerns reality versus imagination. As an exaggerated microcosm of society, the seminary represents suppression; any display of sensuality is censured uncompromisingly by the seminary and selectively (according to gender) by society in general. As a result of such suppression, Julio resorts to imagination and art as a substitute for real sensual gratification.

El convidado de papel is generally labeled an autobiographical novel through which Jarnés attacks his own religious education. Without question, the personal element serves as a point of departure for the social criticism that the novel projects. But the novel is also, one might argue, a novel about literature itself[63] and in that sense an artistic echo of some of Ortega's distinctions between popular versus the new art. The key to how the theme of art itself is conveyed is found in the relationship between the protagonist's vision and the narrator's voice.

In the prologue the voice of the narrator dominates the view of the protagonist, who as a ten-year-old boy has limited experience and analytical capacity. Julio and his childish innocence serve as a sign pointing at a whole society: "vive en esa edad sin historia en la que todo el mundo se le detiene en la piel. Aun no conoce las torturas o el deleite de su mundo interior. Vive hacia fuera"[64] ("he lives in that ahistorical age in which everyone lingers on the epidermal. He still doesn't even know the tortures or the delights of an inner world. He lives outwardly"). The message implicit in this connection between Julio and society concerns childhood itself. Just like the ten-year-old boy, society has not matured to the point of developing its own inner sense of being; it is still at the exclusively tactile stage of experience, one reflection of which is Julio's walking barefoot to school: "Conoce de la piedra sus látigos, sus besos, sus voluptuosos cosquilleos" (p. 21; "As far as rocks are concerned, he knows their lashings, their kisses, and their voluptuous tickling sensations"). In short, there is a metonymic link formed between the ten-year-old Julio and the world in which he was born; since according to the narrator it is a world that has not yet reached the maturity for intellectualizing, cognition does not extend beyond the epidermal level.

Julio's next encounter with sensual experience begins when he knocks on the door of the new teacher for whom he has been asked to serve as guide to the village: "En el umbral hay una mujer, casi desnuda" (p. 21; "At the threshold there is an almost nude woman"). As he waits for her to dress, she offers him chocolates wrapped in gold foil, and the opportunity to fondle the wrapping represents a tactile experience that up to now was forbidden to him: "ese oro que nunca ha visto sino en cálices y aureolas, en las patenas intangibles, en radiantes ostensorios que obligan a llevarse las manos a la espalda para no caer en la tentación de acariciar la divina superficie. El niño siempre vio el oro rodeado de centinelas inflexibles. Nunca lo ha tocado" (p. 23; "that gold that he has never seen except for the chalices and halos, in the intangible medallions, in radiant exhibits where they make you keep your hands behind your back to avoid the temptation to caress the divine surface. The child always saw gold surrounded by stern sentries. He has never touched it"). Now with Eulalia's encouragement he has discovered a new dimension of tactile reality. It is the same visual material that the church used to tempt him, at the same time denying him any physical contact: "obligan a llevarse las manos a la espalda para no caer en la tentación de acariciar la divina superficie." Of course it does not tax the imagination to draw an analogy between the almost nude Eulalia and the forbidden gold. Since the chapter is entitled "Danae," after the mythical goddess who was impregnated by a golden shower, the analogy cannot be ignored. When Eulalia then gives Julio a real golden necklace to replace the foil, there is a progression in the cognitive role of his sensual experience that points to the conclusion of the prologue.

Eulalia's pedagogical role in the prologue culminates when she is forced to leave the town. Her uninhibited sexuality—she is repeatedly called a "llama verde" ("green flame")—becomes a distraction for the entire populace: "Todas las noches están ya llenas de Eulalia. Ríe con tal ímpetu que su alegría brinca sobre el negro torrente de las sombras y tiende de día en día un frenético puente cristalino. Los mozos, en los zaguanes, besan a Eulalia en la boca de las novias" (p. 28; "Every night is filled with Eulalia. She laughs with such force that her happiness bounces over the black torrent of the shadows and stretches a frenzied crystalline bridge over them. The young men, in the doorways, kiss Eulalia on the mouth of their girlfriends"). As a result of the general sensual awakening she inspires—"La fantasía lugareña abre de par en par todas sus ventanas; Eulalia obró el milagro de fertilizar un campo estéril" (p. 29; "The village fantasy opens wide all its windows; Eulalia worked the miracle of making the sterile fields fertile")—the local priest decrees that she is an agent of the devil and must go. At the moment

Julio arrives to say good-bye to her, she is dressed only in a kimono. When the garment slips from her shoulder and she invites the boy to caress her shoulder and breast, he discovers yet a new tactile reality: "El aún no conoce el poder de sus manos, y le sorprende un mundo de pulsaciones nuevas. . . . Julio, atónito, adivina entonces que de sus manos brota un poder maravilloso: el de hacer vibrar la materia, el de arrancarle sus tañidos más dulces. . . . Preciosas manos de infante que han tocado el oro de los dioses llovido sobre la epidermis fugitiva de las rosas humanas" (pp. 32–33; "He still does not know the power of his hands, and he is surprised by a world of new sensations. . . . Julio, astounded, senses then that a marvelous power flows from his hands: the power to make matter vibrate, to bring forth the sweetest notes. . . . Precious infantile hands that have touched the gods' gold sprinkled over the fugitive epidermis of the human roses"). Eulalia has taught her lesson well. Since Julio "vive en esa edad sin historia en la que todo el mundo se le detiene en la piel," the miracle of epidermal reality is fundamental to his learning process. He learns first how the act of touching leads to his own pain and pleasure; then he discovers, thanks to Eulalia's guidance, how his touch also can create in others the miracle of sensual awakening: "Eulalia, caídos los brazos, entornados los ojos, entreabierta la boca, va sumiéndose en una gozosa postración" (p. 33; "Eulalia, her arms at her side, her eyes half-closed, her mouth half-open, falls into pleasurable submission").

As we have seen, pedagogy is the theme of the prologue. It is a theme involving not merely Eulalia as Julio's teacher, but also the narrator as the reader's mentor. The lesson that Eulalia teaches Julio, in other words, is double-voiced, and its message to the reader concerns the pleasure of sensuality and the attempt of society to suppress that physical reaction. In addition, there is a message concerning the role of art in counteracting that taboo: "Y se mira atónito las manos, esas manos tiernas de niño, maravilloso instrumento por quien despiertan en la piedra y en la carne los ímpetus eternos del arte y del amor" (p. 33; "And he looks in amazement at his hands, those soft hands of a child, marvelous instruments capable of awakening in stone and in flesh those eternal impulses of art and love"). Clearly the voice of the extradiegetic narrator conveys a message that goes beyond the comprehension of the ten-year-old Julio as the viewing subject. As it does so, it points the reader to the body of the novel where, in the next phase of Julio's education, the seminary, he turns to art as a substitute for sensual reality.

Julio believes that the compensatory role of art is imposed by the seminary priests. By suppressing any expression of sensuality, the priests force students such as Julio to rely on vicarious pleasures. Julio, therefore, engages in dialogues with a fictitious alter ego to whom he explains how his amorous experiences of the summer will comfort him during the school year: "Exprimiré de cada beso toda la miel que les concede la retórica, y con ella iré punteando de dulce amarillo mi larga teoría de noches solitarias" (p.

42; "I will squeeze from each kiss all the honey that rhetoric will allow, and with it I will dot in sweet yellow my long theory of solitary nights"). If from his own point of view art allows him to transcend the restraints imposed by the seminary, the narrative voice suggests that he has fallen victim to another type of restraint, literary convention itself—"toda la miel que les concede la retórica." In addition to the restraints imposed by a dated literary style, Julio emphasizes purely decorative art: "Con esas pocas palabras forjaré los primeros eslabones de una larga cadena de diálogos, tejeré un largo friso metafórico" (p. 42; "With those few words I will forge the first links of a long chain of dialogues, I will weave a long metaphoric frieze"). Again, whereas from Julio's view art leads to freedom and creativity, the narrative voice refutes that claim as it implies that art as conceived by Julio is but another type of imprisonment.

Julio is imprisoned both by the models he tries to imitate and by his self-consciousness as the imitator: "Sabe que todos los personajes de novela están obligados a seguir el proceso de su mundo interior, y Julio está dispuesto a cumplir fielmente su papel de personaje de novela. En este año académico, su *Diario* recogerá, fase por fase, todas las de su espíritu. Julio pretende en vano ser héroe de novela trascendental. Tendrá que limitarse a escribirla" (p. 53; "He knows that all the characters of a novel are obligated to follow the process of their inner world, and Julio is faithfully prepared to complete his role as a character of a novel. In this academic year, his *Diary* will collect, step by step, all the phases of his spirit. Julio pretends, in vain, to be a transcendent hero of a novel. He will have to limit himself to simply writing it"). Whereas the seminary will prevent him from playing the transcending role to which he aspires, he is confident that he can do it vicariously with his art. This propensity for substituting literature for reality soon becomes his dominant distinguishing characteristic; Julio seems destined to fall victim to his own self-deception and to the suppression of the seminary. Of course the term *transcendence* signals the censuring presence of the posited author, and behind him Ortega and his essay noting an end to conventional art and its transcendent pretensions. Double-voicing, therefore, extends to three levels. Julio's vision projects social criticism, the narrator's doubled voice points at the protagonist's self-deception, and the posited author's, with echoes from Ortega y Gasset, at the issue of literature itself.

Julio soon draws on two very real referents for his literary escape: his friend Adolfo and the woman with whom Julio saw him in front of the seminary gate. Since Julio does not know the name of the mysterious woman, he draws on literary sources and calls her Beatriz. Then, in clear imitation of sentimental literature, he imagines her sitting beside a river under a poplar tree with an open book. In his representation she is remembering a former lover who abandoned her. When the fictionalized Adolfo arrives, and as the two embrace, the book falls into the river. Their love then goes through a series of stages: "Ahora están en la tercera etapa, y mi carta debía ser evocadora, reavivadora de rescoldos. Su pluma haría revivir el río, el chopo, los pájaros . . . . Pero todo esto es aburrido" (p. 56; "Now they are in the third stage, and my letter should be evocative and rekindle the embers. His pen would make the river, the poplar tree, the birds, revive. . . . But all this is boring"). Julio is now a self-conscious creator, and his self-consciousness is hardly reassuring. He recognizes that his efforts to write transcendent art lead merely to triteness. Reinforcing that conclusion is the voice of the extradiegetic narrator imposing itself by means of the image of the unread book that falls into the river. That book, metaphorically, tends to point at the futility of Julio's escapist efforts. Beatriz, although herself a fiction, no longer cares about literary romance once the fictionalized Adolfo appears. In short, the narrator turns Julio's art against him as this would-be author's own creations reject his attempt to substitute art for living. But Julio misses that message and decides the problem is of another nature.

He thinks that his failure is a question of mimesis, and so he goes to Adolfo in an attempt to gather more factual information as a basis for his fictional creation. Adolfo initially complies beyond expectation by explaining that the young woman he was with is his sister. Suddenly Greek tragedy enters the picture as Julio's mind races to construct the formula. Before he can do so, however, Adolfo adds that she is not really a sister, but a step-sister: "La voz *política* es un guijarro que cae en medio del friso haciéndolo añicos. De una a otra palabra ha desfilado por Julio toda la cultura helena. Sófocles, con todos sus camaradas, huye buscando más oportuna adaptación. Ya basta Echegaray" (p. 60; "The word *step-sister* is a boulder that falls in the middle of the frieze, smashing it to fragments. From one word to the other all Hellenic culture has passed over Julio. Sophocles, with all his companions, flees seeking a more suitable adaptation. Now Echegaray will serve"). Julio is caught in a vicious circle. He goes from sentimental to tragic and back to sentimental literature. Rather than being a source of new creative inspiration, Adolfo's story leads him from tragedy to melodrama, from incest to insipidity. Instead of the classical example of Sophocles, we are left with the romantic excess of Echegaray. And by means of such a retrogressive pattern, the narrator's voice mocks Julio and his pretensions.

Julio's pedestrianism responds not only to the worn-out models he follows, but also, at least in part, to the antiheroic nature of contemporary society. For example, Julio tries to equate with a Calderón honor play a scandal he is told concerning an errant priest of the seminary. The title of this chapter is "La siesta de un fauno," and the story that Julio is told concerns a young priest who, while serving in a rural parish, seduces one of the parishioners. But when the aggrieved father learns of the affront to his honor, the prelate's method of persuasion leads to a nontragic solution: "El mal discípulo de Pedro Crespo aceptó villanamente todas las excusas metálicas" (p. 71; "Pedro Crespo's poor excuse for a disciple villainously accepted all his monetary apologies"). Obviously the convention of Calderón's time, when questions of honor involved tragic consequences, no longer applies. As a result, any attempt to draw an analogy between his tragedies and contemporary reality leads to satire. This incident, in which Julio is observer or listener rather than author, allows him to realize that the seminary is an extension rather than an aberration of the society in which he lives. In addition, for the first time he indicates a nascent awareness of how inappropriate past literary models are in his present-day society.

The suggestion of new insight gained from the example of the errant priest is soon corroborated as Julio takes stock of his own life in the seminary: "Siempre la hembra, convidada perenne, ceñida de tropos antiguos, coronada de símbolos nuevos, que se acerca desnuda a enlazarse ardientemente con nosotros, torpes simuladores, eternos escolares, esclavos de fórmulas, de ritos, de metáforas polvorientas. ¡Papel, todo papel, en silencio abrazado, reducido a pavesas por estas ocultas centellicas del instinto!" (p. 74; "Always the female, the perennial guest, besieged by ancient tropes, crowned by new symbols, who approaches in the nude to join arduously with us, awkward pretenders, eternal pupils, slaves of formulae, of rituals, of dusty metaphors. Paper, all paper, embraced in silence, reduced to embers by these hidden flashes of instinct!"). What Julio now seems to realize is that art as he is practicing it does not fulfill its true function. Art that tries to compensate for rather than enrich reality is a fraud, mechanical in the same sense that the errant priest who, in spite of lacking an authentic vocational calling, continues to celebrate a "misa mecánica" (p. 72; "mechanical mass"). But these lessons learned as reader are soon forgotten, and Julio resumes his authorial self-deception.

Julio's failure to remember the message concerning the limitations of art is apparent in his adherence to a church definition of artistic creation: "Bastaba un adjetivo de los que señalaba la Retórica para hacer de un objeto trivial un objeto bello. Podía repartir todas las cosas en tres grupos: lo bello infinito, lo bello sublime y lo bello honesto, donde concurrirían la utilidad y el santo deleite" (p. 78; "An adjective was sufficient, one of those that Rhetoric identified as serving to make a trivial object beautiful. He could separate everything into three groups: infinite beauty, sublime beauty, and honest beauty, where utility and saintly delight could come together"). It soon becomes obvious even to him, however, that this formula for existence involves its own contradiction: it is abstract, albeit symmetrical. A fourth category, ephemeral beauty, poses a threat to the perfect balance of his holy trinity: "Todo lo que en la contemplación de la belleza no tendiese a elevar el espirítu padecía de un cáncer diabólico. Todas las mujeres estaban en ese caso. Ni siquiera a su madre miraban los santos. Julio no podía comprender por qué. Pero una ráfaga de viento se lo hizo adivinar. Ante un poco de carne desnuda de mujer, mecida por un remolino, sintió Julio vacilar toda su fe en los textos" (p. 78; "Everything that in the contemplation of beauty did not tend to raise the spirit suffered from a diabolic cancer. All women fell into this category. The saints did not even look at their mothers. Julio could not understand why. But a gust of wind allowed him to divine it. At the glimpse of a little bit of naked female flesh, thanks to the swaying action of a whirlpool of air, Julio felt all his faith in texts falter").

Julio realizes that he is threatened by a problem confronting all the students in the seminary. The danger concerns learning that is limited to books and abstract ideals. Yet the message concerning the students' collective problem is also double-voiced, and the narrator intrudes to clarify the lesson he wishes to impart: "Cada bella mujer desconocida abre ante ellos un nuevo libro del que sólo leerán la primera página; creen ver entonces en el amor un cuento divino del que sería delicioso ser protagonista. El cuento de Mireya, el cuento de Virginia, el cuento de Pepita Jiménez, otros cien cuentos blancos y azules, o levemente teñidos de rosa. Conocen antes los libros que la vida, antes las copias que el texto, y creen aún en la fidelidad de las copias—algunas tan deplorables" (pp. 79–80; "Every unknown beautiful woman opens before them a new book of which they will only read the first page; they believe that they then see in love a divine story in which it would be wonderful to play the role of protagonist: the story of Mireya, the story of Virginia, the story of Pepita Jiménez, and a hundred other blue and white stories, or tinted slightly pink. They know the books before they know about life, the copies before the original text, and they even believe in the fidelity of the copies—some of them so deplorable"). Not only are these students limited to literary reality, but this reality itself is a copy of another source. On one level the message, conveyed by Julio's consciousness, is that seminary education limits the students' contact with reality; on another level the message concerns literature that merely imitates models that are now exhausted. This double message addresses the Spanish society of 1924–1934, as well as the question of literature itself as practiced by Julio and others who slavishly copy not only previous models, but often imitations, "tan deplorables," of those models.

The narrator most frequently directly attacks imitators whose products reflect sentimental and melodramatic excesses, Zorrilla, Echegaray, and Valera being the names that appear most often. But when Adolfo begins to wax poetic over nature, the narrator can no longer restrain himself and intrudes to voice his criticisms: "Como todo infeliz enamorado, quiere buscar resonancias en la vieja arboleda. . . . Todo romántico doncel suele hablarnos del canto de los pajarillos *pequeños y pintados,* sin percibir nunca la monotonía del aguza-nieve, la alborada molesta de la alondra, la insoportable estridencia del gorrión. Nos habla de arroyuelos y piedrecillas sin haberse detenido nunca a precisar colores. Para él no hay variaciones en ningún tema melódico. Le hace falta solfeo y una agria batuta" (p. 86; "Like all unhappy lovers, he tries to look for echoes in the old tree groves. . . . Every young romantic tends to speak to us of the song of kites, *tiny and painted,* without ever noticing the monotony of the wagtails, the annoying dawn song of the lark, the insufferable stridence of the sparrow. He speaks to us of streams and little pebbles without having paused to detail the colors. As far as he is concerned, there is no variation in any melodic theme. He needs to include the inharmonious sounds of a solfa and baton"). With this example of nonmimetic language, there is no need to decode a message conveyed by Julio concerning society before arriving at the message concerning literature; the narrator, by intruding, assures that his meaning will not be missed. We see a similar example of this type of direct narrative intrusion criticizing romantic excesses when Julio hides a photo of Lucía, which he can consult as a model for his verbal recreations of her (p. 100). So although there is an implicit criticism of mimetic art and its limitations (the photo), there is again a direct attack on the pernicious influence of romantic excesses.

The attack on sentimental and romantic influences culminates when Julio remembers celebrating as a child the end of the nineteenth century:

A este gran siglo le vio Julio marchar una noche de diciembre, muy fría y muy simbólica. Le despidió definitivamente en los umbrales de la catedral, toda resplandeciente de electricidad y de música de Perossi. Sobre el altar ardían las joyas y los cirios de las *grandes solemnidades*. Fue un adiós a toda orquesta, digno del empaque solemne del viajero. Julio, aun niño, vio alejarse tristemente al anciano de las barbas de nieve, curvado como una hoz bajo la carga de unas enormes alforjas atiborradas de ardientes endecasílabos, de turbulentas proclamas y de períodos redondos escogidos en las tribunas y en los púlpitos. Al lento ritmo del *Te Deum* con que se saludaba al Siglo Nuevo desapareció el magnífico anciano por el laberinto de calles de la vieja Augusta. (Fue una bella reproducción de esas estampas que todos los años publican los almanaques ilustrados.) Julio, candorosamente, pensó entonces en un viaje definitivo. Creyó oírle llorar su ruina y hundirse después suavemente en el río. . . . Pero no fue así. Pronto el suicida se convirtió en un espectro. El anciano fue desde entonces un huésped invisible de bibliotecas y colegios. Cuando nadie pensase en él, se deslizaría cautelosamente hasta la mesa de los poetas, resbalaría por las obscuras galerías de los internados, se escondería en las celdas y prendería en las bocas los antiguos nombres sonoros de mujer—Teresa, Manón, Laura o Margarita—; extendería furtivamente sus recortes de periódico—restos de tribuna o de púlpito—sobre las mesas de redacción, en los escaños de las Cámaras, en los saloncillos de los teatros, en los tocadores de las rameras. (p. 127)

(Julio witnessed this grand century pass on one cold and very symbolic December night. He said good-bye to it definitively in the threshold of the cathedral, all aglow with electric lights and the music of Perossi. The jewels and the candles of the *Great Solemnities* flickered on the altar. It was an orchestrated farewell, worthy of the solemn pomposity of the departing guest. Julio, still just a child, watched as the old man faded into the distance, curved like a sickle under the weight of his enormous sacks filled with arduous endecasyllables, of turbulent proclamations and emphatic sentences plucked from church rostrums and pulpits. To the slow rhythm of *Te Deum,* with which they greeted the New Century, the magnificent old man disappeared through the labyrinth of streets of the old section of Augusta. [It was a beautiful reproduction of those stamps that they publish every year in the illustrated almanacs.] Julio, fervently, thought then about a final trip. He thought he heard him bemoan his collapse and then sink softly into the river. . . . But it was not like that. Soon the suicide victim became a ghost. The old man was then an invisible lodger of libraries and schools. When no one was watching, he would carefully slide to the poets' table, he would slip through the dark rooms of the boarding schools, he would hide in cells and place on people's lips the old sonorous names of women—Teresa, Manón, Laura, or Margarita; he would slyly extend his newspaper clippings—the remains from rostrums or pulpits—over the editing tables, on the benches of the staterooms, in the theaters and in the whores' boudoirs.)

The passage begins with Julio's nostalgic memories of this New Year's Eve, 1899. Yet projected over his nostalgia is a hint of the narrator's ironic voice. We become aware of the narrator's presence first by virtue of a stylistic device: the words "*grandes solemnidades*" in italics. Then, with the reminder that Julio was "aun niño," we begin to hear the narrator's voice in the vocabulary. For example, the past century is metaphorically pictured as a traveler outfitted with "enormes alforjas atiborradas de ardientes endecasílabos, de turbulentas proclamas y de períodos redondos escogidos en las tribunas y en los púlpitos." At this point the focus has shifted from Julio's memory to the narrator's voice; rather than the nostalgia of the passing of a century, we hear sarcasm directed at the all-too-typical way the transition was staged on that night. In short, the subject is now literary style, and with the words, "Pero no fue así," the narrator's voice completely obliterates Julio and his memory, and in so doing foregrounds literary codes. With this foregrounding, the characterization of the previous century as an old man becomes a metaphor for certain literary styles which, rather than following the script and doing themselves in, surreptitiously slipped into all levels of the 1920s and 1930s—from the pulpits to the boudoirs of prostitutes. Julio's story once again becomes double-voiced, and projected over the personal and social issue of life in a seminary is the literary question of new versus old forms of expression.

From the prologue up to the memory of New Year's Eve, 1899, there is a marked difference between the protagonist's vision and the narrator's voice. As a victim of seminary life, Julio suffers from suppressed sensual instincts and resorts to hackneyed literary modes of expression to compensate for his frustrations. The narrator, as a result, feels obliged to intrude into the narrative to point out the folly of Julio's literary orientation, inherited from the society in which he lives. Although at an early stage Julio recognizes the abnormality of society's attitude toward sensuality, only near the end of the novel does he achieve a similar understanding of how society perpetuates exhausted literary modes of expression. For example, when Adolfo asserts that every *ismo* is an excess, Julio explains: "—Pero es también un salvavidas. Sólo los *ismos* nos pueden redimir de la enojosa continuidad. El principio de inercia es el principio de la monotonía. Y la inercia—en arte, en la vida, en todo—sólo puede salvarse por un *ismo*, es decir, por un salto" (p.

138; "But it is also a life jacket. Only the 'isms' can save us from the maddening continuity. The principle of inertia is the principle of monotony. And inertia—in art, in life, in everything—can only save itself with an 'ism,' that is to say, by means of a leap"). Here is an unmistakable resonance of the former narrative intrusions criticizing Julio's own enslavement to literary modes from the previous century. As a result, we detect the narrator's voice behind this discourse pronounced by Julio. Unlike the earlier examples, the narrator does not need to intrude with a rejoinder to something expressed by Julio, for now the protagonist is voicing the same attitudes stated earlier by the narrator. In short, Julio's real coming-of-age involves his literary maturation.

Julio's cultural maturity, however, is far from complete, and his old teacher feels obliged to teach him one more lesson. It is presented in the form of a biography that she has written of her relationship with Adolfo. Rather than presenting the lesson in person, she has Adolfo deliver the biography to Julio. Doing so, Adolfo explains, "Te llamamos—Adolfo sonríe tristemente—*nuestro poeta*. Confiamos en que algún día has de escribir nuestra novela: por eso te queremos tanto. Sin ti no seríamos nada. Y ella dice que es preciso informarte bien, para que no nos desfigures. Por eso te envía este borrador que ella no sabe poner en limpio. Dice que eres tú, precisamente, el que has de poner en limpio nuestras vidas" (p. 158; "We call you—Adolfo sadly smiles—*our poet*. We trust that one day you will write our novel: that's why we love you so much. Without you we would be nothing. And she says that it is necessary that you get things straight, so that you do not distort how we are. That is why she sent you this rough copy that she is unable to polish. She says that it is you, precisely, who is to put our lives straight"). Since Eulalia does not speak these words directly, the job of decoding the meaning requires an alert student. In view of all that we have seen of her and given her earthy essence, it is difficult not to read sarcasm into what she says. Eulalia may well be mocking Julio and his penchant for fictionalizing rather than experiencing reality. In the biography she supposedly speaks in vivid detail of how she seduced Adolfo and demonstrates thereby how art can enhance without substituting for reality. This is the final lesson she presents to Julio. If he fails to apprehend it, he condemns himself to continue in his illusion that the word and the referent are one and the same. If, on the other hand, he understands the lesson, he can become a true artist by recognizing the essential distinction between art and reality. And since, as we saw in the prologue, Eulalia is a master teacher, there seems to be no question that sending Adolfo as spokesman forms part of her lesson plan.

Adolfo's role in the exercise becomes clear when he explains why he wants Julio to fictionalize Eulalia: "—Así no envejecerá nunca. Tú le concederás una juventud eterna, que ya iba perdiendo" (p. 158; "In this way she will never grow old. You will grant her eternal youth, since she was beginning to show her age"). Such an explanation suggests that Adolfo, also too much of a child, cannot accept the Eulalia of flesh and blood. He prefers a simulacrum with the illusion of eternal youth to the reality of a woman older than he who is beginning to show her age. Adolfo stands before Julio, therefore, as a living example of the dehumanizing effect inherent in confusing art and reality. Attentive student that he has become, the lesson is not lost on Julio.

When, therefore, Adolfo is expelled from the seminary and Julio does not have an opportunity to talk to him before he departs, and then in addition the young writer discovers that the biography written by Eulalia was censored by the priests when they searched the rooms, Julio is not concerned with the lack of a conclusion to Adolfo's story: "Y nada importaría desconocer el resto de la aventura de Adolfo, porque cualquiera puede reconstruirla holgadamente. Es un *caso* de infinitas soluciones" (p. 165; "And it wouldn't make any difference if the rest of Adolfo's adventure is never known, because anyone can reconstruct it at his leisure. It is a *case study* with infinite solutions"). Thanks to Eulalia's lessons, Julio now realizes that anecdote is but another device for confusing art and reality; anyone can imagine an ending for an anecdote. True art does not try to hide behind the illusion of reality; on the contrary, it strives to keep the two separate. And so Eulalia's real lesson concerns the need to distinguish between fiction and reality, above all the need to experience life in order to become a true artist. Her message calls for a commitment to living.

As noted earlier, pedagogy and its social implications are one of the major themes of *El convidado de papel,* and juxtaposed with the seminary as a negative example is Eulalia as the positive one. Indeed, the major conflict in the novel between art and reality coalesces around Eulalia. She is at once a sign pointing at both reality and art; her sensuality is grounded in earthy essence, but that sensuality is also an artistic creation. Such a combination, then, inspires Julio to leave the seminary: "Rápidamente Julio decide salir al encuentro del destino, suprimir trámites enojosos, evadirse de aquella red disciplinaria. Una mano suave caliente, sedosa—la del convidado de papel, no del de piedra—le arrastra a los infiernos" (p. 166; "Quickly, Julio decides to go meet his destiny, to eliminate maddening half-steps, to evade that disciplinary net. A soft, warm, silky hand—of the paper guest, not of the stone one—drags him down to hell"). Rather than an escape from reality, the concept "convidado de papel" now connotes a confrontation with reality. The implication seems to be that Julio is now the "convidado"; he is being enticed—invited—to experience reality, above all sensuality, as an indispensable step toward understanding the function and limitations of art. And if eternal damnation is the price of all heresy, a hand that is "suave, caliente, sedosa" seems to represent a viable alternative to the conventional one of stone, with its religious connotation.

Finally, "convidado de papel" serves as a sign pointing at the new art. As the novel ends, Julio goes to his favorite spot, a railing overlooking the river. While reflecting on his decision to leave the seminary, he becomes aware of a woman at his side. They go to a cafe, and once inside Julio looks at his new companion: "La muchacha del río está allí, transfigurada, estremecida, sin velos, como en el viejo cuadro . . . ¿Es Eulalia? ¿Es Lucía? Es la heroína sin nombre, nebulosa de Julio, ya sumergido en la deliciosa claridad del siempre anónimo convidado de papel" (p. 171; "The girl from the river is there, transformed, frightened, without veils, just like in the old painting. . . . Is it Eulalia? Is it Lucía? It is the nameless heroine, Julio's nebula, already submerged in the delicious clarity of the ever anonymous paper quest"). His vision has now merged with the narrator's voice to convey the posited author's message: a definition of *arte joven.* Literature is literature and reality is reality. The young woman standing beside Julio is neither Eulalia nor Lucía; she is a fiction, a simulacrum of a person, a product of written language. Art should not pretend to be anything other than what it is, art. Julio is now ready to graduate, to assume his rightful role as a fictional character, as the reader's "convidado de papel."

The theme of reality may seem surprising for a novel so closely identified with the vanguard movement. Yet as the preceding analysis of *El convidado de papel* demonstrates, a protective, almost sacred attitude toward reality is fundamental to the new art. The battle of these artists is not against the real world at all, but against those who would have one believe that verbal simulacra are real. To state it in another way, Jarnés in this novel celebrates reality and art as opposed to the realists who, he implies, distort and therefore denigrate both in their attempt to make them appear as one. That statement, harsh as it may sound, is a fair paraphrase of the vanguard manifestoes. Yet as is the case with most such declarations, few of the works assigned to the offending category fit the mode defined.

As an appropriate finale to this examination of the process initiated in 1902 toward vanguard art, we will now turn to Pedro Salinas and his *Víspera del gozo* of 1926. In this collection of stories Salinas also offers his voice to the battle cry against the phantasm of realism. Although the theme is the same, the tone is much more modulated than what we heard from Gómez de la Serna, and even from Jarnés.

Víspera del gozo

Whereas *El novelista* exhibits many of the excesses inherent in vanguard fiction and *El convidado de papel* (at least in its revised form) was apparently written with the purpose in mind of correcting such immoderations, *Víspera del gozo* offers a felicitous blend of the old and new approaches to fiction. Although recognition has been slow in coming, Pedro Salinas's collection of stories is arguably the best achievement in Spanish prose fiction of a work clearly identified with the *arte joven* movement.

Perhaps the key to *Víspera del gozo* is the first story, "Mundo cerrado," which holds the distinction of having been nominated as the first example of

Hispanic vanguard fiction.[65] In the first part of the story there is a shift of focus from characters and events (conventional art) to literature as its own subject (vanguard art). Such a reorientation of focus, as we have seen, begins somewhat tentatively in 1902 and becomes more pronounced in each of the subsequent two decades, with *El novelista* representing one of the more extreme expressions of the 1920s. In "Mundo cerrado," as well as in the other stories of *Víspera del gozo,* Salinas is not content with a single change of focus. Counterbalancing the new orientation toward art itself is a shift back to a more conventional mode in the second part of virtually each work. In short, Salinas's version of the new art includes an accommodation with the old.

The focus on literature itself in "Mundo cerrado" becomes evident in a summary of the story. It concerns a man on a train en route to visit a former female friend. By his side is a closed book, but instead of opening and reading it, he "reads" the views out the window of the train. As he does so, he encounters an anthology of literary styles, beginning with classicism: "Llegaba, por ejemplo, una página tierna, conmovedora, tan clásica en su sencillez cual la despedida homérica, escrita con cristalina frase por el curso del río"[66] ("For example, a tender, moving page arrived, so very classic in its simplicity, much like a Homeric leave-taking, written with crystalline sentence by the course of the river"). Shortly after, a radically different literary style emerges: "en una página de estación de tercera, donde una vía muerta, con despintados vagones, una pared gris, de depósitos, al fondo, y un cartel: 'Lampistería', por lema componían un 'trozo' asombrosamente realista, eso sí, pero tan pobre e insignificante, que no se le explicaba uno como nacido del mismo autor, sospechando en él una interpolación apócrifa" (pp. 12–13; "on a third-class station page, where there is a side track with unpainted cars, a gray wall, warehouses in the background, and a poster reading: 'Lamp Repair Shop,' composed an astonishingly realistic 'passage,' for sure, but one so poor and insignificant that it did not seem to be born of the same author, leading one to suspect that it is an apocryphal interpolation"). Of course there is also the obligatory passage from romanticism, but just as it appears there is a change in the wind, and "un humo gris y apelmazado, detrás del cual estaba huyendo vertiginosamente, expirando sin remedio, para nosotros, quizá la escena más hermosa del libro" (p. 14; "there appeared a gray and solid cloud of smoke, behind which was rapidly and vertiginously fleeing, hopelessly expiring, perhaps what for us would have been the most beautiful scene of the book"). Finally, his patience with the "author" wears thin: "Y aun lo peor de todo fue aquella vez, cuando se desplegaba en su cimera belleza una descripción de desfiladero abrupto, todo rocas y nácar, y de pronto se cerró bruscamente el relato y quedó el cristal de la ventanilla ilegible, negro, con hosca negrura de túnel, en un túnel" (p. 14; "And worst of all was that time when a description of an abrupt gorge, all rocks and mother-of-pearl, was unfolding in all its crowning beauty, and suddenly the passage ended and the window pane was illegible, black, with the gloomy blackness of a tunnel, in a tunnel").[67]

Irritated by the imposition of the reality of the tunnel on his imaginary literary world, the protagonist abandons the texts of the window and picks up two notebooks, one with the names and addresses of friends, and the other with a list of cities. By matching the names of people he knows with cities he has never visited, the protagonist is able to imagine that he already knows the cities, which then appear before him "por modo mágico y suavísimo, igual que se presenta el cisne de *Lohengrin*" (p. 16; "by a magic and gentle means, just the way the swan is introduced in *Lohengrin*"). He then matches Icosia, his current destination, with the name Lady Gurney, written over an erased Alice Chesterfield. In spite of the reality of the married name of his former friend, the protagonist places that fact under erasure and recreates his moments with Alice. Reality, however, imposes itself as a porter interrupts his reveries to ask him which stop he wants. When he gets off at the central city, there is a letter waiting for him. Unlike the book at the beginning of the story, he cannot ignore this text and upon opening it reads that Alice has died. Art proves to be a feeble and illusory escape from harsh reality in "Mundo cerrado."[68]

From this summary, it is clear how Salinas carried to the next logical phase the examples in the previous two novels of foregrounded literary codes. Beginning with *Sonata de otoño* and extending through the *Novelas poemáticas* and up to an example as contemporary to this collection of stories as is *Doña Inés*, parody serves as a device for indirectly foregrounding literary codes. Salinas, however, makes literary styles the explicit subject of his narrative. In "Mundo cerrado" the story that unfolds beyond the train window is manifestly about literature and nothing else. The emphasis in the second half, nevertheless, shifts primarily to people and events.

Reflecting the conflict in the story between imagination and invention on the one hand, and concrete reality on the other, is the protagonist-versus-narrator relationship. The protagonist Andrés serves as the point of focalization, and so we see his view, while the extradiegetic narrator relates that view, and so we listen to his voice. An example of this view/voice conflict occurs when Andrés realizes that as he looks out the window the train is arbitrarily determining the subject matter of his inventions, that exterior reality is being imposed on him. As a result, he loses interest in this particular creative process: "Ya aquello le cansó, le molestó en su dignidad de aficionado rico y ocioso que lee y goza a su capricho. Y sin hacer caso del silbido con que el tren le invitaba, a la salida del túnel, a reanudar la arbitraria lectura, echó mano al maletín y sacó sus dos abultados cuadernos de señas" (p. 14; "That business now made him tired; it irritated the dignity of his rich and idle hobby of reading and enjoying at his own leisure. And without paying any attention to the whistle inviting him, as the train emerged from the tunnel, to resume the arbitrary reading, he reached in his bag and took out two bulky address notebooks"). Although the point of focalization is Andrés's own mind, we clearly hear the voice of the narrator. That voice, in turn, is responsible for the vocabulary that characterizes Andrés as a somewhat childish dilettante, whose "dignidad de aficionado rico y ocioso" has been offended when the reality of the tunnel interrupts his game and forces him to realize that his inventions were dependent on factors outside himself. Then, in another childlike reaction, he turns to his "abultados cuadernos de señas" in search of a diversion totally in his control and free from the obtrusive influence of reality. When he picks up the notebooks he introduces the second half of the story.

In the new game of matching acquaintances with unfamiliar cities, there is again an underlying contradiction: he must rely on a familiar person living in the city as a point of departure for this particular pastime: "Lo nuevo, lo desconocido, lo temerosamente deseado y distante, tales ciudades, apuntadas en el segundo cuaderno, sólo cobraba movimiento y vida gracias a la rotación que le imprimiera lo sabido, lo familiar, los nombres del cuaderno primero" (p. 15; "What was new, unknown, fearfully desired, and distant, such cities, entered in the second notebook, only achieved dynamism and life thanks to the process of matching them with the known and familiar names of the first notebook"). His spirit of adventure is tempered by the need for a domesticating influence. Rather than truly creating with his imagination, he depends on someone grounded in reality to enable him to familiarize the unfamiliar. Yet he prefers this game to the scenes from the train window, where he was so at the mercy of the train itself. Now it is easier for him to pretend that he is in control, that in effect he is the origin of reality.

The self-deception inherent in his dream of power becomes especially evident when he remembers how he had always been intrigued by a particular city, exotic and inaccessible, until one day in a hotel he met a woman from there: "Y, de pronto, aquel punto lejano se acercaba al alcance de su voluntad, por modo mágico y suavísimo, igual que se presenta el cisne de *Lohengrin,* todo porque una señorita muy blanca, de ademanes ondulosos y menudos, como de pluma, le dijo una tarde: 'Venga usted a pasar unos días. Yo le enseñaré mi pueblo' " (p. 16; "And suddenly that distant point grew nearer to the extension of his willpower, by a gentle and magic means, just like the introduction of the swan in *Lohengrin,* all because a very white lady, with undulating gestures, like a feather, said to him one afternoon: 'Come for a few days. I will show you my town' "). The dialogue that concludes this passage, presented by the narrator and therefore double-voiced by him, underscores the conflict between imagination and reality. Andrés's illusion of power over a world of enchantment and myth was dependent on the reality of their meeting in a hotel; the narrative rendering of his imagination is juxtaposed to the verbal utterance of her invitation. By virtue of these contrasts, the narrator communicates to the reader the protagonist's self-deceiving conviction that he can deny and in effect control exterior reality. That illusion in turn points to the denouement of the story.

As the game of matching names with cities continues, he arrives at the name associated with Icosia: "Junto a Icosia había algo escrito y borrado, cual una esperanza que se abandona y luego, con letra muy reciente: Lady Gurney. Sonrió. Porque, en realidad, a esta amiga, Lady Gurney, que le allanaba el acceso a Icosia, no la conocía. Coqueteaba con esta realidad, la acariciaba sin miedo, como un revólver descargado y de lujo, que no puede hacer daño" (p. 17; "Next to Icosia there was something written and erased, like an abandoned hope, and then in more recent handwriting: Lady Gurney. He smiled. Because in reality, he didn't know this friend, Lady Gurney, who was providing him with easy access to Icosia. He flirted with this reality, and caressed it without fear, as if it were an unloaded showpiece revolver, one that can't hurt anyone"). The refusal to recognize that the Alice he knew is now married and the act of toying with a reality he does not want to accept are loaded with potential danger, which is conveyed by the simile of the revolver. That image is double-voiced, and as Andrés caresses the self-deception, "descargado y de lujo," that he does not know a Lady Gurney, the reader hears the narrator's voice echoing countless newspaper stories of people injured or killed by supposedly unloaded weapons. By virtue of the narrator's voice, the reader anticipates the inexorable and perhaps tragic end to the protagonist's dream.

As the train approaches the city, the conflict between imagination and reality accelerates. First Andrés confesses to himself that Alice Chesterfield is now Lady Gurney, but immediately following that confession his mind begins to drift back to his past with Alice (p. 19). Then the porter jolts him into reality by asking him which stop he wants. That question is followed by visions of an inaccessible fruit (Icosia) being offered to him by Lord and Lady Gurney, and he feels he can already taste its sweet and delicious juice (pp. 19–20). That taste is short-lived, however, when upon his arrival he reads the letter: "Icosia, al primer contacto con los labios, apenas mordida le daba el sabor más amargo de todos, sabor a tierra mortal" (p, 21; "Icosia, at first contact with the lips, when he had hardly taken the first bite, left him a most bitter taste, the taste of mortal earth"). His illusory world is no defense against the ultimate reality of death. Rather than trying to expand and enrich reality by means of invention and imagination, Andrés tries to deny it. As a result, he is totally unprepared for the inexorable "sabor a tierra mortal" when it touches his palate.

"Mundo cerrado" deserves to be ranked as a modern masterpiece of short fiction. It is justifiably recognized as a standard-bearer of vanguard tenets, yet it also counteracts or at least attenuates those very dogmas. While invention predominates in the first half, empirical reality imposes itself in the second half; aesthetics is privileged over plot and character at first, only to give way to the story of Andrés and Lady Gurney as the story approaches its end. That dichotomy projects the posited author's voice as he simultaneously champions the new art and warns of the dangers of its excesses. "Mundo cerrado," therefore, points toward the future as it heralds fiction about fiction, and yet it looks back at the roots from which that new fiction emerged.

In contrast to Gómez de la Serna's expression and to Ortega's explanation, Salinas demonstrates that it is possible to look both at the window and at the scene beyond it. Having established the focus on aesthetics in the first part, that focus is superimposed on the characterization and action presented in the second half. The result is art for art's sake in a story about people and events. In "Mundo cerrado," the old art is not erased by the new; the two are fused.

"Cita de los tres" offers another version of the conflict between imagination and reality. This story is constructed around a series of enigmas as a young man, alternately referred to as "Angel" and "Jorge," goes to the cathedral at six o'clock for a date with Matilde. In addition to the protagonist's name, there is an enigma from the beginning concerning the time. The bells of the various parishes announcing six o'clock begin to toll as early as a quarter till six and continue to do so for over an hour. Notwithstanding this illusion of a synchronic extension of a particular hour, "resultaba que a las siete todavía no se habían acabado las seis" (p. 43; "it turned out that at seven six still had not ended"), the protagonist finally has to concede that Matilde is late and apparently has stood him up. Then he confesses that the date was really not with him after all, but with Alfonso de Padilla, and the protagonist had come at six to take advantage of a situation created by someone else: "Se estaría tendido al borde de la cita, acostado en la ribera de las seis, como se está a la orilla de un rí que no fluye para nosotros, que va a otra cosa" (p. 47; "He would be lying at the edge of the date, resting on the shore of six o'clock, just as one is on the bank of a river that does not flow for us, that is concerned with something else"). When finally the sacristan pulls out his keys to lock the cathedral, Matilde appears. She excuses herself for being late, voices an unconvincing sorrow that there is not time to see Alfonso de Padilla, and she and the protagonist leave the cathedral, which is being locked for the night. In the final paragraph the narrator informs the reader that Alfonso de Padilla is a statue of a page who served the Catholic queen and who, according to a ballad, was killed near Granada fighting against the Moors.

Similar to what happens in "Mundo cerrado," the story begins with an apparent negation of empirical reality: "Cuando Angel entró en la iglesia no eran más que las seis menos cuarto, pero ya empezaban a dar las seis. Porque la ciudad tenía, y ese era su más secreto encanto, la razón de que la vida fuese aquí tan holgada y generosa, un modo descuidado y señoril de contar el tiempo" (p. 37; "When Angel entered the church it was only a quarter to six, but it was already ringing six o'clock. Because the city had a carefree and genteel way of telling time, which was its most secret enchantment, life here was so leisurely and generous"). Such a genteel if haphazard method of dealing with time is a new experience for the protagonist:

Estaba Jorge avezado a vivir en lugares donde esa riqueza inagotable y fugitiva, perfectamente acuñada en diversos tipos de moneda, horas, minutos y segundos, era escrupulosamente medida y administrada, pieza a pieza, por los relojes y por el tráfico, por las faenas humanas y por el alumbrado municipal, de suerte que nunca podía haber error en la cuenta y toda criatura recibía su porción exacta, los sesenta minutos, odiosamente iguales de la hora, a cada hora. (pp. 37–38)

(Jorge was accustomed to living in places where that inexhaustible and fleeing wealth, perfectly minted in diverse types of coins, hours, minutes, and seconds, were scrupulously measured and administered, piece by piece, by clocks and traffic, by human tasks and municipal street lights, with the result that there could never be an error in the account and all creatures received their exact, odiously equal portion of an hour, sixty minutes, on the hour.)

If on the one hand the treatment of time in this city strikes one as excessively capricious and slightly pretentious—"señoril"—the alternative of reducing it to a transaction, "medida y administrada, pieza a pieza . . . de suerte que . . . toda criatura recibía su porción exacta," eliminates all its human element. The initial attack against an empirical reality of objective observation and experiment, then, involves transforming one of our mechanically measured elements—time—into subjective experience.

The process of converting chronometric time into human time begins with its personification. First there is an extension of the financial metaphor. As opposed to the prudence of citizens elsewhere, the protagonist discovers that the people here in Sarracín "se gastaban la hora alegremente, en cualquier cosa, en caprichos, besos o pereza, despilfarrándola en unos minutos, para quedarse en seguida con las manos vacías, sin nada" (p. 38; "happily spent their hour on any old thing, on whims, on kisses or laziness, pilfering it in minutes, only to be left suddenly with empty hands, with nothing"). Of course they have gone broke from living, whereas people in other places enjoy a sterile solvency, "pasando y repasando entre sus dedos exangües, los dorados minutos sobrados, contándolos uno a uno, sin saber qué hacerse con tanto dinero, porque no tenían en qué gastar" (p. 38; "running and rerunning their weak fingers through the golden minutes, counting them one by one, without knowing what to do with so much money, because they had nothing to spend it on"). In its initial pages, then, "Cita de los tres" privileges subjectivity over objectivity, whimsical imagination over exacting documentation. In its next phase, however, the narrator addresses the problem of an imagination that does not merely attempt to enrich reality, but also to replace it. After first undermining the very concept of empirical reality, the story now begins to reaffirm it.

The key to a reaffirmation of the "real" world is the narrator. As in "Mundo cerrado," the focalizing source is the protagonist, while the voice is provided by an extradiegetic narrator. The metaphors, therefore, reflect the narrator's efforts to project the protagonist's vision and feelings as he discovers the enchantment of human time. As his delight increases, he even discovers the sensual dimension of time: "el tiempo estaba desnudo y se comportaba liberal y graciosamente, como en una fiesta báquica el cuerpo que soltó corsé y tirantes, ligas y corchetes, todo lo que le ceñía oprimido y estricto y se muestra ahora desenvuelto y rosado sin dejar ya dudas respecto a su entrega total" (p. 38; "time was naked and behaved freely and delightfully, similar to a bacchanal party at which a woman's body which has shed its corset and ties, garters and snaps, all that held her oppressed and constrained, now shows itself unwrapped and pink, without leaving any doubt concerning her total surrender"). This feminization of time (with its sexist connotations), complete with orgy and seductive striptease, reflects the degree to which the protagonist is attracted by this new concept of reality grounded in feelings and sensuality. And since it is so seductively alluring with its "placeres agraces" (p. 40; "primitive pleasures"), and "delicioso *flirting*" (p. 41), he is more than willing to terminate his previous espousement of pragmatic reality. But in addition to the protagonist's vision we have the narrator's voice undermining Angel/Jorge's enchantment as it points at the ending of the story to explain Matilde's own pragmatic motives for not being "on time."

The narrator's presence begins to assert itself as the protagonist reacts to the bells from the various parishes. With the beginning of their extended announcement of six o'clock, Angel/Jorge begins to characterize each tolling by means of similes. He likens the sound to birds, to the first cherries of the season, and to chords on a piano. Such metaphorization begins to wear thin. The protagonist seems to be forcing his analogies, and what initially was inventive is now becoming mechanical. As a result of these forced analogies, the reader begins to detect the sound of the narrator's overlaid voice, which finally emerges clearly to remind him that inevitably it will be, "las seis de verdad" (p. 40; "the real six o'clock").

"Por fin llegaban las seis, las seis auténticas, justas, legítimas hijas del meridiano" (p. 41; "Finally, six o'clock arrived, the authentic six, punctual, legitimate daughters of midday"). But the actual six o'clock makes an appearance in marked contrast to its apocryphal siblings: "Porque las seis en punto no sonaban, no daban en ningún reloj; las marcaba con sus agujas el único que vivía puntualmente, sin equivocarse nunca, el de la Audiencia, reloj mudo y sin campana, dechado perfecto de una justicia, casi divina, que no yerra nunca y se cumple en secreto" (p. 42; "Because six o'clock on the dot did not make a sound, it was not announced by any clock; the hour was marked by the needles of the only clock that lived punctually, without ever making a mistake, the one on the city hall, a silent clock without bells, a perfect example of almost divine justice, which never errs and carries out its duty silently"). Reality thus makes its appearance without benefit of sonorous charm. Rather than tolling bells, it asserts itself with menacing "agujas," and the consummate symbol of temporal authority, the government. Once again these threatening images represent the protagonist's vision. He is seduced by the invitation to deny time and almost terrified by the implacable reality of it, "porque tenía cita con las seis, a las seis" (p. 42; "because he had a date with six, at six"). His amorous adventure, he seems to believe, is incompatible with reality, so he opts for the illusion of timelessness and with it the safety of inventing and imagining sensual pleasures. Once the real six o'clock arrives, he believes, he will have to admit to himself that Matilde has stood him up, and with that reality he will not be able to sustain his dream of erotic delights.

As reality in the form of the actual six o'clock, and with it Matilde's perfidy, close in on him, even the tolling of the late bells takes on a sinister rather than soothing connotation: "A esas seis retrasadas, el último recurso, que flotaban perezosas en el aire líquido y transparente como restos del naufragio del tiempo, se asió Angel, desesperado, ansioso para no hundirse del todo en la certidumbre hondísima, fría y sin luz, como el fondo del mar, de que ya no vendría Matilde. 'Apenas si son las seis, decía, aún puede venir'. Aunque él sabía que las seis estaban allí hacía diez minutos, como está la muerte, sorda y segura" (p. 43; "As a final recourse Angel clutched at those late six tolls that floated lazily in the liquid and transparent air like splinters from shipwrecked time, desperately, frantic in his effort to avoid sinking totally into the cold and dark depths of certainty, as if it were the bottom of the sea, that Matilde would not come. 'But if it's barely six,' he was saying, 'she can still come,' although he knew that six had been there for ten minutes, just like death, silent and certain"). What before was seductive now is menacing. His own words "Aún puede venir, apenas si son las seis" (p. 44) come back to him as a ghostly echo in response: "Ya no vendrá, ya no vendrá" (p. 45; "Now she will not come, she will not come"). Even a momentary attempt to rationalize that perhaps the date was for seven o'clock, not six, fails miserably. The reality of time can no longer be denied. Behind its alluring makeup, time in Sarracín also hides a gloomy and lethal face; its enchanting capriciousness conceals a fickle duplicity.

With the recognition that six o'clock has passed and the certainty that Matilde is not going to appear, there is a radical change in tone: "Pero, al fin y al cabo, ¿qué más le daba? Porque lo curioso estaba en que esa cita, esperada por él desde el día antes, no era con él" (p. 46; "But, after all, what difference did it make? Because the curious thing was that the date, which he had been waiting for since yesterday, was not with him"). As the narrator reveals the protagonist's thoughts, we learn that Matilde's date was really with Alfonso de Padilla, whom her friends urged her to go see in the cathedral at six. Yet as Angel/Jorge recalls Matilde's response to her friends' importunities, her message contradicts his expression of indifference noted above: "dijo firmemente, mirando derecha a Angel: 'Mañana, a las seis, iré a la catedral'" (p. 47; "she firmly stated, looking right at Angel: 'Tomorrow, at six, I will go to the cathedral'"). There is no question that she is signaling to him that he, not Alfonso, will be the object of her visit. Either he failed to decode that message, or he is pretending that he did not understand it. If the latter is the case, he is deceiving himself, rationalizing to save face from having been stood up. In view of the narrator's structuring hand, here as throughout the story, the reader is inclined to opt for the self-deception interpretation. Angel/Jorge, with his contradictory identity connoting the otherworldly and worldly, can be seen as a sign of the new and old art. At the same time that he represents pure fiction with his celebration of metaphoric renditions of reality, he also signifies the old with his penchant for escapism. In a sense he himself is a metaphor for the conventional reader who latches on to the illusions of fiction and transforms them into a substitute for reality. And as if to demonstrate the attractive force of that process, the narrator lures the reader into the same trap.

The disposition to accept illusion as reality is underscored when the narrator notes the presence in the cathedral of the protagonist's rival: "Alfonso de Padilla se encontraba en la iglesia desde mucho antes que Angel entrara" (p. 47; "Alfonso de Padilla was in the church long before Angel entered"). In view of Angel/Jorge's lack of self-confidence, the reader shares with him a certain misgiving in the face of this expression of aggressiveness and determination by his rival. Then again with the protagonist as the focalizing point, Alfonso is described holding an open book in his hand that he does not bother to read.[69] Apparently he is confidently waiting for his date with Matilde. There are, however, two unusual aspects about him: He is lying down, and he has a dog at his feet. Considering that the setting is a cathedral, his posture and the presence of the dog seem highly inappropriate. Other than these two discordant notes, the reader is convinced that some kind of dramatic showdown is about to occur.

The tension is relieved, however, as the protagonist prepares to abandon the territory to his rival. At that moment there is a flash of light, and the goddess Diana appears in all her pagan splendor. Diana then metamorphoses into Matilde, who unequivocally affirms her grounding in reality by explaining, "Llego muy retrasada, ¿verdad?, qué pena. No podré verle" ("I'm late, right? What a shame. I won't be able to see him"). Then the narrator observes, "Salieron juntos, perseguidos, echados como de un frustrado paraíso, por las llaves y el paso del sacristán. Pero Angel sentía un placer satánico y secreto, porque él se marchaba con Matilde, andando a su lado, de carne y hueso, por una tarde palpitante y verdadera" (p. 50; "They left together, pursued, thrown out as if from a frustrated paradise, by the keys and the steps of the sexton. But Angel felt a secret satanical pleasure, because he was going with the real Matilde at his side, into a palpitating and authentic afternoon").

Again the story has led the reader through a series of stages. First he becomes enmeshed in a world in which subjectivity completely overshadows objective reality. Then, led by the narrator's structuring hand, the reader begins to see the protagonist's self-deception, his use of imagination and invention to escape reality. In the next step, however, the reader himself becomes caught up in a world of illusion as he accepts the protagonist's view of Alfonso de Padilla. Finally, the protagonist is ejected from his frustrated paradise of pure imagination by two overwhelming realities: the seven o'clock closing time of the cathedral and the physical presence of Matilde. At that moment, subjectivity and objectivity, imagination and reality, harmoniously blend as the protagonist, with the Matilde "de carne y hueso" at his side, walks into "una tarde palpitante y verdadera."

Although the enigmas of time, Matilde's tardiness, and the role of Alfonso de Padilla are solved within the text, there still remains that of the title, "Cita de los tres." As the protagonist and Matilde walk into the sunset, and Alfonso de Padilla remains imprisoned in the now-dark cathedral, the story ends with the notice: "deshecha ya la cita de los tres." (p. 50; "the date for three now broken"). It is a classic case of understatement to say that these words resist an unequivocal reading. Yet it seems clear that the broken date involves only Alfonso de Padilla. He is a stone simulacrum, a fiction of a fiction, which no power of imagination can transform more than temporarily into a real character. Within the fictional world of the story, however, the protagonist, thanks to Matilde, does become a "real" person. She enables him to transcend the pitfalls of pure aestheticism, or pure escapism. One possible reading of the title, therefore, is the need to blend aestheticism, escapism, and pragmatic reality. A world of pure fiction, of fiction serving as its own referent, the posited author seems to warn, must be avoided as much as pure escapist literature, or as pure mimetic art. Matilde's arrival demonstrates the solution: "entraban desatados, alegres, como una jauría, un tropel de rayos de sol, dorados, rojos, leonados, aullantes, saltando todos alrededor de una figura encendida y gallarda de mujer, rubia y esbelta, que traía bajo el brazo un carcaj parecido a una sombrilla corta" (p. 49; "a troop of disheveled, happy sun rays entered like a pack of dogs, golden, red, tawny, howling, jumping around an elegant, inflamed figure of a woman, blonde and slender, who was carrying under her arm a quiver that looked just like a short parasol"). She is the nominative form of the verb *citar,* whose principal meanings include: to make reference to, to make a date with, and from its Latin root, to put into motion. By virtue of the root meaning of the verb, Matilde incarnates how literary symbol and carnal reality can be fused into the transcending vitality of a new art.

Whereas "Mundo cerrado" presents a painful affirmation of reality and "Cita de los tres" a blissful one, "Aurora de verdad" offers yet a different process and result. Reality again inevitably asserts itself, but in this case it is a prosaic reality appearing at the expense of idealization.[70]

Anecdotally, the story concerns Jorge, who, upon awakening, discovers that Aurora is not at his side in spite of having spent the night with him. When he prepares to note this disquieting occurrence in his diary, he discovers that the night before he had written another note reminding himself that he has a date with Aurora in the museum this very day at ten o'clock. On his way to the date he begins to recreate Aurora from a series of images he encounters along the way. Yet there are three aspects of Aurora that he cannot capture, that only her presence can fulfill: her gaze, her smile, and her voice. When finally she appears in the Turner Room of the museum, however, rather than fulfilling the image he had been constructing, she destroys it. The Aurora standing before him does not resemble his ideal image at all, but rather "era la vida de hoy, era Aurora de verdad," (p. 69; "she was today's life, she was the real Aurora").

The key word in the story is *Aurora*. As a phenomenon of nature, that word connotes intangible beauty, very often idealized and romanticized, and above all stylized. *Aurora* also has a decidedly literary connotation. As the name of a person it signals a complex reality that above all resists reification in any form. The basic conflict of the story, therefore, is signaled by the word *Aurora*.

The person responsible for interpreting Aurora is Jorge, the point of vision in the story. But Jorge is characterized by the combination of his own actions and by the voice of the extradiegetic narrator. In order to understand Aurora, then, we first must arrive at some kind of understanding of Jorge.

As the story begins, the object of focalization is Jorge's consciousness: "Las citas con Aurora eran siempre por la mañana, porque entonces el día recientísimo y apenas usado es todo blanco y ancho, como un magnífico papel de cartas donde aún no hemos escrito más que la fecha y en cuyas cuatro carillas podremos volcar todas las atropelladas efervescencias del corazón sin que haya que apretar la letra más que un poco, al final, anochecido, cuando siempre falta espacio" (p. 61; "The dates with Aurora were always in the morning, because then the newborn and scarcely used day is all white and wide, like a magnificent stack of paper on which we still have not written more than the date and on those four faces we will be able to empty all the hasty effervescence of the heart without having to squeeze the letters more than a little, at the end, at nightfall, when space is always lacking"). In addition to the play on the word *Aurora,* this passage refers to its own creation, to the act of being written. It offers the reader a simultaneous view of the product and process of the protagonist's creative urge. As he aspires to "volcar todas las atropelladas efervescencias del corazón," we realize that we are in the presence of an artistic soul somewhat lacking in talent. His mode of expression imitates a style buried in the distant past.

His poetic style is not only anachronistic, but basically deficient. For example, when the first thing he discovers on awakening is the absence of Aurora, "iba derecho a la mesa de escritorio, con aquella manía suya de anotarlo todo, para apuntar el primer adverso acontecimiento del día: 'A las ocho y media, pérdida de Aurora' " (p. 62; "he went straight to the desk, with his mania to write down everything, to note the first adverse event of the day: 'At eight thirty, Aurora is gone' "). This new play on the word *Aurora* makes a complete farce of Jorge's artistic pretensions. His mode is deficient, and he seems to be sorrowfully lacking in imagination.

There is yet another side to this would-be romantic writer: He is also prosaically practical. Unlike a true romantic, Jorge is methodical: "Como la hora señalada eran las diez, Jorge se despertaba a las ocho y media" (p. 61; "Since the designated time was ten o'clock, Jorge woke up at eight thirty"). Then when he reads the note written the night before that he has a date today at ten, "que ese mañana de anoche estaba ya logrado y maduro . . . de que ese mañana era hoy" (p. 62; "that the tomorrow of last night had already arrived and was under way . . . that tomorrow was today"), rather than reflecting on the philosophical implications of this temporal paradox, "Abría el balcón, miraba el reloj, en busca de corroboraciones" (p. 62; "He opened the balcony, stared at the clock, in search of corroboration"). And when he realizes that the date is not for another hour and a half, that, as he expresses it, his loved one is on a distant shore separated by ninety minutes, he responds in a very unromantic fashion: "Jorge no se paraba a mirar melancólicamente a aquella ribera distante aún y deseada, sino que, alegre y provechosamente, con el baño, con vestirse y desayunar, suprimía distancias" (p. 63; "Jorge did not stop to look melancholically at that distant and desired shore, but happy and pragmatically showered, dressed, and ate his breakfast, and thus he decreased the distance"). One has to admit that he is certainly careful not to let his artistic aspirations get in the way of some practical daily chores. And so the narrator's voice is telling the reader that Jorge's temperament is that of a pure pragmatist; he is merely bourgeois with some romantic pretensions.

As he sets out for the museum and his date with Aurora, however, a change occurs: "en cuanto salía al bulevar empezaba ya a encontrársela. Porque no hallaba a Aurora de pronto, de una vez, por súbita aparición ante la vista, sino poco a poco, por lentos avances" (p. 63; "as soon as he went out into the boulevard he began to meet her. Because he did not discover Aurora immediately, at one time, by virtue of a sudden apparition before his eyes, but little by little, by slow advances"). Aurora appears in the form of a plethora of spontaneous images; in effect she seems to portray herself: "la sombra de una modistilla transeúnte . . . una imagen en el fondo del estanque . . . un sombrerito de paja de Italia . . . un agua sin forma . . . una postura de torcido reposo, de atormentada estabilidad . . . una ondulación suave del Mediterráneo" (pp. 63–65; "the shadow of a seamstress walking by . . . the image in the bottom of a pool . . . a small Italian straw hat . . . a formless puddle of water . . . a twisted repose, of anxious stability . . . a soft Mediterranean wave"). Rather than imitating hackneyed literary models in a clumsy attempt to portray Aurora, Jorge is now relying on scenes from the real world to inspire him. Of course this is not mimetic art, but sensorial reactions to what the viewer sees. The picture of Aurora that emerges, therefore, is as intangible and vital as reality itself:

Poco a poco la figura aún invisible y distante se formaba por la coincidencia de aquellos abigarrados elementos exteriores que la ciudad le ofrecía sueltos, incoherentes, pero que él, gracias al modelo, a la imagen ejemplar que llevaba grabada en el corazón, iba colocando cada uno en su sitio igual que las piezas de un *puzzle*. Y ya faltaban muy pocas, porque como la ciudad era tan animada y abierta, con perspectivas hondas de mar y de montaña, tan rica de tráfico y abundantísima en razas y variedades indumentarias, formas, líneas, colores de todas clases le salían al paso copiosamente. (p. 65)

(Little by little the still invisible and distant figure was taking form by virtue of the coincidence of those hidden exterior elements that the city offered to him in individual and incoherent examples, but which he, thanks to the model, to the exemplar image that he had engraved in his heart, was gradually putting into place just like the pieces of a "puzzle." And now he just lacked a few pieces, because since the city was so animated and open, with deep vistas of the sea and the mountain, so rich in traffic and so very abundant in races and the variety of clothing styles, forms, lines, all kinds of colors, all these jumped out at him in copious amounts.)

By selecting aspects from exterior reality, Jorge has managed to convey a sense of interior existence. This Aurora is much more than a physical being described in painstaking detail. Because of the images of the city, we experience her human complexity: "perspectivas hondas de mar y de montaña . . . abundantísima en razas y variedades indumentarias, formas, líneas, colores de todas clases." The double-voiced message that emerges from this section seems to say that when art serves reality rather than pretending to supplant it, both art and reality are enhanced. Art imitating art becomes self-parodic; art responding to the real world is creative.

Jorge seems to learn from this contact with the real world, but what he learns merely sends him in search of yet another literary model. Now he feels tied to an empirical approach, which echoes the realistic rather than romantic tradition: "Jorge no podía encontrarse realmente con Aurora entera y cabal hasta que la tuviera delante, porque siempre le faltaban unas cuantas cosas esenciales, huecos que no podría llenar mientras que ella con su primer saludo no le diera, en la sencilla fórmula del 'Buenos días', aquellas tres piezas únicas e insustituibles: mirada, sonrisa y voz" (p. 66; "Jorge could not meet up with the whole and perfect Aurora until he had her before him, because he was always lacking certain essential things, holes that he could not fill until she provided him, by means of a greeting with the simple formula 'hello,' those three unique and nonsubstitutable pieces: gaze, smile, and voice"). As he enters the museum, the protagonist intends to complete his verbal picture by means of mimesis: "poner ojos, dibujar labios e infundir palabra, hacerla obra vivificada y perfecta, cosa que no lograría sino con la colaboración de Aurora, colaboración fácil, y sin pena, simple presencia" (p. 66; "paint eyes, sketch lips, and instill a voice, make her a vivid and perfect work of art, something that he would not achieve except with Aurora's easy collaboration, no pain involved, just her simple physical presence"). The key word in this case is *perfecta*. In spite of insisting on the need for her physical presence, her concrete reality, it is obvious that he has already predetermined what that presence and reality are to be. In short, her role is to complete the picture that he has already formed on the basis of certain artistic models.

The imitative source now is also from the nineteenth century, but from the plastic arts rather than literature. He goes directly to the Turner Room of the museum: "Empujó la pesada puerta y sintió en seguida la atmósfera densa y caliente, de treinta y cinco grados, de aquella pintura. Eva, Aurora, no estaba, la creación se había retrasado" (p. 67–68; "He pushed open the heavy door and immediately felt the dense and warm atmosphere of thirty-five degrees from that painting. Eve, Aurora, wasn't there, the creation had been delayed"). Jorge is no longer waiting for Aurora, but for Turner's Eve. What he conceives as an impending moment of creation promises in fact to be a simple act of imitation. She is supposed to appear as an icon, not as a person.

The inevitable denouement arrives. Aurora appears at his side while he is watching a distant shadowy outline that he is convinced is she. Then the real Aurora speaks: "Vengo un poco tarde, ¿verdad?" (p. 69; "I'm a little late, right?"). When he turns to her, "un asombro inmenso le sobrecogía" (p. 69; "an immense shock overwhelmed him"). He is shocked because she is not playing the role he created for her. She is not wearing the clothes he had imagined she would be wearing, or that his Eve would wear. Instead, "lo que tenía delante, intacta y novísima, en la virginal pureza del paraíso, tendiéndole la mano, contra costumbre sin guante, era la vida de hoy, era Aurora de verdad" (p. 69; "what he had before him, intact and very modern, in the virginal purity of the Turner paradise, stretching out her hand to him, in defiance of custom since she was gloveless, was today's life, was the real Aurora"). The narrator's voice makes it clear that despite Jorge's surprised disappointment, he indeed has before him an Eve, not one modeled after Turner's, but Aurora's own version. And whereas this new rendition fails to meet Jorge's expectations, it should correspond to the reader's, thanks to the images Jorge observed on his way to the museum. This "Aurora de verdad" is not a plastic image, but ephemeral like formless water, fascinating like the undulation of the Mediterranean. She is sea and mountain fused into one. In short, Aurora is at once the new woman of 1926 and the new art of vanguardism. Like so many of his male and literary colleagues, Jorge is apparently ill-prepared to accept the newness of Aurora.

Although *Víspera del gozo* justifiably represents one of the standard-bearers of vanguard art, it also reflects an acute awareness of its artistic roots. In the three stories examined here, and indeed in all the stories of the collection, the concept of reality is a major theme, and through it the realistic tradition serves as an essential subtext. The new art as defined by Salinas in this collection is anything but abstract and dehumanized.[71]

In addition to the explicit presence of the realistic tradition in this fiction, there is the unmistakable trace of the textual strategies developed by the novelists of the Generation of '98. But where the works analyzed from that period tend more to parody as a means of underscoring their break from the conventions of the previous century, Salinas's stories stress satire. The novelists of the generation directed their focus to specific styles and movements, while Salinas directs his to the people who try to imitate past literary traditions. In both cases, and despite Salinas's surprisingly more protective attitude toward the realist tradition, there is the same search for new modes of expression.

The novelists of the vanguard movement, and to a somewhat lesser extent those of the Generation of '98, apparently feeling more threatened by realism than by any other literary movement, pretended to deny that mimetic tradition. Salinas, temporally and perhaps as a poet artistically more removed from that threat, seems disposed to accommodate it. Given the general orientation of the Spanish vanguard movement, Salinas (and to a less effective degree Jarnés in his fiction) provides the formula in *Víspera del gozo* that, had it been espoused by others, might well have disarmed many of the attacks leveled against the new art.[72] As we already saw in the case of Gómez de la Serna, however, realism in any form is anathema to some advocates of the new aesthetic.

Conclusion: 1988

The literary text is dynamic. It consists of an interplay that involves the structural components of the work, the context in which the work was created, and the context in which it is read.[1] If there is a key to that dynamic interplay, it is the readers. Their context (which includes the critical strategies they employ) influences how they read the circumstances in which the work emerged and how they attempt to reify its structural components. All criticism, therefore, like the literature it studies, immediately becomes dated. It is a temporal art, and as such it elicits its own revision; criticism itself constitutes a dynamic process in which each reading is destined to be answered by yet another reading.

Not only does the present determine how we read the past, but the reverse is also true. How we read in a given moment is influenced by how others have read in the past, just as the way literature is currently being written responds to how it has been created over the years (and indeed without question, to how it was structured in its prewritten stage). In a word, the present both determines and is determined by the past—and so, again, the dynamics of literature and literary criticism.

The preceding new readings, then, are also old readings. They are responses to previous interpretations, responses determined by the context of 1988 (which reflects the critical strategies employed in addition to the sociopsychological forces that influence the critic). Of course they date themselves in the very process of coming into existence and thereby invite revisionist responses.

The readings of the four novels published in 1902 reveal the clear imprint of 1988. The focus on voice versus vision, on extradiegetic versus intradiegetic speakers, on authoritative versus nonauthoritative discourse, on reader expectations versus narrative presentation, and of course on the concept of double-voicing itself, all reflect current structural and poststructural critical strategies that even at this point are dated, at least to some extent. In addition, the very thesis of this study reflects the present tendency to discredit the concept of literary generations and to speak in the much broader terms of modernism or postmodernism (the European as opposed to the Hispanic versions of those terms).

As a result of the current context, therefore, the view projected in this study of the period and novels analyzed differs from that offered previously by others. The emphasis here is on innovative techniques designed to renovate the novel form and on how these techniques link two movements which are traditionally viewed as separate. In the case of *Camino de perfección* the techniques involve creating a new concept of realism, in *La voluntad* the emphasis is on a new concept of the role of the protagonist, in *Amor y pedagogía* the strategy involves the *protagonization* of the author, and in *Sonata de otoño* there is a betrayal of conventional reader expectations.

The readings outlined above are new, yet they also reflect the previous philosophical and social emphasis of other critics. The imprints of Nietzsche, Schopenhauer, Kierkegaard, and others, as well as the Generation of '98's concerns over the Spanish nation, all of which has been documented by others, permeate the focus on a subjective view of reality, an effacement of the protagonist, an incorporation of the author into the text, and a new role for the reader. Although I focus attention here on the novelistic process itself, that process has obvious philosophical and social implications. Again, the context in which the work was created helps to define the text, and therefore any textual strategy will reflect that context.

The sociopolitical circumstances of the second decade impose themselves in yet another way. With the notable exceptions of Unamuno and Pérez de Ayala, innovative fictional writing experienced a hiatus during the years 1910–1919. A perusal of the newspapers *El Imparcial, El Heraldo de Madrid, La Epoca,* and even *La Lectura* during the war years reflects the degree to which political concerns overshadow works of fiction. The few reviews that do appear tend to concern literature about the war. In fact, Valle-Inclán's account of his visits to the trenches of the French army, *La media noche: Visión estelar de un momento de guerra,* appeared in serial form in *El Imparcial* in 1916, while that paper did not publish a review of either "Nada menos que todo un hombre" or *Las novelas poemáticas* during the same year.

In spite of the general preoccupation with the war, the Unamuno novel demonstrates a refinement of his strategy initiated in 1902 to redefine the author/character concept. As opposed to his Generation of '98 colleagues, he reaches his artistic peak at the very time Martínez Ruiz and Valle-Inclán suspend their efforts to write fiction. Pérez de Ayala also emerges during the war years with a work that redefines the generic distinction between lyric and prose. These two writers, in short, play fundamental roles in continuing the 1902 campaign, threatened by World War I and perhaps a need for retrospection on the part of some, to renovate novelistic canons.

Finally, the years 1923–1926 represent both the culminating and declining point of the process of rejuvenating Spanish fiction in the first three decades of the twentieth century. Martínez Ruiz in *Doña Inés* refines the process of effacing the protagonist initiated in *La voluntad.* He demonstrates how parody can control without eliminating reader identification and transcendent implications, two features of the new art defined by Ortega and practiced with mixed results by so many others. Valle-Inclán blends his own brand of dehumanization *(esperpento)* with a cubist approach to structure in yet another display of what Ortega likened to an emphasis on art as opposed to theme. Still, both Martínez Ruiz and Valle-Inclán were able to fuse technique and message; they did not have to sacrifice content for the sake of innovation, perhaps because they had been perfecting their new approaches for more than twenty years. By the same token, each unquestionably benefited from some of the vanguard concepts just coming into mode.

In short, these two novelists best represent the fusion of the two movements; *Doña Inés* and *Tirano Banderas* demonstrate the dynamic potential of past and present converging in an artistic endeavor.

The link between 1902 and the other writers studied here is indirect rather than direct. Gómez de la Serna deserves credit for expressing artistically in *El novelista* the essence of what Ortega would popularize expositorily one year later. By the same token, Gómez de la Serna is guilty of many of the inherent excesses of the new art, especially in his insistence that the game itself is supreme. His studied attempt to separate himself from his immediate predecessors limits rather than enhances his efforts. Jarnés, especially in his revised form of *El convidado de papel,* seems more conscious of the limitations of "pure art," and therefore strives for a healthy balance between aesthetic escape and the real world. Salinas, finally, in *Víspera del gozo* reaches the most felicitous accommodation of all the vanguardists examined here between escape and reality, between the game of fiction and the travails of existence.

One is tempted to speculate that the fatal error of the members of the vanguard movement was to lose sight of their immediate predecessors or precursors. The new wave was guilty of beating a dead horse. The members of the Generation of '98 launched an attack that extended over three decades on the canons of realism, yet the vanguard members seemed oblivious to that effort. Of course the continued success of the practitioners of the *novela rosa,* in addition to novelists such as Pío Baroja, in part justified the vanguardists: the group that formed the Generation of '98 obviously failed to finish off the realist tradition. Yet, and again the concept of 1988 enters the picture, we know now that popular literature throughout this century has tended to conform to that same realist tradition. Although Ortega emphatically distinguished between the masses and the elite, the very aesthetic with which he is identified tended to ignore that distinction. The Generation of '98 had already provided models for the elite, and so Ortega's school, one can argue despite the philosopher's own disclaimers, was in fact directed at the masses; the group dedicated to the *arte joven* hoped to impose its art on the very common people whom Ortega himself disdained. The result was, in too many cases, a kind of artistic radicalism that led to solipsism; art for art's sake became a pretext for self-indulgence. Little wonder, therefore, that the movement was dead even before 1936 and the outbreak of the Spanish Civil War.[2] Thanks to our vantage point of 1988 we can see, or at least think we see, a network of associations invisible to the people of those early decades. Future vantage points will inevitably provide still other visions, each one representing a continuation and a departure of the vision that preceded it. Such is the dynamic nature of art and criticism.

Notes

Notes to Introduction

1. *Idle Fictions: The Hispanic Vanguard Novel, 1926–1934*, p. 29.

2. This is precisely what Pérez Firmat does in *Idle Fictions*. He arrives at his definition of vanguard fiction by analyzing statements from people involved in the movement. As a result, his explanation of what the movement proposed is in my mind the best we have, at least from the Peninsular side of the issue. Yet, by ignoring the whole Generation of '98 movement (I found only one passing reference to the Generation of '98 in the entire book), he projects an image of vanguard fiction that lacks an essential contextual element.

3. In addition to Pérez Firmat's book, for examples of the vanguard manifestoes see: *Documents of the Spanish Vanguard*, ed. Paul Ilie; and Ramón Buckley and John Crispin, *Los vanguardistas españoles (1925–1935)*.

4. Jorge Urrutia, *El Novecentismo y la renovación vanguardista*, suggests a somewhat different explanation. According to Urrutia, the fiction of the members of the Generation of '98 was a complete commercial failure, and therefore the new group set out to corner the market, as it were, and prove that their art would become popular. Urrutia's thesis is unusual given the elitist attitude of Ortega, whom Urrutia proposes as one of the leaders of the "novecentistas."

5. Indeed, the novelist has been linked to the European modernist movement heralded by Proust, Joyce, and others. See J. J. Macklin, "Pérez de Ayala y la novela modernista europea," pp. 21–36.

6. At least one prominent critic agrees with my evaluation of the novelettes and specifically of the status of "La caída de los Limones" among the three. See Eugenio G. de Nora, *La novela española contemporánea I*, pp. 467–513.

7. Two particularly fine studies of this novel exist: Frances Wyers Weber, *The Literary Perspectivism of Ramón Pérez de Ayala*; and María del Carmen Bobes, *Gramática textual de "Belarmino y Apolonio."*

8. Perhaps the most convincing champions of these two novels are Julio Matas, *Contra el honor: Las novelas normativas de Ramón Pérez de Ayala*; and Norma Urrutia, *De Troteras a Tigre Juan: Dos grandes temas de Ramón Pérez de Ayala*.

9. "Fiction on a Palimpsest: *Niebla*," in *Beyond the Metafictional Mode: Directions in the Modern Spanish Novel*, pp. 33–44.

10. "Closed World," in *Idle Fictions*, pp. 67–80.

11. The recent study of Roberta L. Johnson, *El ser y la palabra en Gabriel Miró*, provides a penetrating analysis of the ideological background projected by Miró's fiction.

12. In a totally unscientific but nevertheless interesting ranking of the best current novels, *Heraldo de Madrid* asked its readers on January 1, 1926, to rank their seven favorite novelists and novels. Excluding those not yet published at the time of the survey (*Tirano Banderas, El convidado de papel*, and *Víspera del gozo*), the ranking of the works included in this study is as follows:
"Sonata de otoño" or *Las sonatas*—35
"Nada menos que todo un hombre" or *Las tres novelas ejemplares*—28
Doña Inés—10
Camino de perfección—6
La voluntad—6
El novelista—3
"La caída de los Limones" or *Las novelas poemáticas*—2
Amor y pedagogía—1
Considering that the novel was so recently published, the popularity of *Doña Inés* is perhaps most surprising. The responses to the survey were published on the following dates: January 1, 2, 4, 5, 6, 9, 11, 16, 21, 25, 26, 27, February 2, 9, 10, 15, 16, 17, 18, 27, and March 2.

13. Trans. Caryl Emerson and Michael Holquist.

14. The two works central to my approach are Félix Martínez Bonati, *La estructura de la obra literaria: Una investigación de la filosofía del lenguaje y estética*; and Gérard Genette, *Narrative Discourse: An Essay in Method*, trans. Jane E. Lewin.

15. For one of the more recent discussions of the concept of the author/work relationship,

see Gonzalo Navajas, "El autor y el paradigma," in *Mimesis y cultura en la ficción: Teoría de la novela*, pp. 29–36.

16. In *Beyond the Metafictional Mode: Directions in the Modern Spanish Novel,* I proposed a concept of the reader involving three levels—text reader, text-act reader, real reader (pp. 1–17). Within the Bakhtin paradigm, those terms would correspond to narratee, posited reader, and again real reader. Since my focus in that book was necessarily fairly theoretical, I tried to employ consistently the term relating to the level to which I was referring. Since the focus in this study is much less theoretical, generally I will merely use the term *reader* or the pronoun *we*. When I do so, I am referring to the real reader (myself in this case) who tries to identify with and decode the message intended for the posited reader of the work. When I say, therefore, that we (or the reader) react(s) in a given way, I will really be saying that I react in this way in my attempt to play the role of the posited reader as projected by the text itself. Because I believe that all readers fail to one degree or another in their efforts to project themselves into the role of the posited reader, my statements concerning reader reactions do not pretend to dictate how other readers should react to the same passage. Finally, when I refer to the reader I will use the masculine pronoun merely because that happens to reflect my gender.

17. As has been noted so often, Unamuno is inconsistent and often self-contradictory. As a result, one could say that there are as many Unamunos as there are works listing him as author. In short, each work projects its own posited author, and that posited author is but a partial and refracted image of the real Unamuno.

18. Ricardo Gullón, *La invención del 98 y otros ensayos,* advocates such an erasure in the case of the generation. In spite of his plea, one suspects that he also was more interested in opening the category (which he did) than actually erasing it.

Notes to Chapter 1: 1902

1. *Historia de la literatura española, II,* pp. 233–47.

2. The bibliography on the Generation of '98 is extensive and so well known that there seems no need to recreate it here. I will limit myself, therefore, to noting that the fundamental study of the themes is probably Pedro Laín Entralgo, *La generación del 98*; of the history of ideas, Juan López Morillas, *Hacia el 98: Literatura, sociedad, ideología*; of sociopolitical implications, Carlos Blanco Aguinaga, *Juventud del 98* ; of the Generation of '98/modernism debate, Pedro Salinas, *Literatura española siglo XX,* and Ricardo Gullón, *La invención del 98 y otros ensayos*; of novelistic technique, Manuel Durán, "La técnica de la novela y la generación del 98"; and of its reception outside of Spain, Hans Juretschke, "La generación del 98, su proyección, crítica e influencia en el extranjero." In the course of this study I make specific reference to some of these and to other general studies on the generation.

3. For more on these magazines, see the seminal work of Guillermo de Torre, "La generación española de 1898 en las revistas del tiempo." Very similar in content to de Torre's article is that of Germán Bleiberg, "Algunas revistas literarias hacia 1898." More recent and adding new information is Geoffrey Ribbans, "Riqueza inagotada de las revistas literarias modernas." Also see Guillermo Díaz-Plaja, *Modernismo frente al noventa y ocho,* and Luis Fernández Cifuentes, *Teoría y mercado de la novela en España: Del 98 a la República.* Of the magazines listed, one should take special note of *Germinal,* since the group responsible for founding it has been labeled one of the keys to the generation: Rafael Pérez de la Dehesa, *El grupo "Germinal": Una clave del 98.* All works cited refer to other journals and newspapers that played a tangential role in defining the movement.

4. The magazines, of course, were not limited to essays. Baroja, Martínez Ruiz (Azorín), and Valle-Inclán published fictional pieces in these journals. In some cases, but not all, they were excerpts from novels in progress (fragments from *Camino de perfección, La voluntad,* and *Sonata de otoño* appear in various of the magazines and in the last case the newspaper *El Imparcial*). The authors used these journals, in other words, to develop what were to become full-length novels.

5. Fernández Cifuentes, *Teoría y mercado de la novela en España,* says in reference to the role of the journals in defining the new canons for the Generation of '98: "Los escritos sobre novela que aparecieron entonces en esas publicaciones suelen tener en común la manifestación explícita o implícita de un mismo desconcierto: la novela desbordaba los viejos cauces del género, acaparaba fórmulas y procedimientos que le habían sido ajenos y se convertía en

un objeto casi ilimitado, indefinible, incontrolable y muy difícil de juzgar" (p. 38; "The commentaries on novels that appeared then in those publications tended to have in common an explicit or implicit manifestation of concern: these novels broke the old generic boundaries and employed formulas and techniques that had been foreign to the novel form with the result that it became an almost unlimited, undefinable, uncontrollable object that was very difficult to judge").

6. At a banquet held on March 25, 1902, in honor of the publication of *Camino de perfección*, Galdós was one of the prominent invited guests (as reported in *El Imparcial*, March 26, 1902, p. 2). Reviews of the novel are listed in articles by José Ares Montes, "*Camino de perfección* o las peregrinaciones de Pío Baroja y Fernando Ossorio"; and Emilio Miró, "En torno a *Camino de perfección*." Manuel T. Sol, in *Contexto, estructura y sentido de "Camino de perfección" de Pío Baroja*, also discusses early reception of the novel.

7. Domingo Ynduráin, "Teoría de la novela en Baroja," discusses how Baroja increasingly stresses clarity and action at the expense of art in his later works. Unlike Martínez Ruiz, Valle-Inclán, and Unamuno, then, Baroja was closer to what came to be labeled vanguard fiction at the beginning of his career than he was near the end. This point is also made by Ricardo Gullón, "Ramón Pérez de Ayala y la novela lírica," in *La novela lírica, II: Pérez de Ayala, Jarnés*, ed. Darío Villanueva, p. 25.

8. Perhaps the best single source for the variety of views concerning the author's voice in the novel is the special issue, "Homenaje a don Pío Baroja en el centenario de su nacimiento," *Cuadernos Hispanoamericanos* 265–67 (July-September 1972). Subseqent references will be made to individual articles in this collection.

9. See particularly the chapter, "Discourse in the Novel," pp. 259–422 in *The Dialogic Imagination*.

10. Juan Villegas, "*Camino de perfección*, o la superación de la dicotomía y el triunfo aparente del superhombre," in *La estructura mítica del héroe*, pp. 139–75.

11. The distinctions between voice and vision are discussed by Genette in the chapters "Mood," pp. 161–211, and "Voice," pp. 212–62 of *Narrative Discourse*.

12. On the thematic level, Juan Cano Ballesta, *Literatura y tecnología (las letras españolas ante la revolución industrial 1900–1933)*, cites the urban/rural conflict in the novel as pointing toward mechanization and technology, which were to become two fundamental vanguard themes.

13. Genette defines the term *extradiegetic* as a narrative level distinct from the level at which the events recounted occur. *Extradiegetic* refers to the narrating instance. *Intradiagetic*, on the other hand, refers to the product of the narrating instance. A speaker narrating from the intradiegetic level is narrating from the same level as the events recounted. For example, in the case of what is conventionally called a first-person narrative, the narrator is extradiegetic when he or she separates him or herself temporally from the action, and intradiegetic when he or she projects him or herself to the moment of the events being recounted. Genette also distinguishes between the narrating instance, which always involves a fictive author, and the literary instance, which involves the real author of the work. As does Genette, I limit my inquiry to the narrating instance in this study.

14. Pío Baroja, *Camino de perfección*, p. 7. All quotes of the text will come from this edition, with the page number indicated in parentheses.

15. I take issue here with Myrna Solotorevsky and her valuable study, "Notas para el estudio intrínseco comparativo de *Camino de perfección* y *La Voluntad*," who maintains that Fernando's character responds to influences that are naturalistic in essence: "El narrador a que hacíamos mención , en una conversación con Ossorio, expone a éste las dificultades existentes en captar la real personalidad de Fernando, aparentemente tan contradictoria y polifacética. Es éste un pretexto para que el personaje fundamente su propia complejidad con un criterio marcadamente naturalista" (p. 117; "The narrator to which we alluded, in a conversation with Ossorio, explains to the latter the difficulties in capturing the real personality of Fernando, apparently so contradictory and many faceted. This is a pretext to enable the character to establish his own complexity by means of clearly naturalistic criteria"). There is no question that Fernando's explanation of how his parentage, environment, and historical circumstances determined his character sounds naturalistic; however, contrary to naturalism, there is no attempt to document how these forces influenced him. If anything, the mention of this naturalistic element serves to underscore the degree to which *Camino de perfección* departs from naturalism and its documented cause-and-effect case-study approach to reality.

16. Others have seen in descriptions of this nature traces of modernism, romanticism, or impressionism that diminish if not disappear in Baroja's later works. The best analyses of Baroja's style are José Alberich, "Algunas observaciones sobre el estilo de Pío Baroja"; Domingo Ynduráin, "Teoría de la novela en Baroja," and Biruté Ciplijauskaite, *Baroja, un estilo.* For studies dedicated to Baroja's use of description, see Robert E. Lott, "El arte descriptivo de Pío Baroja"; Fay R. Rogg, "Aspectos psicosimbólicos del paisaje en *Camino de perfección*"; María Salgado, "El paisaje animado en *Camino de perfección*"; and Manuel T. Sol, *Contexto, estructura y sentido de "Camino de perfección" de Pío Baroja.* Laura Rivkin, "Pain and Physiological Form in Baroja's *Camino de perfección,*" draws interesting analogies between the style and structure of the novel and Baroja's medical essays on pain and happiness.

17. This passage seems to support Rivkin's thesis that much of the description of the novel relies on a lexicon associated with physiological suffering, and that the rhythm of the novel reflects a constant movement from brief moments of happiness to predominant periods of pain, suffering, and images of death. A similar example occurs in Chapter 13 when Fernando imagines the bishop of Segovia lying in his tomb:

> Estaría allí abajo con su mitra y sus ornamentos y su báculo, arrullado por el murmullo de la fuente. Primero, cuando lo enterraran, empezaría a pudrirse poco a poco: hoy se le nublaría un ojo, y empezarían a nadar los gusanos por los jugos vítreos; luego el cerebro se le iría reblandeciendo, los humores correrían de una parte del cuerpo a otra y los gases harían reventar en llagas la piel; y en aquellas carnes podridas y deshechas correrían las larvas alegremente. . . .
>
> Un día comenzaría a filtrarse la lluvia y a llevar con ella sustancia orgánica, y al pasar por la tierra aquella sustancia, se limpiaría, se purificaría, nacerían junto a la tumba hierbas verdes, frescas, y el pus de las úlceras brillaría en las blancas corolas de las flores. (p. 91)
>
> (He would be there, underground, with his mitre and its ornaments and his staff, lulled in his sleep by the murmur of the fountain. First, when they bury him he would start to rot bit by bit: today an eye would disappear, and the worms would start to swim in the slimy juices; later his brain would soften, the vapors would float from one part of the body to another and the gases would be vented through his ulcerated skin; and larvae would happily run through the rotten and decaying muscles. . . .
>
> One day the rain would start to filter through and carry with it the organic sustenance, and passing through the earth with this sustenance it would be clean and be purified, and the tomb would bear green, fresh weeds and the pus of the ulcers would sparkle in the white petals of the flowers.)

18. Solotorevsky, "Notas para el estudio intrínseco," argues convincingly that Laura represents unnatural rather then natural instinct, and for that reason Fernando senses that she is a threat rather than a solution to his search for a natural and meaningful existence.

19. In addition to Solotorevsky's, Sol's, and Villegas's structural analyses of the novel, see Mary Lee Bretz, *La evolución novelística de Pío Baroja,* and Joaquín Casalduero, "Sentido y forma de 'La vida fantástica' " in *Pío Baroja,* ed. Javier Martínez Palacio.

20. For an analysis of the Nietzschean ideas espoused in the novel, and for an identification of the referent for Schultze, see Gonzalo Sobejano, "Componiendo *Camino de perfección.*"

21. Sobejano, "Componiendo *Camino de perfección,*" p. 479.

22. It should be obvious from this example that double-voicing is also subject to infinite deferral. That is to say, there must be yet another voice behind every voice identified. If Nietzsche's voice is behind that of the posited author, obviously there is another voice behind Nietzsche. But since my interest is the literary text, in this study I direct my efforts to defining the implicit message to the posited reader, rather than to identifying philosophical sources of the message.

23. See especially Solotorevsky,"Notas para el estudio intrínseco," for views on Dolores versus the other women Fernando encounters in his quest. The significance of the name *Dolores* in this case is more equivocal than directly ironic as it was with Ascensión.

24. Solotorevsky makes the following observation in reference to the ending: "Se mantiene, por lo tanto, absolutamente, en el desenlace de la novela, el conflicto que ha existido a través de toda la obra: pugna entre la voluntad y la inteligencia" (p. 140; "Therefore the conflict that has existed throughout the work, a struggle between willpower and intelligence, is

absolutely maintained in its denouement"). Whereas I would stress religion rather than intelligence as the opposing force to creative willpower, I agree with Solotorevsky's thesis that the two conflicting forces represent the structuring motivation in the novel.

25. Zeda (pseud. for Francisco Fernández Villegas) in *La Lectura* 11 (June 1902), 264–66. Eduardo Gómez Baquero, in *El Imparcial*, July 21, 1902, writes almost exactly the same review, again stating that some will not consider *La voluntad* a novel. In an earlier edition of *La Epoca*, "El problema de la voluntad," June 17, 1902, Gómez de Baquero, in an obvious reference to the Martínez Ruiz novel, wrote an editorial attacking the current intellectuals' preoccupation with willpower, or more precisely the lack of it. Even Juan Ramón Jiménez, in a review of *Antonio Azorín*, *Helios* 1 (1903), 497–99, deplores the gloomy world view of *La voluntad* along with that of the newer novel he is reviewing. Inevitably such criticisms cite passage of the philosophical discussions rather than the ending or general structural patterns of the novels.

26. Although not mentioning *La voluntad*, Leon Livingstone, "Novel and Mirror, the Eye and the I," in *Homenaje a Azorín*, ed. Carlos Mellizo, offers an excellent analysis of how Azorín employs imagery to convey the viewer's state of mind. Alonso Zamora Vicente, "Una novela de 1902 (Notas a una lectura apresurada)" in *La novela lírica, I: Azorín, Gabriel Miró*, ed. Darío Villanueva (Madrid: Taurus, 1983), pp. 98–110, offers some interesting comments on how descriptions of nature in this novel contrast with those in nineteenth-century realistic novels.

27. In *Idle Fictions*, Pérez Firmat labels one of his chapters "Decharacterization," pp. 81–99, since he considers what I am calling the effacement of the protagonist as one of the distinguishing characteristics of vanguard fiction. As Pérez Firmat notes, the term *descaracterización* was coined by Esteban Salazar y Chapela in reference to Ramón Gómez de la Serna's *Chao* (*El Sol*, February 7, 1934, p. 7).

28. To avoid unnecessary confusion I refer to the protagonist as Antonio in this essay, even though in the novel he is most often called Azorín.

29. According to Joaquín de Entrambasaguas, "José Martínez Ruiz (Azorín)," in *Las mejores novelas contemporáneas (1900–1904)*, the referent for Yuste is Francisco Pi y Margall, while that for Olaiz, who appears in Part 2, is Pío Baroja (pp. 641–42).

30. In spite of focusing on point of view to demonstrate how Azorín represents a departure from the realistic tradition, Antonio Risco, *Azorín y la ruptura con la novela tradicional*, essentially dismisses *La voluntad* as a conventional third-person narrative interrupted only by an equally conventional epistolary form in the final part. Robert E. Lott, "Sobre el método narrativo y el estilo en las novelas de Azorín," holds a similar view and refers to the traditional third-person narration in the novel. Sergio Beser, "Notas sobre la estructura de *La voluntad*," in *La novela lírica, I*, pp. 111–21, and Myrna Solotorevsky, "Notas para el estudio intrínseco comparativo de *Camino de perfección* y *La voluntad*," following Kayser's definition, argue that *La voluntad* is a "character novel": it is structured around the personality of the protagonist. Beser and Solotorevsky are right insofar as Kayser's formula is valid. The danger in following Kayser's terminology, however, is the tendency to force into a single category works that may be fundamentally different in spite of surface similarities. As an example, I will be arguing that whereas *La voluntad* appears to be a character novel about Antonio, in the final analysis he is but a vehicle by which the posited author expresses his own view of life and especially of art.

31. José Martínez Ruiz (Azorín), *La voluntad*, ed. E. Inman Fox, pp. 57–58. Subsequent quotations will come from this edition, with the page numbers indicated in parentheses.

32. In the introduction to his critical edition of the novel, Fox notes that all the statistical material in the prologue is accurate and can be verified in the Casa Museo de Azorín in Monóvar.

33. See Emile Benveniste, "The Correlations of Tense in the French Verb," in *Problems in General Linguistics*, trans. Mary Elizabeth Meek, pp. 205–15.

34. For more comments on the prologue, with emphasis on its thematic connection to the Generation of '98, see Andrés Amorós, "El prólogo de *La voluntad* (Lectura)." Kathleen M. Glenn, *Azorín (José Martínez Ruiz)*, also offers some useful comments on the thematic implications of the prologue.

35. In a very general sense my use of the term *distance* conforms to the term as defined by Edward Bullough, "'Psychical Distance' and a Factor in Art and an Esthetic Principle," in *Aesthetics: Lectures and Essays*.

36. In spite of a tendency on the part of some to identify the character Yuste with the author

Martínez Ruiz, the same kind of distance is created between that character and the reader, and again by means of a mocking tone. Roberta Johnson makes this point in her paper, "*La voluntad*: Azorín's Post-modern Novel."

37. For a discussion of the concept of narrative authority vis-à-vis narrators versus characters, see Félix Martínez Bonati, *La estructura de la obra literaria*.

38. I must take issue with Solotorevsky's reading when she insists that the novel characterizes intelligence as subordinate to willpower. In arriving at such a reading, she fails to take into adequate consideration the epilogue and the manipulation of narrative voices (Solotorevsky pointedly excludes these narrative switches since she argues that they are not relative to her critical approach).

39. The author expressed on many occasions and in essay form his opposition to the institution of marriage, and he has often been accused of misogynistic attitudes. See, for example, Poncela Serrano, "Eros y tres misóginos (Unamuno, Baroja, Azorín)," in *El secreto de Melibea*, pp. 139–67.

40. Beser, "Notas sobre la estructura," sees the function of the epilogue as more conventional: "Dentro de la arquitectura de la novela el contraste más marcado es el existente entre el 'epílogo' y el resto del libro, contraste que supera a lo novelesco al introducir en el mundo imaginario de Antonio Azorín y el real de J. Martínez Ruiz y Pío Baroja, transformando en realidad lo que hasta ese momento era recibido por el lector como imaginario. La novela se convierte así en historia, en reportaje" (pp. 112–13; "Within the novel's architecture the most notable contrast is that appearing between the 'epilogue' and the rest of the book, a contrast that transcends fiction by introducing into the imaginary world of Antonio Azorín the real world of J. Martínez Ruiz and Pío Baroja, thus transforming into reality what up to this moment the reader conceived as imaginary. In this way the novel is transformed into history, into journalism").

41. Critics are in almost total agreement that *Diario de un enfermo* (1901) is a prenovel rather than an actual novel. The basic study on José Martínez Ruiz's novelistic development continues to be Leon Livingstone's *Tema y forma en las novelas de Azorín*. In addition to works mentioned earlier, also important are José María Valverde, *Azorín*—it should be noted that Valverde labels *La voluntad* as a "narrativa de vanguardia" (p. 190); José Martínez Cachero, *Las novelas de Azorín*; and Anna Krause, *Azorín, the Little Philosopher: Inquiry into the Birth of a Literary Personality*.

42. What I am labeling *transparent narrating* qualifies as one popular definition of metafiction. For various other definitions of that concept, see my *Beyond the Metafictional Mode*.

43. Paul R. Olson, "The Novelistic Logos in Unamuno's *Amor y pedagogía*." Olson also notes how some people do not even classify *Amor y pedagogía* as a novel. The quotation is the initial sentence of the article (p. 248).

44. Typical of this reaction is Zeda, in *La Epoca*, July 7, 1902, p. 1. Zeda classifies *Amor y pedagogía* as a satirical novel and even suggests that it is a parody. Having thus removed it from the conventional category, Zeda praises the intellectual focus and limits his criticism to what he feels is an excessive repetition of vocabulary. Also voicing a favorable reaction to the novel's intellectual content, constituting a welcome relief from the all-too popular *novela rosa*, but criticizing the epilogue, is R. D. Perés in *La Lectura* 2 (July 1902), 400–402. Adolfo Posada, on the other hand, writing in the *Heraldo de Madrid*, August 4, 1902, p. 4, refuses to be intimidated by Unamuno's reputation as a philosopher: "*Amor y pedagogía*, más que novela en sí, parece ser un desahogo psicológico, no sé si del buen humor o del otro, del sabio y original autor de *Tres ensayos*" ("*Amor y pedagogía*, more than a novel, seems to be a psychological vent, whether of good humor or the other kind I'm not sure, by the learned and original author of *Tres ensayos*"). Posada then writes a parody of a review, or perhaps an antireview, for what he clearly considers an anti- or even non-novel.

45. "A lo que salga," in *Ensayos*, pp. 121–44.

46. Critics almost universally accept Unamuno's self-evaluation in this case. See, for example, Francisco Ayala, "El arte de novela en Unamuno"; Ricardo Gullón, *Autobiografías de Unamuno;* Juan López Morillas, "Unamuno y sus criaturas: Antolín S. Paparrigópulos"; Geoffrey Ribbans, *Niebla y soledad*; and Mario J. Valdés, *Death in the Literature of Unamuno*. See the "Prólogo-epílogo" added to the 1934 edition, pp. 15–22, for Unamuno's own statement concerning the seminal role of *Amor y pedagogía* in his novelistic development.

47. Bakhtin in *The Dialogic Imagination* distinguishes between what he calls authoritative discourse, whose authority must be accepted immediately and totally, and internally per-

suasive discourse, which slowly persuades us by virtue of its artistic development. Although interesting, Bakhtin's point here on authoritative discourse is one of his less convincing arguments. For a more productive alternative, see Martínez Bonati's concept of mimetic versus nonmimetic language in his *Estructura de la obra literaria.*

48. See particularly Olson, "The Novelistic Logos," on this point. Also very helpful is the López-Morillas article, "Unamuno y sus criaturas," Gullón's chapter in *Autobiografías,* and Manuel García Blanco, "*Amor y pedagogía,* nivola unamuniana."

49. Although one can argue that the "Prólogo-epílogo" added to the 1934 edition should also be considered part of the novel, I consider it a comment on rather than a segment of the work. For this study, therefore, I am referring to the first edition and limiting my comments to the original prologue. (A review of the 1934 edition that appears in *Indice Literario* 5 [May 1934]: 102–3, discusses the content of the added prologue-epilogue.) In the few cases where critics have addressed the problem of the frame, they have argued that Unamuno uses it as a device to posit his aesthetic ideas directly to the reader. See especially Ricardo Gullón in *Autobiografías,* and Ricardo Diez, *El desarrollo estético de la novela de Unamuno.*

50. Miguel de Unamuno, *Amor y pedagogía,* p. 7. Subsequent quotations from the text will come from this edition, with the page numbers indicated in parentheses.

51. This passage has been cited as the key to Don Fulgencio's contradictory role in the novel; at times he is a caricature, but he also seems to serve as authorial spokesman. See, for example, D. L. Fabian, "Action and Idea in *Amor y pedagogía* and *Prometeo*"; Gullón in his *Autobiografías;* and Ribbans in his *Niebla y soledad.* López-Morillas, on the other hand, argues that Fulgencio represents a character in total opposition to Unamuno's views ("Unamuno y sus criaturas").

52. For example, in his review, R. D. Perés, *La Lectura,* praises everything in the novel but the epilogue, whereas Adolfo Posada, *Heraldo de Madrid,* in his review-parody says with biting irony that the prologue is the best part of the novel. In both cases we find real readers indicating that they consider the frame extraneous to the "novel."

53. In the "Prólogo-epílogo" added to the 1934 edition, Unamuno has the following to say regarding the dedication:

> Al frente de la primera edición de esta obra, la de 1902, aparecía esto, que se reproduce ahora: "Al lector, dedica esta obra, *El autor.*" Al lector y no a los lectores, a cada uno de éstos y no a la masa—público—que forman. Y en ello mostré mi propósito de dirigirme a la íntima individualidad, a la individual y personal intimidad del lector de ella, a su realidad, no a su aparencialidad. Y por eso le hablaba a solas los dos, oyéndonos los respiros, alguna vez las palpitaciones del corazón, como en confesonario. (p. 18)
>
> (At the beginning of the first edition of this work, that of 1902, this passage appears: "The author dedicates this work to the reader." To the reader and not to the readers, to each and every one and not to the mass—public—that they form. And by this means I illustrated my purpose of directing myself to the intimate individuality, to the individual and personal intimacy of the reader of this work, to his reality, not to his apparent reality. And for that reason I spoke to him in private, listening to one another's breathing, and occasionally our heartbeats, just like in the confessional.)

54. See the article by Manuel García Blanco, "*Amor y pedagogía,* nivola unamuniana."

55. Geoffrey Ribbans, in *Niebla y soledad,* has very astutely analyzed the dichotomy in Don Fulgencio's character. It is generally accepted that this personage was intended as a caricature of Menéndez y Pelayo.

56. Miguel de Unamuno, *Del sentimiento trágico de la vida,* p. 266. One could argue, of course, that even these words cannot be attributed to the true Unamuno, but rather to the persona (posited author) of this book of essays. Such an argument becomes even more persuasive if we accept the author's claims that *Del sentimiento trágico de la vida* is also a novel.

57. Olson in "The Novelistic Logos" also notes the role of language in the novel: "In linguistic terms it appears as the problem of the individuation of the novelistic logos from the continuum of language as a whole, both in the dimension of actualized speech and in that of the potential for the generation of new forms" (p. 266).

58. Ramón del Valle-Inclán, *Sonata de primavera, Sonata de estío, Sonata de otoño, Sonata de invierno: Memorias del Marqués de Bradomín,* ed. Allen W. Phillips (Mexico: Porrúa, 1979), p. 2.

Further quotations will be taken from this edition, with the page numbers indicated in parentheses. In her landmark study of the genesis of *Sonata de otoño, De "Sonata de otoño" al esperpento: Aspectos del arte de Valle-Inclán* (London: Tamesis, 1968), Emma Susana Speratti-Piñero notes that in the newspaper serial form in which the nucleus of the story first appeared, this passage served as a conclusion. In the first 1902 edition of the novel, however, it had been changed to serve as an epigraph. Eliane Lavaud, in "La genèse des Sonates" (*Valle-Inclán du journal au roman* [Dijon: Klincksieck, 1979]), traces the evolution of the stories originally published in newspapers and magazines. Unfortunately, no one to date has documented the changes that appear in the various editions of the *Sonatas*.

59. The primary source for reception aesthetics and the concept of horizons of reader expectations is Hans Robert Jauss in *Toward an Aesthetic of Reception*, trans. Timothy Bahti (Minneapolis: University of Minnesota Press, 1982). See particularly Chapter 1, "Literary History as a Challenge to Literary Theory," pp. 3–45.

60. For a more detailed discussion of first-person narration and the difference between the speaker ("the narrating self") and the protagonist ("the experiencing self"), see Franz Stanzel, *Narrative Situations in the Novel: Tom Jones, Moby Dick, The Ambassadors, Ulysses*, trans. James P. Pusack (Bloomington: Indiana University Press, 1971). Briefly, Stanzel notes that although they seem to be the same person, the narrating self is older and therefore presumably wiser than the experiencing self. When the narrator projects himself into his past being, we are not aware of his present, narrating being. When, on the other hand, the narrator switches to the present tense, we become completely aware of the narrating self and lose sight of the experiencing self—the protagonist. Of course, without resorting to the present-tense verb form, the narrating self is revealed indirectly by what can be called stylistics (vocabulary, syntax), structure (the order in which events are narrated), and by the very nature of the events narrated. Roberta L. Salper de Tortellá, "La dimensión temporal y la creación del Marqués de Bradomín," *Insula* 237–38 (1966): 15 and 26, analyzes the temporal levels and author/character relationships in "Bajo los trópicos" (an essay), "La niña Chole," *Sonata de estío*, and *El marqués de Bradomín*.

61. Nor should one ignore the sexual connotations of the name *Concha* and the self-referential implications of the labyrinth. In an important study, Georges Güntert, "La fuente en el laberinto: Las *Sonatas* de Valle-Inclán," *Boletín de la Real Academia Española* 53 (1973): 543–67, equates the labyrinth with the "enredo verbal" ("verbal entrapment") of the novel. Güntert argues that the *Sonatas* represent an "alegoría del acto de escribir" (p. 558; "an allegory of the writing process").

62. José Alberich, "Ambigüedad y humorismo en las *Sonatas* de Valle-Inclán," *Hispanic Review* 33 (1965): 360–82, also notes parody in these works. According to Alberich, Valle-Inclán not only parodies romanticism (I discuss this aspect later in the analysis), but also the very modernism that the *Sonatas* are supposed to represent.

63. When the marquis questions Florisel concerning which master he prefers to serve, the boy answers: "—Al que sabe ser humilde, en todas partes le va bien" ("One who knows how to be humble gets along well everywhere"), to which the speaker notes: "Había nacido para vivir en un palacio, educar los mirlos, amaestrar los hurones, ser ayo de un príncipe y formar el corazón de un gran rey" (p. 98; "He was born to live in a palace, train blackbirds, domesticate ferrets, be a prince's guardian, and help shape the heart of a great king").

64. Noel Valis, in an unpublished essay, "The Novel as Feminine Entrapment: Valle-Inclán's *Sonata de otoño*," studies the image of women projected in the novel. She argues that in the final analysis Bradomín's male attitude toward women has to be seen as a direct extension of the author. George Güntert, "La fuente en el laberinto," on the other hand, separates the two: "El autor de las *Sonatas* se sitúa definitivamente fuera de su obra, puesto que como consciencia que vive en el tiempo no le es posible penetrar en un mundo 'sin alma y sin edad' " (p. 565; "The author of the *Sonatas* places himself definitively outside his work since as a conscious being living in his time it is impossible for him to penetrate a world 'devoid of a soul and a time frame' ").

65. For two other views on the religious theme in this work, see Eliane Lavaud, *Valle-Inclán du journal au roman*, and Robert Marrast, "Religiosidad y satanismo, sadismo y masoquismo en la *Sonata de otoño*," *Cuadernos Hispanoamericanos* 199–200 (1966): 482–92.

66. The seduction of the reader could be seen as an expression of *épater le bourgeois*. For a fascinating study of this concept, see Gonzalo Sobejano's *Forma literaria y sensibilidad social (Mateo Alemán, Galdós, Clarín, el 98 y Valle-Inclán)* (Madrid: Gredos, 1967). That same idea is

noted by Ildefonso Manuel Gil in "El disputado '¡Viva la bagatela!': Baroja, Azorín y Valle-Inclán," *Cuadernos Hispanoamericanos* 226–27 (1968): 451-65.

67. A similar point is made by Valis, "Valle-Inclán's *Sonata de otoño*: Refractions of a French Anarchist," *Comparative Literature Studies* 22 (1985): 218–30: "We read the work with a divided mind, seeing in it an aesthetic exercise and, at the same time, a veiled and cynical comment on the corrupted nature of man and society. It is as though there were two texts thrust upon us in a single reading, and we were at a loss as to which was the real one" (p. 228). My only difference with Valis's perceptive exegesis is that the two texts fuse to constitute one text. I would argue that it is not a question of choosing one over the other but of accepting the contradiction created by the two as yet another text, something resembling the "real text," perhaps. Stated in another way, the aesthetic exercise in effect constitutes the message of "the corrupted nature of man and society." I would also like to call attention to Valis's use of the word *refractions* in her title. When she analyzes how Valle-Inclán borrows from Octave Mirbeau's *Le Journal d'une femme de chambre,* then completely subverts the message of Mirbeau's work, she is in effect also studying a case of double-voicing, although she does not use Bakhtin's term.

68. Since the *Sonatas* are generally identified with Hispanic modernist canons, the emphasis on sensuality can be seen as an escape. The "modernistas" used exotic scenes as an evasion of reality, and it is generally agreed that such an escape conveyed an implicit criticism of a bourgeois society. Rather than in exotica, Valle-Inclán expresses his criticism by means of the glorification of sensuality. See José F. Montesinos, "Modernismo, esperpentismo o las dos evasiones," *Revista de Occidente* 44–45 (1966): 146–65, for some interesting views on how, even in these early works, Valle-Inclán rejected mimetic renditions of reality so as to arrive at deeper levels of the problems of society.

69. José Antonio Maravall, "La imagen de la sociedad arcaica en Valle-Inclán," *Revista de Occidente* 44–45 (1966): 225–56, also makes the point that there is a fusion in Valle-Inclán's overall work between aesthetics and social messages. Obdulia Guerrero Bueno, "Vocación histórica y realismo en la obra literaria de Valle-Inclán," *Insula* 236–37 (1966): 22, on the other hand, limits the definition of realism in the author's works to extratextual referents that she identifies.

70. Amado Alonso, "Estructura de las *Sonatas* de Valle-Inclán," in *Materia y forma en poesía* (Madrid: Gredos, 1977), pp. 222–57.

71. The most recent and insightful of these studies showing how Valle-Inclán artistically modified his models is Valis's "Refractions." In addition, see Amado Alonso, *Materia y forma en poesía,* and Alonso Zamora Vicente, *Las Sonatas de Valle-Inclán* (Madrid: Gredos, 1983). Carol S. Maier presented the same thesis in reference to *La lámpara maravillosa*: "Valle-Inclán's Literary Relations: The Creation of Context," paper presented at the annual meeting of the Modern Language Association, Washington D.C., December 1984. The issue of literary borrowing with a plagiaristic connotation was first raised in 1916 by Julio Casares in his *Crítica profana* (Madrid: Imprenta Colonial, 1916), where he says the ending of *Sonata de otoño* was in effect stolen from Barbey d'Aurevilly's *Le Rideau Cramoisi.* Barbara A. Terry, "The Influence of Casanova and Barbey D'Aurevilly on the 'Sonatas' of Valle-Inclán," *Revista de Estudios Hispánicos* 1 (1967): 61-88, while not accusing Valle-Inclán of plagiarism, does argue that the influence of others in his work is direct rather than refracted.

72. For one of the more negative evaluations of the *Sonatas,* based largely on what the critic believes is a failure to reflect social reality, see Enrique Anderson Imbert, "Escamoteo de la realidad en las *Sonatas de Valle-Inclán,*" in *Crítica interna* (Madrid: Taurus, 1960), pp. 211–28.

73. Two who have recognized this tie without trying to demonstrate its artistic expression by means of a textual analysis are Allen W. Phillips, "Estudio Preliminar," pp. vii-lxii in the edition cited in this study, and Rafael Conte, "Valle-Inclán y la realidad," *Cuadernos Hispanoamericanos* 199–200 (1966): 53–64.

Notes to Chapter 2: 1916

1. See the study by Jorge Urrutia, *El Novecentismo y la renovación vanguardista.*
2. See Carlos Blanco Aguinaga, *Juventud del 98.*
3. Quoted by Juan Marichal in "Los intelectuales y la guerra."

4. Miguel de Unamuno, "A lo que salga," in *Ensayos,* pp. 121–44.
5. Miguel de Unamuno, *Niebla,* p. 149.
6. *La estructura de la obra literaria.*
7. For an enlightening analysis of Augusto's existential search, see Juan Villegas, "*Niebla*: una ruta para autentificar la existencia," in *Spanish Thought and Letters in the Twentieth Century,* ed. Germán Bleiberg and E. Inman Fox.
8. Miguel de Unamuno, "Nada menos que todo un hombre," in *Tres novelas ejemplares y un prólogo,* p. 113. Subsequent quotations from the text will come from this edition, with the page number indicated in parentheses.
9. The concept of language as a façade for reality is one of the themes of *Niebla.* For example, Augusto's dog Orfeo makes the following comment in the epilogue concerning human speech: "La lengua le sirve para mentir, inventar lo que no hay y confundirse" (p. 164; "Language serves for lying, for inventing what does not exist and for creating confusion").
10. In the prologue to *Tres novelas ejemplares,* Unamuno defines nonbeings with the terms "querer no ser" ("wanting not to exist") and "no querer no ser" ("not wanting not to exist"). He then adds, "De uno que no quiere ser difícilmente se saca una criatura poética, de novela" (p. 17; "From one who does not want to exist it is difficult to create a poetic creature").
11. As linguists have pointed out, negatives are inherently ambiguous and paradoxical: they tend to make visible what they pretend to erase, to suggest what they seem to negate, and to promote what they claim to prohibit. Exceptionally useful for my understanding of this concept was Bertrice Bartlett, "Negatives and the Reader"; also see Floyd Merrell, *Pararealities: The Nature of Our Fictions and How We Know Them*; and Mary Louise Pratt, *Toward a Speech Act Theory of Literary Discourse.*
12. Frank Durand, "Search for Reality in *Nada menos que todo un hombre,*" argues persuasively that Julia is the real *agonista* of the novel. Ricardo Gullón, "Cómo se hace un hombre," in *Autobiografías de Unamuno,* pp. 178–93, also sees Julia and not Alejandro as the main character. Offering an opposing view is Angel del Río, "Las 'novelas ejemplares' de Unamuno," who insists that Alejandro is the only real character in the novel. Focusing on the theme of a tragic class struggle is Carlos Blanco Aguinaga, "Aspectos dialécticos de las *Tres novelas ejemplares.*" Mario Pinto, "*Todo un hombre,* de Miguel de Unamuno," offers interesting comments concerning the stage production of the novel. Finally, for one of the more negative reactions, we have Francisco Ayala, "El arte de novelar en Unamuno,": "en lugar de 'todo un hombre', su Alejandro Gómez resulta ser todo un fantoche, al que ni siquiera el suicidio final consigue redimir del ridículo" (p. 356; "rather than a 'real man,' his Alejandro Gómez turns out to be a nonentity whose final suicide doesn't even succeed in saving him from being ridiculous").
13. José María Monner Sans, "Unamuno, Pirandello y el personaje autónomo," concurs that "desde 1914 a Unamuno le es imposible desentenderse de este Pérez, neurótico y perseguidor" (p. 399; "Ever since 1914 Unamuno cannot separate himself from this neurotic and ever-present Pérez"). Geoffrey Ribbans, to the contrary, in *Niebla y Soledad,* rejects the link between *Niebla* and Unamuno's subsequent novels: "Las novelas posteriores siguen una técnica a todas luces diferente de la de *Amor y pedagogía* y *Niebla*" (p. 105; "The later novels obviously follow a completely different technique than that of *Amor y pedagogía* and *Niebla*"). Ribbans argues that whereas the characters of the two novels cited develop and become viviparous, the characters of the later novels are already completely formed when they appear. Although Ribbans's thesis has a certain degree of validity, in view of the changes that Alejandro and Julia undergo in "Nada menos que todo un hombre," one must conclude that the point is overstated. But even granting that characters such as Alejandro are more "formed" than an Apolodoro of *Amor y pedagogía,* or an Augusto of *Niebla,* I would continue to argue that there is a direct and essential link between Augusto Pérez and Alejandro Gómez on the one hand, and Julia on the other: It is the link formed by the evolving relationship of a particular creator (Unamuno) to his creations. It also is significant that the original title of *Amor y pedagogía* was in fact "Todo un hombre"—see Manuel García Blanco, "*Amor y pedagogía,* nivola unamuniana." Joseph E. Gillet's classic study, "The Autonomous Character in Spanish and European Literature," discusses Unamuno's technique within the general European context.
14. The benchmark study on this work is Armando F. Zubizarreta, *Unamuno en su nivola.* Ricardo Gullón, "La novela personal de don Miguel de Unamuno," calls the work a novelized autobiography.

15. Ricardo Gullón, "Ramón Pérez de Ayala y la novela lírica," in *La novela lírica, II,* pp. 25–33, also argues that Pérez de Ayala belongs in the same category of innovators as Martínez Ruiz, Unamuno, and Valle-Inclán. It should be noted that Gullón basically rejects the Generation of '98 label, anyway (see his *La invención del 98 y otros ensayos*), and indeed in his more recent study *La novela lírica* he proposes a definition that spans, as I am attempting here, the conventional boundaries that separate the generation and vanguardism.

16. As noted earlier, J. J. Macklin, "Pérez de Ayala y la novela modernista europea," places Pérez de Ayala's innovations on the same level with those of Joyce, Woolf, Mann, Gide, and Proust.

17. Miguel Angel Lozano Marco, *Del relato modernista a la novela poemática: La narrativa breve de Ramón Pérez de Ayala,* argues that the *Novelas poemáticas* represent a contribution to Spanish literary history equal to Valle-Inclán's *esperpento* and Unamuno's *nivola,* and that they are "del más genuino y original arte narrativo ayaliano" (p. 228; "of the most genuine and original of the author's narrative artistry"). Also ranking the *Novelas poemáticas* as Pérez de Ayala's best artistic achievement are Eugenio de Nora, "Ramón Pérez de Ayala," in *La novela española contemporánea,* pp. 467–513; and Andrés Amorós, *La novela intelectual de Ramón Pérez de Ayala,* pp. 236–289. Julio Matas, *Contra el honor: Las novelas normativas de Ramón Pérez de Ayala,* discusses how the collection forms a bridge between the author's early works and his later, more innovative ones.

18. Amorós, *La novela intelectual,* notes that when they were originally published as separate items, neither "Luz de domingo" nor "La caída de los Limones" contained the poems.

19. The function of the poems has attracted considerable critical attention: María Dolores Rajoy Feijóo, "Poesía y narrativa en R. Pérez de Ayala (Lectura de *Las novelas poemáticas*)," in *Homenaje a Ramón Pérez de Ayala,* ed. María del Carmen Bobes Naves, pp. 45–66, offers the most comprehensive discussion as she analyzes each poem in the collection. Angeles Prado, "Las novelas poemáticas de Ramón Pérez de Ayala," discusses how they create a metaphysical perspective. Mario Baquero Goyanes, "Contraste y perspectivismo en Ramón Pérez de Ayala," in *Perspectivismo y contraste,* pp. 171–244, notes their contrastive effect with the narrative accounts. Eugenio de Nora, *La novela española,* sees their function as that of a Greek chorus. Frances Wyers Weber, *The Literary Perspectivism of Ramón Pérez de Ayala,* discusses how the poems set the stories apart from contemporary reality. Pelayo H. Fernández, *Ramón Pérez de Ayala: Tres novelas analizadas,* notes how the poems of "La caída de los Limones" point to the anecdotal content of the narratives. Beth Noble, "The Descriptive Genius of Pérez de Ayala," although focusing her analysis on "La caída de los Limones," makes only passing reference to the poems.

20. Although critics differ widely on which of the three novelettes is best, Eugenio de Nora, *La novela española,* states unequivocally that "La caída de los Limones" represents the "obra maestra" ("masterpiece") of the collection.

21. The referent for this incident was a famous murder committed in 1902 and labeled the "Don Benito crime." Andrés Amorós, *La novela intelectual,* quotes a newspaper report of the crime written by Baroja (pp. 272–74).

22. Ramón Pérez de Ayala, "La caída de los Limones," in *Prometeo, Luz de domingo, La caída de los Limones,* p. 90. Further quotations of the text will come from this edition, with the page number indicated in parentheses.

23. Rajoy Feijóo, "Poesía y narrativa," suggests a similar reading of the poems in the whole collection when she says that "su forma—¿voluntariamente?—descuidada presenta un aspecto abandonado, incluso prosaico" (p. 48; "their form—voluntarily?—disordered presents a neglected aspect, which is even prosaic"). Yet Rajoy Feijóo treats them as serious lyric poetry in her analyses and never really deals with the question she raises of the prosaic, neglected form. Andrés Amorós, *La novela intelectual,* commenting on this initial poem, even goes so far as to claim that "el poema es hermoso, con ribetes de arcaísmo" (p. 280; "the poem is beautiful, with an archaic touch").

24. This less refracted correspondence in Chapter 2 between the poem and the narrative is really the only example in the novelette that justifies the explanation so often offered that the poems function independently, as it were, to lend greater profundity and universality to the work. In effect, if viewed in isolation, the effect of the poems often is the opposite. The key to their function is the voice and message that emerges from their juxtaposition with the narrative accounts.

25. Although he does not mention this novelette, Mariano Baquero Goyanes, "La novela

como tragicomedia: Pérez de Ayala y Ortega" in *Perspectivismo y contraste*, pp. 161–70, offers some important comments on how the author blends comedy and tragedy in his novels. Again, that blend has generally been recognized in the narratives of the *Novelas poemáticas* but ignored in the poems, and especially in the effect created by the juxtaposition of the two genres. The social criticism implicit in "La caída de los Limones," as well as that in the other novelettes of the collection, is very much in the spirit of the Generation of '98.

26. Angeles Prado, "Las novelas poemáticas," offers a very useful summation of the author's comments. Prado's article, however, focuses primarily on the stories of *El ombligo del mundo*.

Notes to Chapter 3: 1923–1926

1. See Paul Ilie, *Documents of the Spanish Vanguard*, for the most comprehensive list of these magazines.

2. Ignacio Soldevila Durante, "La problemática del nacionalismo en los prosistas de la Generación de 1923 (1918–1931)," in *Nation et nationalités en Espagne XIXe-XXe S.*, pp. 249–59, makes the following statement in reference to the manner in which the magazines scrutinized the credentials of their contributors: "Si algún joven estudiante de derecho, aún con el pelo de la provincia (a donde llegaban con cierto retraso los giros de orientación), se permitía publicar un par de novelas con una problemática politizada muy evidente, como fue el caso de Francisco Ayala entre 1925 y 1926, para entrar en la sala de redacción de la revista, donde se operaba la magia dehumanizada, hubo de hacer enmienda honorable" (p. 254; "If some young law student, with his provincialism still intact [the new trends reached the provinces a little late], was permitted to publish a couple of novels with very evident political themes, as was the case of Francisco Ayala between 1925 and 1926, in order to get into the publishing house door, where the dehumanization magic was spinning its web, he had to pay his appropriate dues").

3. *Teoría del arte de vanguardia*, trans. Rosa Chacel.

4. See especially Guillermo de Torre, *Historia de las literaturas de vanguardia*, and Paul Ilie, *The Surrealist Mode in Spanish Literature*.

5. *Idle Fictions*.

6. Víctor Fuentes, "La narrativa española de vanguardia (1923–1931): Un ensayo de interpretación."

7. Juan Cano Ballesta, *Literatura y tecnología: (Las letras españolas ante la revolución industrial 1900–1933)*.

8. For the titles of the major full-length studies of José Martínez Ruiz's (Azorín's) opus, most of which consider the concepts of time, structure, and style, see the bibliography. Essays focused specifically on time in his work include Miguel Enguídanos, "Azorín en busca del tiempo divinal"; Jorge García Gómez, "Notas sobre el tiempo y su pasar en novelas varias de Azorín"; Leon Livingstone, "Tiempo contra historia, en las novelas de José Martínez Ruiz," in *La novela lírica, I*, ed. Darío Villanueva, pp. 49–63; "José Antonio Maravall, "Azorín. Idea y sentido de la microhistoria"; M. Montes Huidobro, "Un retrato de Azorín: *Doña Inés*"; Marguerite Rand, "Más notas sobre Azorín y el tiempo"; and José B. Vidal, "El tiempo a través de los personajes de *Doña Inés*."

9. Studies focused on stylistics include Carlos Blanco Aguinaga, "Especticismo, paisajismo y los clásicos: Azorín o la mistificación de la realidad," pp. 3 and 5; Mariano Baquero Goyanes, "Elementos rítmicos en la prosa de Azorín"; Roberto González Echevarría, "El primitivismo de Azorín"; Robert E. Lott, "Sobre el método narrativo y el estilo en las novelas de Azorín"; and Julián Marías, "*Doña Inés*."

10. See Joseph E. Gillet, "The Autonomous Character in Spanish and European Literature"; Leon Livingstone, "The Pursuit of Form in the Novels of Azorín"; and Thomas C. Meehan, "El desdoblamiento interior en *Doña Inés*."

11. The subtitle unfortunately does not appear in all the editions. For this study I quote from the most recent one, Azorín, *Doña Inés (Historia de amor)*, ed., intro. and notes by Elena Catena. Catena, with the exception of the beginning of Chapter 7, faithfully follows the initial 1925 edition of the novel.

12. Since Don Juan is commonly employed as a stereotype, giving that name to the lover is another example of a play on convention.

13. Offering an opposing view is Elena Catena, "Lo azoriniano en *Doña Inés*," who says that *Doña Inés* is a "novela rosa en la mejor tradición del género," and that it "es una novela ejemplar a la manera decimonónica" (p. 266; "a sentimental or romantic novel in the best tradition of the genre," and that it "is an exemplary novel of the nineteenth-century tradition").

14. Perhaps Don Pablo, Doña Inés's uncle, is the best example of a satirized type in the novel. In spite of the commonly held opinion that he represents the real author's alter ego in the novel, he is the target of some satiric censoring. For example, when he is first introduced, the narrator notes: "El caballero se nos aparece alto y recio; en algunos momentos, de pie, erguido, con la mano puesta en la abertura de la levita, semeja un doctrinario francés" (p. 109; "The gentleman seems tall and strong; on occasion, standing, proud, with his hand in the opening of his coat, he looks like a French doctrinaire"). His Napoleonic pose becomes even more ironic given his indolent nature. In fact, when he finally promises to intervene on his niece's behalf in the face of opposition to her by the entire community, his intentions are sabotaged by the force of his *abulia*: "Tomada esta resolución—resolución de aplazamiento—don Pablo queda tranquilo. Ya puede seguir el curso sereno y normal de su vida. Hasta dentro de cuatro días—habíamos dicho tres o cuatro—no habrá que pensar en el problema" (p. 205; "Having resolved to do this—a resolution of postponement—Don Pablo is calm. He can follow a serene course and a normal life. Until four days have passed—we had said three or four days—he will not have to think about the problem"). Although this is humorous, there is a certain biting irony also directed at his failure to come to the aid of Doña Inés. As the narrator informed his reader earlier, Don Pablo harbors a hidden resentment: "desdén quizás a causa de la ingratitud del amigo y de la inconsciencia de la muchedumbre. Los ojos de tío Pablo, a pesar del íntimo desdén, miran con indulgencia" (p. 110; "disdain perhaps because of the ingratitude of the friend and the insensitivity of the masses. Uncle Pablo's eyes, in spite of an intimate disdain, gaze with indulgence"). In light of his failure to help his niece, his resentment toward the ingratitude displayed toward him by others is more than slightly hypocritical. Finally, then, these examples demonstrate the danger of identifying the real author with this or any character in a work of fiction. In spite of expressing some opinions that echo those voiced by the author himself in his essays, Don Pablo is not José Martínez Ruiz; Don Pablo is a fictional character who plays a key structural role in the novel. At most he is a refracted image of the author, as are all the other characters in one way or another.

15. Elena Catena, in a footnote to the edition of the novel being cited in this study (p. 118). Catena's analogy, to which she expresses surprise, supports my basic thesis linking *Doña Inés* to the vanguardist movement, a movement with which Gómez de la Serna is closely identified.

16. Elena Catena (p. 142) identifies the source as "Romance del prisionero," found in Menéndez Pidal's *Flor nueva de romances viejos*.

17. Leon Livingston, *Tema y forma* and "The Pursuit of Form," is the name most associated with this term. See also the articles of Gillet, "The Autonomous Character," and Meehan, "El desdoblamiento interior."

18. The focus on literature itself, or the foregrounding of literary codes, is one type of metafiction. For a definition of this expression as opposed to others, see my *Beyond the Metafictional Mode*.

19. José Ortega y Gasset, *La deshumanización del arte*. I should note, however, that the essay appeared in a newspaper in serial form the year before.

20. Emil Staiger, *Conceptos fundamentales de poética*, trans. Jaime Ferreiro Alemparte.

21. Ramón del Valle-Inclán, *Tirano Banderas: Novela de tierra caliente*, intro. Antonio Valencia, p. 112. All subsequent quotes from the text will come from this edition with the page numbers indicated in parentheses.

22. Valle-Inclán defines this term, which technically he coined for his theatrical works, as a view of reality by means of a concave mirror; whereas *Doña Inés* can be seen as an impressionist painting in prose, *Tirano Banderas* would be expressionist. Perhaps the best analysis we have of *esperpento* as it applies to *Tirano Banderas*, a mode the author connects to surrealism, is Paul Ilie, *The Surrealist Mode in Spanish Literature*. The work most often cited on the subject of *esperpento* in general is probably Rodolfo Cardona and Anthony N. Zahareas, *Visión del esperpento*.

23. Luis Fernández Cifuentes, *Teoría y mercado de la novela*, pp. 360–70, offers an informative summary of critical opinion at the time the novel appeared. He notes that the novel was

unusually successful, with 10,000 copies sold in the first three months. Reviewers above all tended to praise the sociohistorical dimension of the novel, but they also noted its connection with the "arte nuevo."

24. Ignacio Soldevila Durante, "Valle-Inclán y las vanguardias literarias: la composición de *Tirano Banderas* como novela cubista," drawing primarily on essays of Alfonso Reyes and an exchange of letters between him and Valle-Inclán, documents Valle's conscious effort to incorporate vanguard aesthetic principles into his novel. In the same symposium, Darío Villanueva, "Valle-Inclán renovador de la novela," draws interesting parallels between the novelistic innovations in *Tirano Banderas* and the postmodernist technique of Joyce in *Ulysses*. Villanueva focuses primarily on how the two authors condense time and disrupt its conventional diachronic representation, and how each creates his own hybrid language. Gonzalo Díaz Migoyo even goes so far as to incorporate the postmodernist label in the title of his paper, "*Tirano Banderas* o la posmodernidad novelesca española," where he concentrates on the problematic relationship between past and present, the question of which is product of which, and how that conflict is reflected in the temporal/spatial composition of the novel.

25. See particularly Ricardo Gullón, "Técnicas de Valle-Inclán"; Virginia Milner Garlitz, "Teosofismo en *Tirano Banderas*"; Dru Dougherty, "The Question of Revolution in *Tirano Banderas*"; and Peggy Lynne Tucker, *Time and History in Valle-Inclán's Historical Novels and "Tirano Banderas"*.

26. Susan Kirkpatrick, "*Tirano Banderas* y la estructura de la historia"; and Gonzalo Díaz Migoyo, *Guía de "Tirano Banderas,"* and his paper "la posmodernidad novelesca."

27. This schematic pattern was first proposed by Oldrich Belic, *La estructura narrativa de "Tirano Banderas,"* and virtually everything said since on the subject of structure in the novel has been some kind of amplification of Belic's model.

28. This point is made by Susan Kirkpatrick in her excellent analysis of the novel, "La estructura de la historia."

29. Kirkpatrick, "La estructura de la historia," and Díaz Migoyo, *Guía*, both offer numerous other examples of this mirror effect of reverse action.

30. Virginia Milner Garlitz, "Teosofismo," offers an insightful analysis of the concept of numbers (particularly three and seven) and moral responsibility as they relate to the theme of theosophy in the novel.

31. The focalizing strategy noted here represents another dimension to the Díaz Migoyo thesis, *Guía*, that the narrator of *Tirano Banderas* is basically invisible; that is, he tends to avoid any direct expression of his attitude and opinions concerning the characters and events of the novel. In this case and the one to follow, the narrator does so by using another character as the focalizing source. Antonio Risco, *La estética de Valle-Inclán: En los esperpentos y en "El ruedo ibérico"*, makes the same point on the invisibility of the narrator, but unlike Díaz Migoyo, Risco does not provide the supporting analysis of how the effect is achieved.

32. The role of Tirano and Don Roque as binary opposites is further underscored by Don Roque's reaction to the stars. Whereas Tirano sees in them only the threat of eternal damnation, Don Roque stresses a different although related message: "La responsabilidad eterna de las acciones humanas le asombraba con el vasto soplo de un aliento divino" (p. 174; "The eternal responsibility of human actions overwhelmed him with the vast puff of a divine breath").

33. The most recent example is Díaz Migoyo, *Guía*, who analyzes the narrator's method of characterizing all the main personages except Zacarías. It should also be noted that Díaz Migoyo's thesis is that the narrator is invisible and that all the characterization is done by the personage himself, or by other personages. As we will see, that thesis does not work so well in the case of Zacarías.

34. In his frequently quoted introductory remarks to his war diary, *La media noche: Visión estelar de un momento de guerra* (1917), Valle offers an explanation of his structural goal in that work, which could well define what he achieved in *Tirano Banderas*: "Yo, torpe y vano de mí, quise ser centro y tener de la guerra una visión astral *fuera de geometría y de cronología*, como si el alma, desencarnada ya, mirase la tierra desde su estrella" (p. 8, emphasis is mine; "Awkward and vain as I am, I tried to be the center and to achieve an astral vision of the war, a vision beyond geometry and chronology, as if my soul, separated from my flesh, were observing the earth from a star").

35. Juan Villegas, in "La disposición temporal de *Tirano Banderas*," was the first critic to elucidate the temporal complexity of the novel. And although Villegas's essay has served

justifiably as something of a model on this aspect of the novel, he assigns all the action of the prologue to the same chronological sequence, as do by direct statement or implication Peggy Lynne Tucker, *Time and History*, Verity Smith, *Valle-Inclan: "Tirano Banderas"*, and most recently, Díaz Migoyo, *Guía*, who goes so far as to insist that the only repeated temporal lapse of the novel occurs within the middle section (see "La bisagra temporal," pp. 111–20).

36. In his stimulating paper presented at the symposium on Valle-Inclán, Díaz Migoyo, "*Tirano Banderas* y la posmodernidad," after first "deconstructing" the framed section of the novel, argues that the frame itself "reconstructs" and imposes closure on the linear sequence of events; the body of the novel reveals fragmented, nonchronological, and contradictory action, while the prologue and epilogue correct that structure by means of a sequential, chronological, and conclusive set of events. Disregarding what some might consider a philosophical inconsistency in such an argument, I believe that the flaw in his thesis is his insistence on the absolute chronological sequence of the events in the frame. As our analysis has demonstrated, the novel does not justify such a closed reading of that section. Manuel Durán, "Actualidad de *Tirano Banderas*," also argues that the novel is ambiguous or open-ended.

37. This is a technique similar to the one that Valle-Inclán's Galician countryman Camilo José Cela employs so masterfully in his novel *La colmena*. A basic difference between the two, however, is that this novel seems to contain a repetition of the same event but not necessarily of the same scene, while with Cela the scene itself is repeated with variations. For more on Cela's use of this technique, see my "Documentación y transformación en *La colmena*," in *La novela española de posguerra: Creación artística y experiencia personal*, pp. 94–130.

38. Susan A. Handelman, *The Slayers of Moses: The Emergence of Rabbinic Interpretation in Modern Literary Theory*, in an interesting if controversial thesis, argues that the present century is characterized by a shift from visual to verbal modes of thought and literary expression. After centuries of Greek influence during which imagery and spatial patterns were the primary modes of expression, now we are turning to the Rabbinic emphasis on language and contiguity; the Greeks believed in the visual power of language while the Rabbis trusted in its sounds. "The movement from image to language is also the movement of the twentieth-century novel, which turns around the problems of its own articulation in a space and time which are preeminently verbal, not visual" (p. 79). *Tirano Banderas* would seem to be representative of the shift that Handelman defines.

39. In a letter to Alfonso Reyes, reported by Emma Susana Speratti-Piñero in her *De "Sonata de otoño" al esperpento*, p. 201. In their exchange of letters, Valle-Inclán expresses his concern, based on Reyes's reports, about the ultimate success of the Mexican Revolution, and states that he decided to change his original idea for *Tirano Banderas* of having the revolution led by the Indians. For some of his other views on Mexico and the revolution, see Dru Dougherty, *Un Valle-Inclán olvidado: entrevistas y conferencias*, and *Valle-Inclán y la Segunda República*. In the latter study Dougherty documents Don Ramón's liberal optimism from the beginning of the republic in 1931 until the author's death in 1936. Whereas one could argue that such an attitude tends to contradict the reading I am proposing for *Tirano Banderas*, it is important to note the difference in time and subject matter between the novel and the political situation in Spain examined in Dougherty's study. Speratti-Piñero and Díaz Migoyo identify many of the referents for the anecdote of *Tirano Banderas*, as does José Extramiana, "A propósito de algunas fuentes de *Tirano Banderas* en un intento de interpretación de la novela." It should be stressed, however, that although Valle-Inclán's reliance on specific referents for his novel is indisputably documented, those referents are transformed by the novel into universal signs.

40. Paul Ilie, *The Surrealist Mode in Spanish Literature*, p. 152.

41. Harold Bloom, *The Anxiety of Influence: A Theory of Poetry*. Within the Bloom scheme, Unamuno and Gómez de la Serna would constitute the "strong novelists" of their respective movements, and Don Ramón's novelistic approach could be seen as a "swerving away" from that of Unamuno. In spite of some strong reservations concerning Bloom's paradigm, I do see a great deal of validity in this concept of "strong poets," and I believe that concept applies to the two Spanish novelists being discussed.

42. That role is certainly championed by Rafael Cansinos Assens, himself one of the high priests of the movement, who credits Gómez de la Serna with bringing a new will and enthusiasm to revitalize art after the members of the Generation of '98 had spent their energies. In fact, Cansinos Assens alleges that the members of the Generation of '98 were intellectuals and critics, not artists, and Don Ramón represents a renaissance of pure art. See "La no-

vísima literatura" in *La nueva literatura, II: Las escuelas (1898 1900–1918)*, pp. 353–375. In a somewhat forced analogy, Ramón Buckley and John Crispin, *Los vanguardistas españoles*, equate Gómez de la Serna's importance to the formation of vanguard prose with the discovery of Góngora to vanguard poetry (p. 12). Finally, Melchor Fernández Almagro, "La generación unipersonal de Gómez de la Serna," pp. 10–11, likens the role of Ramón in the new art to that of Azorín to the Generation of '98 art.

43. Although critics do not agree on which are Gómez de la Serna's best novels, certainly *El novelista* ranks as one of them. Eugenio G. de Nora, *La novela española contemporánea*, is the most vociferous defender of that novel, while José Camón Aznar, *Ramón Gómez de la Serna en sus obras*, conveys its importance by virtue of the space he dedicates to it. Gaspar Gómez de la Serna, *Ramón (obra y vida)*, on the other hand, avoids singling out any novel as the author's best or most important. For other general comments on the novelistic style of Ramón Gómez de la Serna, see Melchor Fernández Almagro, "La generación unipersonal de Gómez de la Serna"; Julián Marías, "Ramón y la realidad," pp. 2 and 8; Rodolfo Cardona, *Ramón: A Study of Gómez de la Serna and His Works*; Francisco Umbral, *Ramón y las vanguardias*; Carolyn Richmond, "Gómez de la Serna novelista," in *La Quinta de Palmyra*, pp. 20–29; and Manuel Lacarta, *Madrid y sus literaturas: De la Generación del 98 a la posguerra*.

44. Genette, *Narrative Discourse*, labels this text within a text *metadiegetic*, or a narrative in the second degree (p. 228). In view of the connotation that the prefix *meta-* has in literary studies, numbering the levels seems less confusing than adding another technical term to the discussion.

45. The term *game*, of course, is borrowed from *La deshumanización del arte*.

46. Ramón Gómez de la Serna, *El novelista*, p. 164. Further quotations from the text will be from this edition, with page numbers indicated in parentheses.

47. For the reader unfamiliar with the *novela rosa* formula, Andrés Amorós provides a somewhat elementary definition in his *Sociología de una novela rosa*. In his review of *Amor y pedagogía*, R. D. Perés, *La Lectura* 2 (July 1902), 400–402, offers the following summary of the genre that Unamuno and his colleagues were opposing: "Con su condimento necesario de amoríos más o menos pecaminosos y bien preparados para que resalten y sirvan de cebo; con sus escenas, ora francamente patéticas, ora regocijadas de veras; con sus páginas de brillantes descripciones, su mujerío incitante y su interés hábilmente sostenido que se procura arrastre la atención" (p. 400; "With the necessary flavor of romance, more or less erotic and well arranged to serve as bait; with its scenes, frankly sometimes pathetic, sometimes overdone; with its pages of brilliant descriptions, its exciting female and a plot designed to capture and sustain attention"). It is significant that the Perés 1902 definition also applies in 1924, further evidence that both the Generation of '98 novelists and the vanguardists were opposing the same foe.

48. As noted earlier, Esteban Salazar y Chapela, in a review of Gómez de la Serna's *Chao, El Sol*, 7 February 1934, p. 7, coined the term *descaracterización* to describe how the novelist subverts the conventional sense of characterization. Pérez Firmat incorporates that term as the title of one of his chapters defining the vanguard novel, *Idle Fictions*, pp. 81–99.

49. My reading of the importance of this particular novel within the novel is not shared by Carolyn Richmond, in her introduction to *La Quinta de Palmyra*, who argues that "El inencontrable," with Lisbon as a setting, is the key interpolated work.

50. The concept of violating narrative levels basically follows Genette's explanation, pp. 234–37. See also my introduction to *Beyond the Metafictional Mode*, pp. 1–17.

51. This is another example of what Martínez Bonati, in *Estructura de la obra literaria*, calls mimetic language, or the language that establishes the "truth" of a fictional work.

52. Jorge Urrutia, *El novecentismo y la renovación vanguardista*, also stresses Gómez de la Serna's attempt to eliminate all sentimentalism and social commitment from his fiction.

53. Noël Valis, in "*El novelista*, por Ramón Gómez de la Serna, o la novela en busca de sí misma," the introduction to her forthcoming critical edition of *El novelista*, analyzes very perceptively several dichotomies in the novel, including the one noted here concerning tone.

54. Fernández Cifuentes, *Mercado*, p. 336, makes a similar point.

55. Pedro Salinas, *Literatura española siglo XX*, expresses the author's contradictory tone in the following way: "Al encontrarse Gómez de la Serna con esta verdad de su espíritu, la no importancia del hombre, su situación marginal en el Universo, la actitud que toma es una actitud de desesperación alegre, de lento y jocundo suicidio" (p. 154; "When Gómez de la Serna discovers this spiritual truth, man's lack of importance and his marginal position in the

Universe, Don Ramón assumes an attitude of happy desperation, of a slow and jocular suicide").

56. Evelyne López Campillo, *La Revista de Occidente y la formación de minorías,* offers an informative overview of the major contributors to the journal and a summary of the views expressed. Significantly, Jarnés and Gómez de la Serna were the two most frequent contributors during the first epoch of the journal.

57. For two of the more enlightening studies of this aspect of Jarnés's novels see Paul Ilie, "Benjamín Jarnés: Aspects of the Dehumanized Novel" (Ilie's essay focuses on *Locura y muerte de nadie*); and María Pilar Martínez Latre, *La novela intelectual de Benjamín Jarnés.*

58. Víctor Fuentes, "La dimensión estético-erótica y la novelística de Jarnés" and "La narrativa española de vanguardia (1923–1931)"; also Marion W. O'Neill, "The Role of the Sensual in the Art of Benjamín Jarnés."

59. See Gustavo Pérez Firmat, "The Novel as Mattress," in *Idle Fictions,* pp. 121–37; and my own "Codes versus Modes: *Locura y muerte de nadie* and *La novia del viento*" in *Beyond the Metafictional Mode,* pp. 45–57.

60. Interestingly, one of the first to recognize this blend in Jarnés's art was Pedro Salinas himself in "Benjamín Jarnés."

61. I have used the date of publication for all the other works in this study, but in this case there is such an insistence on 1924, which not only appears at the end of the novel, but is also noted by the author in his "Advertencia" to the 1934 edition, that it seems more appropriate than 1928. And although the edition I am using is based on the 1934 revised version, Jarnés's emphasis on the date when he wrote the novel seems the most appropriate one to follow for this study.

62. Emilio de Zuleta, *Arte y vida en la obra de Benjamín Jarnés,* carefully documents all the changes between the 1928 and 1934 editions. As Zuleta states, the modifications in general reflect a desire to give more coherence to the work, to develop characterization further, or to sharpen the social criticism. In a word, the changes are designed to make the novel a bit more "realistic." Zuleta's study, of course, lends support to those who argue that the Spanish vanguard movement had spent itself by the early 1930s. The other general work on Jarnés is J. S. Bernstein, *Benjamín Jarnés.*

63. Víctor Fuentes, "La sociedad y lo social en la obra de Benjamín Jarnés," pp. 13–14, although stressing the social focus, also points out that one of the constants in Jarnés's novels is a criticism of art itself.

64. Benjamín Jarnés, *El convidado de papel,* p. 19. Further quotations will come from this edition, with the page number indicated in parentheses.

65. Gustavo Pérez Firmat, *Idle Fictions,* p. 70. Pérez Firmat focuses primarily on structural characteristics, while Juan Cano Ballesta, *Literatura y tecnología,* emphasizes the metaphorization of technology and prosperity in the stories as he singles out this collection as one of the prime examples of the new art.

66. Pedro Salinas, *Víspera del gozo,* p. 12. Further quotations will come from this edition, with the page number indicated in parentheses.

67. Pérez Firmat, *Idle Fictions,* likens this sequence to a metaphor of a metaphor: "It turns out that Salinas's transposition of words and objects is itself a transposition into a fictional key of a metaphor from *La deshumanización del arte.*" Pérez Firmat goes on to explain that Ortega's metaphor involves a scene viewed through a windowpane. In conventional art the scene is the focal point and the windowpane is not noticed. In the new art advocated by Ortega, the focus is shifted to the panes and the scene behind it is in effect erased from vision. In Salinas's case, so argues Pérez Firmat, the equation is reversed as the protagonist of "Mundo cerrado" transforms the scenes beyond the train window into literary texts. Ortega also insists that this is an either/or choice. If one opts to focus on the scene beyond (conventional art), it is impossible to look also at the pane (new art), and vice versa. I believe these Salinas stories challenge that aspect of Ortega's thesis.

68. Pérez Firmat argues that the title refers primarily to vanguard art as a closed system, and secondarily and perhaps contradictorily to the nineteenth-century novel, which closed the reader within it. Although conceding the presence of realistic elements in the story, Pérez Firmat insists that the novel should be read as vanguardist in intent and that intent is privileged over any realist concessions. While I concede that vanguard techniques are of primary importance in the collection, I place more importance than does Pérez Firmat on the concessions to realist canons.

69. Again there is an echo from "Mundo cerrado" and what Pérez Firmat sees as an analogy between the unread book and vanguard literature with its emphasis on the nonevent.

70. I offer a reading of this story focused somewhat differently in an essay entitled, "Realidad prosaica e imaginación transcendente en dos cuentos de Pedro Salinas" in *Pedro Salinas*, ed. Andrew P. Debicki.

71. Ortega's term "dehumanization of art" was probably one of his more infelicitous word choices. Although his explanation makes plain that the dehumanized form he was defining was designed to lead to deeper and more authentic inquiries into human existence, the tendency has been to accept the literal meaning of the term and to label as dehumanized any art from that period that was nonmimetic. For example, Andrew P. Debicki, *Estudios sobre poesía española contemporánea: la generación de 1924–1925*, was the first successfully to challenge and in effect to revise the prevailing wisdom that the poetry of that generation was abstract and dehumanized. As Debicki's perceptive analyses demonstrate, the poetry of Alberti, Guillén, Lorca, Alonso, and of course Salinas, is anything but dehumanized. As we have just seen, the same is true of Salinas's fiction.

72. Salinas published two other works of fiction: a novel, *La bomba increíble*, and another collection of short stories, *El desnudo impecable y otras narraciones*. For an analysis of one of the latter, see my essay, "La gloria y la niebla" in *Pedro Salinas*.

Notes to Conclusion: 1988

1. See, for example, Roland Barthes, "From Work to Text," in *Textual Strategies* ed. Josué Harari (Ithaca: Cornell Univ. 1979), pp. 73–81.

2. Guillermo de Torre, *Historia de las literaturas de vanguardia*, cites a 1930 issue of *La Gaceta Literaria* proclaiming the vanguard spirit is dead. Paul Ilie, *Documents of the Spanish Vanguard*, also accepts the 1930 date as the end of the movement. Pérez Firmat, *Idle Fictions*, on the other hand, argues that it continued until 1934, while Ramón Buckley and John Crispin, *Los vanguardistas españoles*, extend it until 1935 (although they label the 1930–1935 period as a second phase).

Bibliography

Alberich, José. "Algunas observaciones sobre el estilo de Pío Baroja." *Bulletin of Hispanic Studies* 41 (1964): 169–85.

———. "Ambigüedad y humorismo en las *Sonatas* de Valle-Inclán." *Hispanic Review* 33 (1965): 360–82.

Alonso, Amado. *Materia y forma en poesía*. Madrid: Gredos, 1977.

Amorós, Andrés. "El prólogo de *La voluntad* (Lectura)." *Cuadernos Hispanoamericanos* 226–27 (1968): 339–54.

———. *La novela intelectual de Ramón Pérez de Ayala*. Madrid: Gredos, 1972.

———. *Sociología de una novela rosa*. Madrid: Taurus, 1968.

Anderson Imbert, Enrique. *Crítica interna*. Madrid: Taurus, 1960.

Ares Montes, José. "*Camino de perfección* o las peregrinaciones de Pío Baroja y Fernando Ossorio." *Cuadernos Hispanoamericanos* 265–67 (1972): 481–516.

Ayala, Francisco. "El arte de novelar en Unamuno." *La Torre* 9 (1961): 329–59.

Bakhtin, M.M. *The Dialogic Imagination: Four Essays by M. M. Bakhtin*. Trans. Caryl Emerson and Michael Holquist. Austin: University of Texas Press, 1985.

Baquero Goyanes, Mariano. "Elementos rítmicos en la prosa de Azorín." *Clavileño* 3 (1952): 25–32.

———. *Perspectivismo y contraste*. Madrid: Gredos, 1963.

Barthes, Roland. "From Work to Text." *Textual Strategies: Perspectives in Post-Structuralist Criticism*. Ed. Josué V. Harari. Ithaca: Cornell University Press, 1979.

Bartlett, Bertice. "Negatives and the Reader." Paper presented at Mellon Faculty Development Seminar, University of Kansas, February 1984.

Belic, Oldrich. *La estructura narrativa de "Tirano Banderas"*. Madrid: Nacional, 1968.

Benveniste, Emile. *Problems in General Linguistics*. Trans. Mary Elizabeth Meek. Coral Gables: University of Miami Press, 1971.

Bernstein, J.S. *Benjamín Jarnés*. New York: Twayne, 1972.

Blanco Aguinaga, Carlos. "Aspectos dialécticos de las *Tres novelas ejemplares*." *Revista de Occidente* 7 (1964): 51–70.

———. "Escepticismo, paisajismo y los clásicos: Azorín o la mistificación de la realidad." *Insula* 247 (1967): 3 and 5.

———. *Juventud del 98*. Madrid: Siglo XXI de España, 1970.

Bleiberg, Germán. "Algunas revistas literarias hacia 1898." *Arbor* 11 (1948): 464–80.

Bloom, Harold. *The Anxiety of Influence: A Theory of Poetry*. London: Oxford University Press, 1975.

Bretz, Mary Lee. *La evolución novelística de Pío Baroja*. Madrid: José Porrúa Turanzas, 1979.

Buckley, Ramón, and John Crispin. *Los vanguardistas españoles (1925–1935)*. Madrid: Alianza, 1973.

Bullough, Edward. *Aesthetics: Lectures and Essays*. London: Bowes and Bowes, 1957.

Camón Aznar, José. *Ramón Gómez de la Serna en sus obras*. Madrid: Espasa-Calpe, 1972.

Cano Ballesta, Juan. *Literatura y tecnología (Las letras españolas ante la revolución industrial 1900–1933)*. Madrid: Orígenes, 1981.

Cansinos Assens, Rafael. *La nueva literatura, II: Las escuelas (1898 1900–1918)*. Madrid: Paez, 1925.

Cardona, Rodolfo. *Ramón: A Study of Gómez de la Serna and His Works*. New York: Eliseo Torres and Sons, 1957.

Cardona, Rodolfo, and Anthony N. Zahareas. *Visión del esperpento*. Madrid: Castalia, 1970.

Carmen Bobes, María del. *Gramática textual de "Belarmino y Apolonio"*. Madrid: CUPSA, 1977.

Casalduero, Joaquín. "Sentido y forma de 'La vida fantástica.' " *Pío Baroja*. Ed. Javier Martínez Palacio, pp. 285–353. Madrid: Taurus, 1974.

Casares, Julio. *Crítica profana*. Madrid: Imprenta Colonial, 1916.

Catena, Elena. "Lo azoriniano en *Doña Inés*." *Cuadernos Hispanoamericanos* 226–27 (1968): 266–91.

Ciplijauskaite, Biruté. *Baroja, un estilo*. Madrid: Insula, 1972.

Conte, Rafael. "Valle-Inclán y la realidad." *Cuadernos Hispanoamericanos* 199–200 (1966): 53–64.

Debicki, Andrew P. *Estudios sobre poesía española contemporánea: La generación de 1924–1925*. Madrid: Gredos, 1968.

Díaz Migoyo, Gonzalo. *Guía de "Tirano Banderas"*. Madrid: Fundamentos, 1984.

———. "*Tirano Banderas* o la posmodernidad novelesca española." Paper presented at the Simposio Internacional: Valle-Inclán y su tiempo, Madrid, May 1986.

Díaz-Plaja, Guillermo. *Modernismo frente al noventa y ocho*. Madrid: Espasa-Calpe, 1979.

Diez, Ricardo. *El desarrollo estético de la novela de Unamuno*. Madrid: Playor, 1976.

Dougherty, Dru. "The Question of Revolution in *Tirano Banderas*." *Bulletin of Hispanic Studies* 53 (1976): 207–13.

———. *Un Valle-Inclán olvidado: Entrevistas y conferencias*. Madrid: Fundamentos, 1983.

———. *Valle-Inclán y la Segunda República*. Valencia: Pre-Textos, 1986.

Durán, Manuel. "Actualidad de *Tirano Banderas*." *Mundo Nuevo* 10 (1967): 49–54.

———. "La técnica de la novela y la generación del 98." *Revista Hispánica Moderna* 23 (1957): 14–27.

Durand, Frank. "Search for Reality in *Nada menos que todo un hombre*." *Modern Language Notes* 84 (1969): 239–47.

Enguídanos, Miguel. "Azorín en busca del tiempo divinal." *Papeles de Son Armadans* 15 (1959): 13–32.

Entrambasaguas, Joaquín de. *Las mejores novelas contemporáneas (1900–1904)*. Barcelona: Planeta, 1971.

Extramiana, José. "A propósito de algunas fuentes de *Tirano Banderas* en un intento de interpretación de la novela." *Bulletin Hispanique* 69 (1967): 465–86.

Fabian, D.L. "Action and Idea in *Amor y pedagogía* and *Prometeo*." *Hispania* 41 (1958): 29–34.

Fernández, Pelayo H. *Ramón Pérez de Ayala: Tres novelas analizadas*. Gijón: Yepes, 1972.

Fernández Almagro, Melchor. "La generación unipersonal de Gómez de la Serna." *España* 9 (1923): 10–11.

Fernández Cifuentes, Luis. *Teoría y mercado de la novela en España: Del 98 a la República*. Madrid: Gredos, 1982.

Fuentes, Víctor. "La dimensión estético-erótica y la novelística de Jarnés." *Cuadernos Hispanoamericanos* 235 (1969): 26–37.

———. "La narrativa española de vanguardia (1923–1931): Un ensayo de interpretación." *Romanic Review* 53 (1972): 211–18.

———. "La sociedad y lo social en la obra de Benjamín Jarnés." *Insula* 256 (1968): 13–14.

García Blanco, Manuel. "*Amor y pedagogía,* nivola unamuniana." *La Torre* 9 (1961): 13–14.

García Gómez, Jorge. "Notas sobre el tiempo y su pasar en novelas varias de Azorín." *Cuadernos Hispanoamericanos* 226–27 (1968): 292–338.

Genette, Gérard. *Narrative Discourse: An Essay in Method.* Trans. Jane E. Lewin. Ithaca: Cornell University Press, 1980.

Gillet, Joseph E. "The Autonomous Character in Spanish and European Literature." *Hispanic Review* 24 (1956): 179–90.

Glenn, Kathleen M. *Azorín (José Martínez Ruiz).* Boston: Twayne, 1981.

Goméz de la Serna, Gaspar. *Ramón (obra y vida).* Madrid: Taurus, 1963.

González Echevarría, Roberto. "El primitivismo de Azorín." *Revista de Occidente* 76 (1969): 95–103.

Guerrero Bueno, Obdulia. "Vocación histórica y realismo en la obra literaria de Valle-Inclán." *Insula* 236–37 (1966): 22.

Gullón, Ricardo. *Autobiografías de Unamuno.* Madrid: Gredos, 1964.

———. *La invención del 98 y otros ensayos.* Madrid: Gredos, 1969.

———. "La novela personal de don Miguel de Unamuno." *La Torre* 35–36 (1961): 93–115.

———. *La novela lírica.* Madrid: Cátedra, 1984.

———. "Las técnicas de Valle-Inclán." *Papeles de Son Armadans* 43 (1966): 21–86.

Güntert, Georges. "La fuente en el laberinto: Las *Sonatas* de Valle-Inclán." *Boletín de la Real Academia Española* 53 (1973): 543–67.

Handelman, Susan A. *The Slayers of Moses: The Emergence of Rabbinic Interpretation in Modern Literary Theory.* Albany: State University of New York Press, 1982.

Ilie, Paul. "Benjamín Jarnés: Aspects of the Dehumanized Novel." *Publications of the Modern Language Association* 76 (1961): 247–53.

———. *Documents of the Spanish Vanguard.* Chapel Hill: University of North Carolina Press, 1969.

———. *The Surrealist Mode in Spanish Literature.* Ann Arbor: University of Michigan Press, 1968.

Jauss, Hans Robert. *Toward an Aesthetic of Reception.* Trans. Timothy Bahti. Minneapolis: University of Minnesota Press, 1982.

Johnson, Roberta L. *El ser y la palabra en Gabriel Miró.* Madrid: Fundamentos, 1985.

———. "*La voluntad*: Azorín's Post-modern Novel." Paper delivered at the 20th Century Spanish Literature Division, MLA, New York, December 1986.

Juretschke, Hans. "La generación del 98, su proyección, crítica e influencia en el extranjero." *Arbor* 11 (1948): 517–52.

Kirkpatrick, Susan. "*Tirano Banderas* y la estructura de la historia." *Nueva Revista de Filología Hispánica* 24 (1975): 449–68.

Krause, Anna. *Azorín, the Little Philosopher. Inquiry into the Birth of a Literary Personality.* Berkeley: University of California Press, 1948.

Lacarta, Manuel. *Madrid y sus literaturas: De la Generación del 98 a la posguerra.* Madrid: El Avapiés, 1986.

Laín Entralgo, Pedro. *La generación del 98*. Madrid: Espasa- Calpe, 1959.

La novela lírica, I: Azorín, Gabriel Miró and *La novela lírica, II: Pérez de Ayala, Jarnés*, edited by Darío Villanueva. Madrid: Taurus, 1983.

Lavaud, Eliane. *Valle-Inclán du journal au roman*. Dijon: Klincksieck, 1979.

Livingstone, Leon. "Novel and Mirror, the Eye and the I." *Homenaje a Azorín*. Ed. Carlos Mellizo, pp. 51–73. Laramie: University of Wyoming, 1973.

———. "The Pursuit of Form in the Novels of Azorín." *Publications of the Modern Language Association* 77 (1962): 116–33.

———. *Tema y forma en las novelas de Azorín*. Madrid: Gredos, 1970.

López Campillo, Evelyne. *La Revista de Occidente y la formación de minorías*. Madrid: Taurus, 1972.

López Morillas, Juan. *Hacia el 98: Literatura, sociedad, ideología*. Barcelona: Ariel, 1972.

———. "Unamuno y sus criaturas: Antolín S. Paparrigópulos." *Cuadernos Americanos* 40 (1948): 234–49.

Lott, Robert E. "El arte descriptivo de Pío Baroja." *Cuadernos Hispanoamericanos* 265–67 (1972): 531–36.

———. "Sobre el método narrativo y el estilo en las novelas de Azorín." *Cuadernos Hispanoamericanos* 226–27 (1968): 192–219.

Lozano Marco, Miguel Angel. *Del relato modernista a la novela poemática: La narrativa breve de Ramón Pérez de Ayala*. Alicante: Universidad de Alicante, 1983.

Macklin, J. J. "Pérez de Ayala y la novela modernista europea." *Cuadernos Hispanoamericanos* 367–68 (1981): 21–36.

Maier, Carol S. "Valle-Inclán's Literary Relations: The Creation of Context." Paper delivered at Modern Language Association convention, Washington, D.C., December 1984.

Manuel Gil, Ildefonso. "El disputado '¡Viva la bagatela!': Baroja, Azorín y Valle-Inclán." *Cuadernos Hispanoamericanos* 226–27 (1968): 451–65.

Maravall, José Antonio. "Azorín. Idea y sentido de la microhistoria." *Cuadernos Hispanoamericanos* 226–27 (1968): 28–77.

———. "La imagen de la sociedad arcaica en Valle-Inclán." *Revista de Occidente* 44–45 (1966): 225–56.

Marías, Julián. "*Doña Inés*." *Insula* 94 (1953): 1.

———. "Ramón y la realidad." *Insula* 123 (1957): 2 and 8.

Marichal, Juan. "Los intelectuales y la guerra." *El Paí Semanal*, June 15, 1986.

Marrast, Robert. "Religiosidad y satanismo, sadismo y masoquismo en la *Sonata de otoño*." *Cuadernos Hispanoamericanos* 199–200 (1966): 482–92.

Martínez Bonati, Félix. *La estructura de la obra literaria: Una investigación de la filosofía del lenguaje y estética*. Barcelona: Seix Barral, 1972.

Martínez Cachero. *Las novelas de Azorín*. Madrid: Insula, 1960.

Martínez Latre, María Pilar. *La novela intelectual de Benjamín Jarnés*. Zaragoza: Institución Fernando el Católico, 1979.

Matas, Julio. *Contra el honor: Las novelas normativas de Ramón Pérez de Ayala*. Madrid: Seminario y Ediciones, 1974.

Meehan, Thomas C. "El desdoblamiento interior en *Doña Inés*." *Cuadernos Hispanoamericanos* 237 (1969): 644–68.

Merrell, Floyd. *Pararealities: The Nature of Our Fictions and How We Know Them*. Amsterdam/Philadelphia: Purdue University Monographs in Romance Languages, 1983.

Milner Garlitz, Virginia. "Teosofismo en *Tirano Banderas*." *Journal of Spanish Studies Twentieth Century* 2 (1974): 21–29.

Miró, Emilio. "En torno a *Camino de perfección*." *Cuadernos Hispanoamericanos* 265–67 (1972): 517–30.

Monner Sans, José María. "Unamuno, Pirandello y el personaje autónomo." *La Torre* 35–36 (1961): 387–402.

Montes Huidobro, M. "Un retrato de Azorín: *Doña Inés*." *Revista de Occidente* 81 (1969): 362–72.

Montesinos, José F. "Modernismo, esperpentismo o las dos evasiones." *Revista de Occidente* 44–45 (1966): 146–65.

Navajas, Gonzalo. *Mimesis y cultura en la ficción: Teoría de la novela.* London: Tamesis, 1985.

Noble, Beth. "The Descriptive Genius of Pérez de Ayala." *Hispania* 40 (1957): 171–75.

Nora, Eugenio de. *La novela española contemporánea I.* Madrid: Gredos, 1973.

Olson, Paul R. "The Novelistic Logos in Unamuno's *Amor y pedagogía*." *Modern Language Notes* 84 (1969): 248–68.

O'Neill, Marion W. "The Role of the Sensual in the Art of Benjamín Jarnés." *Modern Language Notes* 85 (1970): 262–68.

Ortega y Gasset, José. *La deshumanización del arte.* Madrid: Revista de Occidente, 1925.

Pérez de la Dehesa, Rafael. *El grupo "Germinal": Una clave del 98.* Madrid: Cuadernos de Taurus, 1970.

Pérez Firmat, Gustavo. *Idle Fictions: The Hispanic Vanguard Novel, 1926–1934.* Durham: Duke University Press, 1982.

Phillips, Allen W. "Estudio Preliminar." *Sonata de primavera, Sonata de estío, Sonata de otoño, Sonata de invierno: Memorias del Marqués de Bradomín* by Ramón del Valle-Inclán. Mexico: Porrúa, 1979.

Pinto, Mario. "*Todo un hombre,* de Miguel de Unamuno." *Nosotros* 50 (1928): 424–30.

Poggioli, Renato. *Teoría del arte de vanguardia.* Trans. Rosa Chacel. Madrid: Revista de Occidente, 1964.

Prado, Angeles. "Las novelas poemáticas de Ramón Pérez de Ayala." *Cuadernos Hispanoamericanos* 367–68 (1981): 41–70.

Pratt, Mary Louise. *Toward a Speech Act Theory of Literary Discourse.* Bloomington: Indiana University Press, 1977.

Rajoy Feijóo, María Dolores. "Poesía y narrativa en R. Pérez de Ayala (Lectura de *Las novelas poemáticas*)." *Homenaje a Ramó Pérez de Ayala,* edited by María del Carmen Bobes Naves. Oviedo: Publicaciones del Departamento de Crítica Literaria, 1980.

Rand, Marguerite. "Más notas sobre Azorín y el tiempo." *Hispania* 49 (1966): 23–30.

Ribbans, Geoffrey. *Niebla y soledad.* Madrid: Gredos, 1964.

———. "Riqueza inagotada de las revistas literarias modernas." *Revista de Literatura* 13 (1958): 30–47.

Richmond, Carolyn. "Gómez de la Serna novelista." *La Quinta de Palmyra.* Madrid: Espasa-Calpe, 1982.

Río, Angel del. *Historia de la literatura española, II.* New York: Holt, 1963.

———. "Las 'novelas ejemplares' de Unamuno." *Revista de la Universidad de Buenos Aires* 5 (1960): 22–34.

Risco, Antonio. *Azorín y la ruptura con la novela tradicional*. Madrid: Alhambra, 1980.

———. *La estética de Valle-Inclán: En los esperpentos y en "El ruedo ibérico"*. Madrid: Gredos, 1975.

Rivkin, Laura. "Pain and Physiological Form in Baroja's *Camino de perfección*." *Symposium* 39 (1985): 207–16.

Salgado, María. "El paisaje animado en *Camino de perfección*." *Hispania* 99 (1966): 404–9.

Salinas, Pedro. "Benjamín Jarnés." *Indice Literario* 3 (1934): 21–24.

———. *Literatura española siglo XX*. Madrid: Alianza, 1979.

Salper de Tortellá, Roberta L. "La dimensión temporal y la creación del Marqués de Bradomín." *Insula* 237–238 (1966): 15 and 26.

Serrano, Poncela. *El secreto de Melibea*. Madrid: Taurus, 1959.

Smith, Verity. *Valle-Inclán: "Tirano Banderas"*. London: Grant and Cutler, 1971.

Sobejano, Gonzalo. "Componiendo *Camino de perfección*." *Cuadernos Hispanoamericanos* 265–67 (1972): 463–80.

———. *Forma literaria y sensibilidad social (Mateo Alemán, Galdós, Clarín, el 98 y Valle-Inclán)*. Madrid: Gredos, 1967.

Sol, Manuel T. *Contexto, estructura y sentido de "Camino de perfección" de Baroja*. Xalapa: Universidad Veracruzana, 1985.

Soldevila Durante, Ignacio. "La problemática del nacionalismo en los prosistas de la Generación de 1923 (1918–1931)." *Nation et nationalités en Espagne XIXe-XXe S.: Actes du colloque international organisé du 28 au 31 mars 1984, à Paris, par la Fondation Singer-Polignac*. Paris: Editions de la Fondation Singer-Polignac, 1984.

———. "Valle-Inclán y las vanguardias literarias: La composición de *Tirano Banderas* como novela cubista." Paper delivered at the Simposio Internacional: Valle-Inclán y su tiempo. Madrid, May 1986.

Solotorevsky, Myrna. "Notas para el estudio intrínseco comparativo de *Camino de perfección* y *La voluntad*." *Boletín de Filología* 15 (1963): 111–64.

Speratti-Piñero, Emma Susana. *De "Sonata de otoño" al esperpento: Aspectos del arte de Valle-Inclán*. London: Tamesis, 1968.

Spires, Robert C. *Beyond the Metafictional Mode: Directions in the Modern Spanish Novel*. Lexington: University Press of Kentucky, 1984.

———. *La novela española de posguerra: Creación artística y experiencia personal*. Madrid: CUPSA, 1978.

———. "Realidad prosaica e imaginación transcendente en dos cuentos de Pedro Salinas." *Pedro Salinas*, edited by Andrew P. Debicki, pp. 249–57. Madrid: Taurus, 1976.

Staiger, Emil. *Conceptos fundamentales de poética*. Trans. Jaime Ferreiro Alemparte. Madrid: Rialp, 1966.

Stanzel, Franz. *Narrative Situations in the Novel: Tom Jones, Moby-Dick, The Ambassadors, Ulysses*. Trans. James P. Pusack. Bloomington: Indiana University Press, 1971.

Terry, Barbara A. "The Influence of Casanova y Barbey D'Aurevilly on the 'Sonatas' of Valle-Inclán." *Revista de Estudios Hispánicos* 1 (1967): 61–88.

Torre, Guillermo de. *Historia de las literaturas de vanguardia*. Madrid: Guadarrama, 1974.

———. "La generación española de 1898 en las revistas del tiempo." *Nosotros* 6 (1941): 1–38.

Tucker, Peggy Lynne. *Time and History in Valle-Inclán's Historical Novels and "Tirano Banderas"*. Valencia: Hispanófila, 1980.

Umbral, Francisco. *Ramón y las vanguardias*. Madrid: Espasa- Calpe, 1978.

Unamuno, Miguel de. *Del sentimiento trágico de la vida*. New York: Las Americas, n.d.

———. *Ensayos*. Madrid: Publicaciones de la Residencia de Estudiantes, 1917.

Urrutia, Jorge. *El Novecentismo y la renovación vanguardista*. Madrid: Cincel, 1980.

Urrutia, Norma. *De Troteras a Tigre Juan: Dos grandes temas de Ramón Pérez de Ayala*. Madrid: Insula, 1960.

Valdés, Mario J. *Death in the Literature of Unamuno*. Urbana: University of Illinois Press, 1964.

Valis, Noël. "The Novel as Feminine Entrapment: Valle-Inclán's *Sonata de otoño*." Forthcoming article.

———. "*El novelista,* por Ramón Gómez de la Serna, o la novela en busca de sí misma." *El novelista*. Forthcoming critical edition.

———. "Valle-Inclán's *Sonata de otoño*: Refractions of a French Anarchist." *Comparative Literature Studies* 22 (1985): 218–30.

Valle-Inclán, Ramón del. *La media noche*: *Visión estelar de un momento de guerra*. Madrid: Clásica Española, 1917.

Valverde, José María. *Azorín*. Barcelona: Planeta, 1971.

Vidal, José B. "El tiempo a través de los personajes de *Doña Inés*." *Cuadernos Hispanoamericanos* 226–27 (1968): 220–38.

Villanueva, Darío. "Valle-Inclán renovador de la novela." Paper delivered at the Simposio Internacional: Valle-Inclán y su tiempo, Madrid, May 1986.

Villegas, Juan. "La disposición temporal de *Tirano Banderas*." *Revista Hispánica Moderna* 33 (1967): 299–308.

———. "*Niebla*: una ruta para autentificar la existencia." *Spanish Thought and Letters in the Twentieth Century*. Ed. Germán Bleiberg and E. Inman Fox. Nashville: Vanderbilt University Press, 1966.

———. *La estructura mítica del héroe*. Barcelona: Planeta, 1973.

Wyers Weber, Frances. *The Literary Perspectivism of Ramón Pérez de Ayala*. Chapel Hill: University of North Carolina Press, 1966.

Ynduráin, Domingo. "Teoría de la novela en Baroja." *Cuadernos Hispanoamericanos* 233 (1969): 355–88.

Zamora Vicente, Alonso. *Las Sonatas de Valle-Inclán*. Madrid: Gredos, 1983.

Zubizarreta, Armando F. *Unamuno en su nivola*. Madrid: Taurus, 1960.

Zuleta, Emilio de. *Arte y vida en la obra de Benjamín Jarnés*. Madrid: Gredos, 1977.

Reviews Cited

El Imparcial, July 21, 1902

El Sol, February 7, 1934

Helios I (1903)

Heraldo de Madrid, August 4, 1902

Indice Literario 3 (May 1934)

La Epoca, June 17, 1902, and July 7, 1902

La Lectura 2 (June 1902) and (July 1902)

Madrid Cómico, July 7, 1902
Nuestro Tiempo 2 (1902)

Editions of Works Analyzed

Baroja, Pío. *Camino de perfección*. Madrid: Editorial Caro Raggio, 1972.
Gómez de la Serna, Ramón. *El novelista*. Madrid: Espasa-Calpe, 1973.
Jarnés, Benjamín. *El convidado de papel*. Zaragoza: Guara Editorial, 1979.
Martínez Ruiz, José (Azorín). *Doña Inés*. Ed. Elena Catena. Madrid: Castalia, 1982.
———. *La voluntad*. Ed. Inman Fox. Madrid: Castalia, 1982.
Pérez de Ayala, Ramón. *Prometeo, Luz de domingo, La caída de los Limones*. Buenos Aires: Losada, 1967.
Salinas, Pedro. *Víspera del gozo*. Madrid: Alianza, 1974.
Valle-Inclán, Ramón del. *Sonata de primavera, Sonata de estío, Sonata de otoño, Sonata de invierno: Memorias del Marqués de Bradomín*. Ed. by Allen W. Phillips. Mexico: Porrúa, 1979.
———. *Tirano Banderas*. Ed. Antonio Valencia. Madrid: Espasa- Calpe, 1984.
Unamuno, Miguel de. *Amor y pedagogía*. Barcelona: Imprenta de Henrich, 1902.
———. "Nada menos que todo un hombre." *Tres novelas ejemplares y un prólogo*. Buenos Aires: Espasa-Calpe, 1963.

Index